Notes on the Art of Life

Haim Shapira
Translated by Linda Yechiel

WATKINS
Sharing Wisdom
Since 1893

Notes on the Art of Life
Haim Shapira

First published in the UK and USA in 2023 by
Watkins, an imprint of Watkins Media Limited
Unit 11, Shepperton House, 83–93 Shepperton Road
London N1 3DF

enquiries@watkinspublishing.com

Translated by Linda Yechiel
Typeset by Lapiz

A CIP record for this book is available from the British Library

ISBN: 978-1-78678-773-6 (paperback)
ISBN: 978-1-78678-800-9 (eBook)

10 9 8 7 6 5 4 3 2 1

Printed in United Kingdom by TJ Books Ltd

www.watkinspublishing.com

MIX
Paper from
responsible sources
FSC® C013056

To Emanuel and Michaela,
Tal and Inbal, and Daniela

Contents

Chapter 1: In the Beginning: The Poetics
of Science   1

Chapter 2: Pen, Ink, and Fine-quality Paper:
The Art of Wonder   7

Chapter 3: Zhuang Zhou's 'Crazy Wisdom'   15

Chapter 4: The Arithmetic of Life and Death   35

Chapter 5: The Sound of Silence   45

Chapter 6: A Harvest of Regrets   51

Chapter 7: Tender Complaints   69

Chapter 8: Dudeism and Daoism   79

Chapter 9: Aristotle's Blog on *Eudaimonia*   117

Chapter 10: The Secret of the Virtues:
Aristotle's Art of Finding Balance   143

Chapter 11: The Appeal of Socrates: What
is Philosophy Supposed to Deal With?   189

Chapter 12: Tips from Epicurus: The Great
Art of Small Pleasures   195

Chapter 13: What is Wisdom?   203

Chapter 14: The Inner Citadel: Stoic Philosophy   211

Chapter 15: On Happiness and Other
Small Things of Absolute Importance   233

Chapter 16: A Few Words about Love   283

Endnotes   298
Acknowledgments   302
Bibliography   304
Books by Haim Shapira   306

CHAPTER 1

In the Beginning:
The Poetics of Science

At the start of his book *Astrophysics for People in a Hurry*, American astrophysicist Neil deGrasse Tyson writes that in the beginning, around 14 billion years ago, all space and all the matter and energy of the universe as we know it today were trapped in a volume that was less than one trillionth of that of the period or full stop that ends this sentence.

I'd been aware for some time of the minuteness of our universe when it was in the cosmic incubator. For some reason, however, the comparison drawn by Tyson to the period at the end of a sentence affected me so much that I had to stop reading for a while. I started staring at the period on the page and tried to imagine a dot a million times smaller than that dot. Then I mentally divided that new dot, which I could not even imagine, into a million. The size now was completely impossible to fathom. Then I tried to comprehend how everything that is in the universe – or was or ever will be in the universe – was once jammed into this cosmic wonder of a dot so small that it was practically nonexistent. In other words, billions of years ago (if we take the scientists' word for it), this tiny point of infinite density contained all quarks, leptons, bosons, and electrons, all atoms and molecules, all particles and all forces – and me and you, and all the babies that were born yesterday and all people who have already left this Earth, and all giraffes, elephants, dolphins, and blue whales, and all skyscrapers and their occupants, all trains and planes, the Pyramids of Giza, the Sahara Desert, and the Hanging Gardens of Babylon, all tsunami waves and the Mariana Trench, and the laws of mathematics, the Hammurabi Code, and the amazing rules of chess, and this book and all the books that have ever been published and will ever be published, and all cherry blossom and all languages, all smiles and hugs, tears of joy and sorrow, and rivers of happiness and oceans of suffering, and spontaneous acts of goodwill and cruelty, and the stardust from which humankind was created, and the Andromeda dust, and all thoughts, hopes, and disappointments, and Lake Como and all the towns on its shores, and all ships, pencils, birds of prey, and airports, and Earth, Mars, Neptune, Uranus, the Sun, the Milky Way, the star of Antares, and some 320 sextillion huge stars that play their part in the wonderful cosmic dance, whose names no one knows, because they are still waiting to be named ...

And all this was in the form of some kind of energy ensconced within a point so tiny that essentially it didn't exist at all, and no one knows who or what created it, or how or why.

Nothingness: a Buddhist-style thought experiment

Imagine that at the push of a button, within a fraction of a split second, you could end the existence of the universe. A little click, and then poof! … everything human, animal, vegetable, and mineral disappears into oblivion. This will happen so abruptly that no one will feel any pain and no one will know anything about what has happened. One push and there will be nothing left. Not even the teeniest thing, the merest speck. And there will be no more suffering. There will *be* no anything at all.

Tempting? Perhaps. But the butterflies will also disappear …

1,000 ways to be happy

Near one of the entrances to the Great Wall of China, near the city of Tianjin near Mao's Garden, stands a wall displaying 1,000 Chinese characters denoting various possible gateways to happiness/joy/contentment/delight/satisfaction/pleasure/delight/enjoyment/serenity. These are there to remind people of all aspects of life's meaning and value.

Images of the 'Wall of Happiness', easily accessed on the Internet, show how the wall teems with beautifully mysterious red characters. I haven't the slightest inkling of what they really mean, but as an avid aficionado of lists (as you may have already guessed) I've drafted a modest compilation of my own moments of contentment.

My list is unapologetically personal, sentimental, nostalgic, romantic. Here it is:

*A mother's embrace; the first time I was called 'Dad'; the
first time I was called 'Grandpa'; the gurgling giggles
of a baby; laughing to the point of tears; a morning
shower in a strong, warm jet of water; the aroma of
apple pie just before it's taken from the oven; my
granddaughter lying on my daughter who was lying
on the sofa in my living room, both of them dozing; the
dance of snowflakes in the light of street lamps; being
helpful to someone; knowing you have a friend; knowing
someone knows you are their friend; travelling along
the backroads in Tuscany; diving alongside smart and
lovable dolphins; skinny-dipping at night; witnessing my
favourite basketball team win the championship final by
throwing a half-court shot right before the final buzzer;
daydreaming; hiking new trails; riding in a buggy car
among the Buddhist temples in Bagan and seeing them
in a bird's-eye view from a hot-air balloon; waking
up next to the woman I love; sharing morning coffee
with her in our garden; being a pioneer and innovator;
being part of something important; holding a fresh-
off-the-press copy of one of my books for the first time;
watching the aerobatic display of a flock of cranes;
chatting with friends; having an eye-to-eye conversation
with a small child; hearing the doctor say there's no
need for surgery; sunset in Sedona, Arizona; beating the
heat with an ice-cold drink; petrichor after the first rain
in ages; saying 'I love you'; hearing 'I love you'; coming
across an elderly couple sitting on a bench speaking
Yiddish in my grandparents' dialect; Friday night meals
with all the family; sitting in a chair by the sea where the*

waves meet the shore; an Ayurvedic massage in a room redolent of incense and sesame oil; falling into blissful slumber after a gruelling day; my dog jumping for joy when I return home from work; any act of love …

The German social psychologist and psychoanalyst Erich Fromm (1900–1980) asks the question, who can tell whether 'one happy moment of love, or the joy of walking on a bright morning and smelling the fresh air' is worth all the anguish and effort life requires of us? As of today, I'd certainly put my hand up and say '*I* can', and I hope this will always be the case.

* * *

After my highly personal Buddhist-style thought experiment, you might like to compile your own list of blessings, drawing deep from your life experiences. Keep the list by you – turn it into a mood board, collage-style, if you wish, to remind you of what makes your challenges worthwhile.

CHAPTER 2

Pen, Ink, and Fine-quality Paper: The Art of Wonder

I should like to introduce you now to some lists of happy and sad things compiled by a unique woman around a thousand years ago, in ancient Japan.

Sei Shōnagon (*c.*966–*c.*1025), writer and poet, served as lady-in-waiting to Empress Teishi (Sadako), around the year 1000, in the period known as the Heian. Japanese scholars incline to translate 'Heian' as 'peace and quiet'. Not much is known about Sei Shōnagon. We do know she was an expert on Japanese and Chinese literature, and we know she had a bitter rival, Mrs Murasaki Shikibu, a member of the Japanese nobility and also a writer. One of Murasaki's works is *The Tale of Genji*, considered by many experts to be the first Japanese novel and, in fact, one of the first novels ever. Murasaki Shikibu described Sei Shōnagon – and we all know that a rival's opinion is often more accurate than that of friends – as a witty woman who never missed an opportunity to display her wisdom.

Sei Shōnagon left her mark on literature with one special book, which is essentially a personal journal. *The Pillow Book* is a collection of reflections, anecdotes, opinions, and lists, and it has been casting its magic on me for many years. Below is a taster from this book by a remarkable weaver of lists from the Land of the Rising Sun.

My version is a jazz-like improvisation based on a good number of sources, and you'll note that I frequently deviate from the accepted scale.

When I read these items, I try to envision each of her descriptive details as a story in miniature that I embellish with what I imagine might be unwritten. Try doing this yourself – it's a pleasurable exercise.

Beautiful, pleasing things that I love	Displeasing things that sadden me
A piece of Chinese embroidery	Sailing in a boat with a torn sail
A sword inside a scabbard decorated with exquisite artwork	Being disappointed by a sequel to a book I really loved
Discovering a treasure trove of stories no one has yet read	A fence that blocks the mountains and trees, hiding a beautiful view
Receiving a gift of an exquisitely bound book that is the sequel to a book that I enjoyed reading	A baby crying in its carriage and no one coming to soothe them
	An empty baby carriage
The Empress calling for me, signalling all the courtiers to make way for me, and me then walking toward her, aware of all the jealous stares	An overturned ox cart – I would expect such a thing to remain always upright
	Cleaning a fancy comb I received as a gift and discovering a tooth is broken

Autumn leaves on a statue of the Buddha	Hearing the raven's kraa at dawn and realizing I've been waiting all night for someone who failed to appear – and I was so certain he would arrive ...
Flowering branches of wisteria in wonderful hues of mauve and yellow spiralling around a pine	The hand of a samurai archer trembling so badly that the arrow misses its mark
A small boy eating strawberries, getting so delightfully messy	People who are not at all smart but think they know everything and can't stop trying to spice up their talk with the names of important people – to the point where their wearisome prattle becomes excruciatingly boring
A letter, filled with lovely words from a dear man, arriving on a gloomy, rainy day	A tree torn out of the ground in a storm and lying on its side with its roots exposed to all
Writing on some fine paper I received from the Empress as a gift, using an incredibly fine brush	A dog intentionally barking at a lover whose visit was supposed to be secret Two men beating a dog – this is really awful
	People who sneeze during prayer
	A lover so intoxicated that he endlessly repeats himself
	A man dear to my heart extolling one of his former lovers
	And the saddest thing in this world: knowing no one loves you

I've noticed in these two lists that the things that sadden, annoy, or infuriate her outnumber the things she particularly admires or finds pleasing, elegant, amusing, or exciting.

Sei Shōnagon compiled other lists too, on almost every topic imaginable (and even some unimaginable). Here are some examples:

Things that deserve to be painted	Things not appropriate for painting
Pine trees, fields in autumn, a village in the mountains, paths in the forest, storks and deer, a particularly cold winter scene	Roses, cherry blossoms, women and men who were extolled for their beauty in a story I read

The near becoming distant	The distant becoming near
Relationships between brothers and sisters and other relatives in a family that has broken apart	Love between a man and a woman

Extremely rare things
A father-in-law who praises his son-in-law
A bride who loves her mother-in-law
A servant who does not gossip about his master
A flawless man
Friendship between a man and a woman
Friendship between a woman and a woman

Sei's views of the world seem as accurate now as they were in her own day. It seems there really isn't much that's new under the sun.

When I read her notes, she feels like an old friend of mine. Sometimes I even get a feeling that, if asked, I could recount from personal memory her encounters in the court of Empress Sadako Teishi during the Heian dynasty.

In truth, this book you are holding in your hands is a kind of 'pillow book' too – an honest and trustworthy companion.

Before we bid farewell to this author, this is how *The Pillow Book* begins:

The seasons

In springtime, it is dawn. As day approaches, the sky at the edge of the mountains has slowly begun to clear and the thin clouds trailing behind the light are mauve in colour.

In summer, it is night. Everyone knows that looking at the moon in the night sky is delightful, but on a dark night it is no less delightful to observe the innumerable fireflies swirling in flight. You can feel the magic even when only one or two fireflies pass by, giving the night a delicate glow. Even rainy nights are delightful.

In autumn, it is evening. How pleasing to watch the setting sun approach the mountains and the ravens rushing back to their nests in threes and fours or sometimes in pairs. No less pleasant is the sight of a flock of geese flying by high in the sky. And then, after sunset, the chirruping of insects that sound like distant cries, and the rustle of the wind, whose magic requires no embellishment with words.

In winter, it is early morning. Obviously it is wonderful when the snow is falling, but it is also delightful to see a pure white frost without snow. The way everyone hurries to light a fire and bring sputtering coals into all the rooms – this is very appropriate for the season.

As the day continues and the cold gradually loses its bite, the rooms warm up and become filled with the aroma of winter food. This is so agreeable and good.

I was planning to finish here but my powers of restraint are not impressive, so here's one of my favourite passages:

> *I remember one bright morning during the ninth moon. The torrential rains had not abated throughout the night, even briefly, but in the morning the sun came out to replace the rain. Caught by bright rays of sunshine, beads of rain dripped to the ground from the chrysanthemum leaves in the garden. I saw the remnants of cobwebs on the bamboo fence, where raindrops were clinging to the torn threads like a white pearl necklace. My spirit soared and I was content. As the day became sunnier, the dew that had until recently lain so heavily on the plants disappeared.*
>
> *I later described to people how beautiful all this was. What particularly struck me was that they were not at all impressed.*

In my opinion, the most important message one can take from Sei is that no matter what happens or where we are, the here and now is beautiful and exhilarating if we can just bring ourselves to pay attention.

> I always want eyes
> to see the beauty of the world
> and to praise this wonderful beauty
> that is without flaw,
> and to praise the one who made it so
> beautifully praiseworthy and complete,
> so complete, beautiful.
> **Nathan Zach**[1]

Have you see the movie *American Beauty* (1999)? Do you recall the scene with the flying plastic bag?

Ricky Fitts is a strange boy, in the good and beautiful sense of the word. He wants to be a filmmaker, but in the meantime divides his time between three passions: filming anything he finds beautiful (which is pretty well almost everything), smoking marijuana, and his beloved Jane. One day Ricky asks Jane if she wants to see the most beautiful thing he's ever filmed. It turns out that this isn't Iguazu Falls or Antelope Canyon; it isn't a superb animal or weather effect or art installation. It's a completely ordinary plastic bag swirling and dancing in the wind for a number of long minutes. Playing in the background is a wonderful melody by Thomas Newman, an exceptional composer who can conjure grand emotion with only a few notes. Ricky says that sometimes there's so much beauty in the world that he feels he can't contain it.

We can also find great beauty in the movie *The Pillow Book* (1996) by British director Peter Greenaway, a great fan of Sei Shōnagon. This is a wonderfully aesthetic and elegant drama about erotica and books ('sex and text', in Greenaway's words). It's often closely related to the diary of this special and inspiring Japanese woman who knew how to see beauty in every drop of dew and in every whorl of needles on a cypress tree … or in every spectacular painting of a mythical hero or heroine or of a flower.

* * *

After this brief excursion into the movies, and back via one of them to Sei Shōnagon in Japan, the time has come to return to China.

CHAPTER 3

Zhuang Zhou's 'Crazy Wisdom'

Chinese philosopher Zhuang Zhou, who according to sinologists lived around the 4th century BCE, is my favourite Chinese sage. Zhuang Zhou's 'crazy wisdom', which he expressed in his short stories, has always delighted me. It has motivated me to look at things from a slightly different angle – and with a dash of humility and humour.

Below are some of the Chinese philosopher's stories I'm particularly fond of. The translations come from many sources in various languages, not including Chinese. (What can I do? – Chinese is Greek to me. The great Austrian Jewish philosopher Martin Buber retold some of Zhuang Zhou's tales and I've been inspired by his efforts.)

As usual, I've allowed myself broad artistic license. By the way, Zhuang Zhou actually gave his prophetic approval to my version by commenting that he'd no intention of reading even one line of anything written by others … and that's good, because I'm also adding some interpretation – something entirely contrary to the spirit of this witty Chinese sage.

The wise man and the frog

Just as there is no point in discussing the great ocean with a frog living in a well (it is trapped within the confines of the well) and just as there is no point in discussing snow and glaciers with summer moths (they are limited to their one and only one season), so too there is no point in discussing the ways of the world with a learned man – he is similarly bound to his own theories and ideas.

One of the great philosophers of the 20th century, Ludwig Josef Johann Wittgenstein (1889–1951), made the point more concisely:

The limits of my language are the limits of my world.
Ludwig Wittgenstein, *Tractatus Logico-Philosphicus*, 1922

All human beings are imprisoned in a well whose five walls are our senses. We cannot imagine anything outside this well. Even when we imagine fictional creatures such as unicorns or centaurs or flying witches, they are still fabricated from elements taken from our own world – horses, horns, people, brooms, and so on. German philosopher Arthur Schopenhauer (1788–1860) wrote that each person accepts the boundaries of their imagination as the boundaries of the world, and it's clear to me that each person has their own personal well. Some have a well that's narrow and shallow, while others have a well that's wide and deep. But for both these categories of people, being unaware of the well and its walls is a form of ignorance.

A saying attributed to the Buddha is that a person's opinion of the world is not much different from that of a chick that hasn't yet hatched from its shell. One way or another, the world is probably stranger and more complex than anything our imagination is capable of envisaging, and this is true regardless of the intensity of our imagination ... or our originality as artists.

A mewing dog

Fire is hot and ice freezes the hands. The morning breeze is felt in my hair and snowflakes melt on my face. An apple falls from the tree. A bird takes wing to the sky. Why are things like this? Why are things not different? What gives the four winds of heaven their direction?

Everyone knows that the dog barks and the cat mews, but no one knows why the dog barks and the cat mews ... or why the dog does not mew and the cat does not bark.

I don't know why the dog barks or the cat mews or the donkey brays. However, I've felt a strong desire to compile a list of things I do not know but would be happy to know. During the task of assembling this list, I've tried not to forget what Spanish-American philosopher George Santayana (1863–1952) said: 'Nature has done us a great kindness in that for most of the questions we do not know how to answer, we also do not know how to ask.' So here are some questions for which nature has not done me any favours.

I do know how to ask, but I really have no idea where the answers lie.

- Is there a God or isn't there?
- For what purpose were the blessed peace and eternal rest of nothingness disturbed? For what reason did God (or the Big Bang) create Earth and the heavens and all the multitudes of creatures, including humankind?
- Why is there anything at all? (Not *how* is it that there is something but *why*? Yet there's almost no doubt that the how and the why are somehow connected to each other, perhaps in some convoluted way.)
- Is there really a Creator/Architect of the world (some sublime wisdom that transcends human understanding) or has everything been created by chance and we are just wondering and wandering and wrong – forlorn and forsaken in an endless cosmic darkness?
- What is awareness and how did it evolve?
- Is life an 'accidental and unnecessary gift', as Pushkin said, or an infinite grace for which we should express thanks every morning of every day?
- Who am I and what's my purpose? How should I live and behave? Does my life have meaning? And where does my longing for meaning come from?
- Why should I be a 'good person'? Exactly what *is* a 'good person'?
- Why are we Death's clients?
- What happens to us after death? Should I hope for some kind of existence after my death or is it better to reside in the hospice of absolute nothingness?
- How is it that there's so much beauty in the world?

- How is it that there's so much evil in the world?
- Where does love come from?
- Is there any meaning to questions about meaning?
- What is faith? Is it possible to have love without faith? Is it possible to have faith without love? As soon as one separates faith from love, does faith separate from faith? Is faith possible without doubt?
- Can we *choose* to want the things we desire?
- Why are bad thoughts more common than good thoughts? (Is there an evolutionary advantage to pessimism?)
- Can the 'pleasure principle', based on pursuit of pleasure and escape from pain, serve as a guide to life?
- Have I ever thought a thought of my own?
- Where does our knowledge of good and evil come from?
- What is happiness? Is the purpose of life to be happy?
- Can there ever be a life without regrets?
- Would I be willing to relive my life over and over again exactly as I've lived it up to the moment of writing this line?

Two wise quotations occur to me now I've reached the end of my list (which, of course, could easily be extended) and before I sample Zhuang Zhou again:

The difficulty in philosophy is to say no more than we know.
Ludwig Wittgenstein, *The Blue Book*

Accustom your tongue to say: 'I do not know.'
Tractate Berakhot, page D, side A, Talmud

Meaning in a trap

A trap is needed to fish, but once you have caught the fish, the trap is no longer needed. A trap is needed to capture a mouse, but once you have captured the mouse, the trap is no longer needed. Words are necessary to grasp meaning, but once the meaning is flowing, there is no longer a need for words. Who will grant me a person who has grasped this meaning so we may exchange a word or two?

Wittgenstein's *Tractatus Logico-Philosophicus* ends like this: 'Whereof one cannot speak, thereof one must be silent.' Yet I've a great desire to talk about things that cannot be talked about: love, God, faith, infinity … Zhuang Zhou helps me to voice such transgressive thoughts:

A butterfly's dream

One night I, Zhuang Zhou, dreamed I was a butterfly fluttering back and forth, floating over fields and tree tops and enjoying the warmth of the sun's rays. All of a sudden I woke up and asked myself how I could possibly know if I am Zhuang Zhou dreaming he's a butterfly or a butterfly dreaming he's Zhuang Zhou?

When people dream, they do not know they are dreaming. Sometimes they dream a dream within a dream. Only when they wake up can they discover they've been in the dream world all this time.

Only with the arrival of the great awakening – death – will a person realize that their whole life has been one big dream. Only those who are feeble-minded believe they are awake now.

The story of Zhuang Zhou and the butterfly is probably one of the best-known tales in philosophical literature worldwide. The anecdote is both entertaining and intriguing, but I think it's a little less mysterious than it seems at first glance. After all, it's clear to us all who is writing the story: Zhuang Zhou. Not one anthology of Chinese philosophy nor any single philosophical or other scholarly source attributes this story to … the butterfly.

In his later notebooks (collected into a volume entitled *On Certainty*, 1969), Ludwig Wittgenstein revisited the subject of dreams, which had occupied him philosophically many times. His point was quite a brain-teaser: 'The argument, "I may be dreaming," is pointless for the following reason: If I am dreaming, then the statement 'I am dreaming', alongside any claim that these words have meaning, must be part of my dream.'

Pisces

Zhuang Zhou and Hui Tzu were once walking along a creek. They climbed onto a bridge to observe the fish swimming in the creek's clear waters below.

'Look how happy the fish are!' Zhuang Zhou exclaimed to his friend.

'You are not a fish. So how do you know whether the fish are happy or not?' retorted Hui Tzu.

'You are not me. So how can you know if I know what makes fish happy?' With that, Zhuang Zhou ended the argument, and the two friends passed over to the other side of the creek.

Fania Pascal, Wittgenstein's friend, tells of the time following a tonsillectomy when she was feeling just awful. The Austrian philosopher called to ask how she was, and she replied that she felt like a dog that had been run over by a truck. Wittgenstein was furious. He yelled that she couldn't possibly know how a run-over dog felt. Commentators disagree as to whether the wrath of the great Ludwig was real or just a philosopher's dash of humour.

I have no opinion on this matter. But I do know that Wittgenstein took the subject of pain – and each person's conception of what that means – very seriously. In section 293 of his book *Philosophical Investigations,* published posthumously in 1953, the philosopher suggests a fascinating thought-experiment with the unusual name of 'beetle in a box.' It works like this. Imagine seven people standing in a circle. Each is holding a small box. Everyone understands that the thing inside their box is called a 'beetle' but each of them can only look at what is inside their own box: no one is allowed to look at the contents of anyone else's box. Any box may contain an insect corresponding in appearance to the average beetle as we conceive it. However, any box *could* hold a key to a safe at the World Bank or a rare stamp or strawberry jam or anything else. It's possible one of the boxes is empty. It's even possible that *all* the boxes are empty.

Now, let's imagine the boxes are actually brains. Inside the box/brain is the thing we call 'pain'. Clearly, the definition, perception, and experience of pain will differ from one person to another. Also, no one can really share their pain with anyone else. It might be possible to understand that someone is 'in pain', because they say so or because we see them writhing or moaning, but there's nobody who can experience another's pain. The closest we can get is to feel empathy.

What I've related so far is merely a taste of the concept. There are hundreds of articles and discussions online concerning the beetle experiment. Just type 'beetle in the box' into your search window. (You could also try searching for 'private language argument'.) Satisfaction guaranteed.

Now, imagine that the thing that's in the box is what everyone calls 'happiness'. Do we all mean the same thing by this? Clearly not. Must there be any similarity in the content of the various boxes? Are there any *empty* boxes? I leave it to you to develop the analogy. It's an important topic for the remainder of this book.

Here is another riddle/statement from *Philosophical Investigations* (section 223) – one that's directly connected to Zhuang Zhou's story:

Even if the lion could talk, we still could not understand what he is saying.

Food for thought. In any case, it seemed to me that Ludwig Wittgenstein was eager to interpret Zhuang Zhou's anecdotes (which arouse in me a strong desire to write a short essay bearing the long title 'Zhuang Zhou meets Ludwig Wittgenstein for an almost rational conversation about an utterly insane perception.')

> I sit with a philosopher in the garden. He says over
> and over, 'I know it's a tree,' pointing to a tree near
> us. Suddenly a man passes by us and hears our
> conversation. And I tell him, 'This guy is not crazy.
> We are simply dealing with philosophy.'
> Ludwig Wittgenstein, *On Certainty*

Knowledge that doesn't know

If a centipede were to know it has so many legs, its legs would get tangled with each other and it wouldn't be able to take a single step. If a fish were to know that it's a fish, it would sink in an instant to the bottom of the sea. The centipede, the fish, the butterfly, the mountain, and the river know themselves through unconscious knowledge – knowledge that doesn't know. Only humans try to know themselves through conscious knowledge. Therefore, a person fails to be a person in the same simple way that a centipede is a centipede, a fish a fish, a butterfly a butterfly … and so on.

My interpretation follows. Warning! It will be quite lengthy!

I have no wish to transform into a centipede, and neither does the idea of being even a butterfly arouse any yearning in my heart. Nevertheless, this story by Zhuang Zhou prompts quite a few reflections about all the superfluous thoughts I've had. We are forced to pay a very high price for conscious knowledge. Very high. What's even worse, we often pay for this by unnecessarily and annoyingly *overthinking*.

I often try to understand myself in terms of 'conscious knowledge'. To be honest, I believe that inside my head there's a tiny man who talks a lot, analyzing and criticizing everything I think and do – in fact, I think it's the same for most people. This little chap doesn't know the meaning of a holiday – he's a diligent worker to the point of being extremely annoying. To my relief, and to the relief of most people, the articulations made by these minuscule people cannot be heard by others – although there are some unlucky people whose mumblings are indeed perfectly audible in public.

Had she known about Zhuang Zhou, I'm pretty sure my late grandmother would have loved him, not only because she had a fine sense of humour but also because one of her favourite expressions in Yiddish (which she liked to repeat over and over again) was '*der grester sauna fun a mentsh iz di eygene mkhshebus*' – 'a person has no greater enemy that their thoughts.' I would be very happy if I could have, now and then, periods of absolute rest and total freedom from my thoughts. A.A. Milne, of Winnie-the-Pooh fame, expresses this much better than I can: 'Did you ever stop to think, and forget to start again?'

* * *

The author of *Ecclesiastes* wrote, 'For with much wisdom comes much sorrow; the more knowledge, the more grief' (1:18). And the Kotzker Rebbe stated that the knowledge justifies the pain – a human being wants and even needs to know.

Is awareness a type of disease? Russian novelist Fyodor Dostoevsky (1821–1881) amused himself with this idea now and again. Indeed, is a horse or a monkey happier than a human being? How did our emergence as conscious beings even come about? After all, if we believe that our building-blocks – atoms and molecules – are devoid of consciousness, where does our consciousness come from?

How was it created? There's a stream in philosophy called panpsychism, which presumes that everything in our world – from the smallest elementary particles upward, including the planet itself – has a soul. The concept of panpsychism was already known by the earliest philosophers – that is, in the time of Thales of Miletus (c.620–c.546 BCE). It was mentioned by 17th-century German mathematician and philosopher Gottfried Wilhelm Leibniz (1646–1716) and noted by British mathematician and philosopher Alfred North Whitehead (1861–1947). The great mathematician-physicist-statistician Freeman John Dyson, who left this world as recently as February 2020, also held the view that atoms have some form of consciousness (even though this is, of course, completely different from human consciousness), and that the entire cosmos also has consciousness (ditto). Dyson's view was that while we might be trying, perhaps even with some success, to explore the consciousness of elementary particles, we are unlikely to fathom the consciousness of the cosmos in the foreseeable future. In the opinion of this notable scientist, we can, if we like, call this cosmic consciousness 'God'.

A butterfly is at least as mysterious as a superstring.
Freeman Dyson, *Infinite in All Directions*, 1988[2]

According to legend, the ancient Greek aphorism *ΓΝΩΘΙ ΣEAYTON* (*gnothi seauton*), meaning 'Know thyself', was inscribed in the forecourt of the Temple of Apollo at Delphi. There are several interpretations of this maxim. One is to know your place in the world and not to overestimate your importance. This interpretation seems quite logical when one considers that another maxim inscribed on the temple wall read, 'Nothing to excess.' However, I prefer a different reading. My favourite interpretation was formulated by Socrates and has become one of the most popular quotes on the English-language web: 'The unexamined life is not worth living.'

Socrates was aware of two conflicting desires – for knowledge ('conscious knowledge') and for ignorance. It was his belief that the quest for knowledge was the ultimate good, whereas wanting to remain ignorant was absolute evil. For Socrates it was inappropriate to live an unexamined life: better to 'Know thyself!' He called on the youth of Athens to question δόξα (*doxa,* or prevailing public opinion): 'Do not,' he entreated, 'believe in anything without examining it closely!'

Clearly, not everyone has agreed with Socrates, and other views abound. For example, 16th-century French philosopher Michel de Montaigne (1553–1592) believed that a significant part of humankind's misery stems from our tendency to overthink all sorts of things in a variety of ways, including some rather strange ones. In his opinion, happiness does not require high intelligence and repeated self-examination. It requires wisdom – not knowledge, note, but wisdom! – and life experience. He recommended spending less time on examining and analyzing our lives. Instead we should devote most of our time to achieving the best life possible. We should stop worrying about what others think of us, accept ourselves as we are, do our best to accept other people as *they* are (even those who are culturally different from us and do not think or behave like us), and most importantly strive to become wise. Michel de Montaigne believed with all his heart that a wise man has two separate traits: a good heart and a good mood.

A joyful heart makes a cheerful face; a sad heart
makes a despondent mood.
Proverbs, 15:13

Like French philosopher Montaigne (and in contrast to our
famous Greek philosopher Socrates), German poet Johann
Wolfgang von Goethe (1749–1832) did not consider in-
depth self-analysis to be such an amazing concept. *Faust*'s
author stated, 'I do not know myself, and God forbid that I
should. Because then I would want to escape from myself.
But where would I escape to? I carry myself everywhere.'

Solaris, a novel by Stanisław Lem (1921–2006), one of
the greatest science fiction writers, perfectly illustrates the
danger of a person encountering themselves. The heroes
of this book are forced to confront aspects of their pasts
they had buried and locked away deep within their minds
– things they really had no intention of exposing. Their
encounters with these experiences end up being traumatic,
to the point where some lose their sanity and some even
commit suicide.

There's a story in Greek mythology that parallels this
idea. One day an extremely arrogant and exceedingly
handsome young man is walking along a trail in a forest. This
is Narcissus, son of the nymph Liriope, who mated with a
river god. Liriope asks Tiresias the seer if her son will live
a long life, and the prophet responds, 'Your son will live a
long life only if he does not end up "knowing himself".' We
witness here a reversal of the time-honoured Greek ideal.

On the other hand, it is written in the *Bhagavad Gita,*
the ancient Hindu scripture, that anyone who reaches true,
deep self-knowledge will never know suffering.

And what do *I* think? In my opinion, the best way to live is Aristotle's middle way. I'll deal further with this idea from the great Greek philosopher in a chapter devoted entirely to it (pages 143–87). At the moment, I'll just note that we need to try to find the difficult balance between, on the one hand, over-examination and over-analysis of every little thing; and, on the other, completely ignoring any impetus to think and know – which is, after all, a key part of the greatness of humankind.

The time has come to allow Friedrich Nietzsche (1844–1900) his say. In note 48 in his book *The Dawn of Day* (1881), Nietzsche wrote that the directive 'Know thyself' refers to scientific exploration: 'Only when we shall have acquired a knowledge of all things will we be able to know ourselves.' According to Nietzsche, knowing the world and knowing oneself are one and the same. Nietzsche's attempt to fulfil the age-old commandment 'Know thyself'' was fanatical, uncompromising, and uninhibited.

Let us return to Zhuang Zhou. Suppose a person does want to know themselves in the sense of 'conscious knowledge'. On what should they concentrate their minds? On their feelings? On their thoughts? On their actions?

The brilliantly insightful Jane Austen, in her novel *Sense and Sensibility*, wrote, 'It isn't what we say or think that defines us, but what we do.' Many good people agree with her. Clearly it's hard for a person to know or understand themselves – because a human being is a rather complex creature. Therefore, if we're so eager to know something about ourselves, perhaps we should focus on our deeds rather than on our thoughts or emotions, because the latter are endlessly confused and we cannot fully understand them.

Once, at the end of one of my lectures, an ultra-Orthodox fellow approached me. (The ultra-Orthodox don't commonly attend my lectures, but the topic of this one was Ecclesiastes.) He told me that Rabbi Yehuda HeHasid (Judah ben Samuel of Regensburg) (1150–1217) taught that if a person wants to know who they really are, they should ask their friends. Why? A person's own opinion of themselves will not be very accurate, because people judge themselves based on their thoughts; whereas their friends will judge them solely by their deeds, which are the true reality.

What did I answer? I told him I think there's a problem with Rabbi Yehuda HeHassid's opinion, because friends can only know some (sometimes very few) of my deeds, while I myself know everything I've done, and these deeds lead me to do quite a lot of thinking.

We kept talking and the guy told me that he liked the idea that it's easier to do good deeds than to think good thoughts. He even added that the Baal Shem Tov (1698–1760), regarded as the founder of Hassidic Judaism, had an indicator to know whether or not someone is a false Messiah. If the person claims he knows how to stop someone from thinking sinful thoughts, then he *is* a false Messiah: sinful thoughts leave us only out of mercy.

(Actually, based on this criterion proposed by the Baal Shem Tov, all those motivators who say they can advise us how to rid ourselves of harmful thoughts and replace them with positive thinking and gratitude for our blessings – a topic I deal with below – are false messiahs.)

It's clear that all these reflections give only a basic approach to knowing oneself, but I hope this brief discussion has opened a gateway that can lead to some interesting questions.

At this point I have some recommended viewing for you. Swedish director Ruben Östlund dedicated two fascinating films, *Force Majeure* (2014) and *The Square* (2017), to examining the connection between a person's thoughts and their actions and between how they see themselves and how they are seen by others.

> Réné Descartes: *I think, therefore I am.*
> Zhuang Zhou: *When a person ceases to think, he can begin to live.*

(No one ever actually heard Zhuang Zhou make this statement, but then he probably didn't actually pen most of the stories attributed to him. Even so, I have no problem spending quality time in his company.)

Let's move on to another story from the ancient Chinese philosopher. We'll then return to Socrates.

Spring, summer, autumn, and winter

Zhuang Zhou's wife passed away. When his friend Hui Tzu came to express his condolences, he was surprised to see Zhuang Zhou drumming on a tin and singing loudly.

'You both lived for many years under one roof, you grew old together, you raised children. Perhaps you are not required to cry at the time of her death ... but to sing!' Thus Hui Tzu scolded his friend, the new widower. 'Aren't you exaggerating your contentment?'

'You don't understand anything,' answered Zhuang Zhou. 'When my wife died I felt such a stab to my heart that I wanted to scream and cry.

'But then I looked back at the time before my wife was born. Not just before she was born, but even before she was in the womb ... before she even had a soul. At some point, a combination of wonder and mystery brought about a miraculous change that led to the creation of my wife's soul. Another change, and her embryo was created. And then she was born. And now, another change. She has died.

'There's a time for everything. Everything passes. Just like the change of seasons. Spring, summer, autumn, winter. Now she's lying peacefully in a large chamber. If I were to scream and cry, it would prove that I don't understand anything about destiny; that I don't understand the necessity of change.

'So I stopped myself. How do I know that my love of life was not an illusion? No one knows when a change is for the better and when it's for the worse. Perhaps death is preferable to life? Perhaps someone who despises death is like a young man who has left his home and forgotten the way back?'

Everyone has heard the adage that it's impossible to step into the same river twice: you are no longer the same you, and the water isn't the same water, the second time around. Everything is constantly in flux. No matter how hard you try to hold on to something, it will change before your eyes or be taken from you. This maxim was devised by the Greek pre-Socratic philosopher Heraclitus, who was also known as 'the Obscure' and 'the Riddler'. It is – at one and the same time – both the most trivial and most profound of concepts. It is also, apparently, the most complicated and most important message that life is trying to teach us.

Everything vanishes from between our fingers. Moments of joy, of creativity, of wonder, and of peace – all slip through.

But so too do moments of physical pain, of heartbreak, and days of mourning for the loss of a loved one or for a vanished dream. These things all start to fade away at that exact same moment we become aware of them.

A girl's smile, the world's empires and kingdoms, butterfly wings and autumn leaves, sunrises and sunsets, ideas we adored and people we despised, our first kiss and our last embrace, all of history, all of the cosmos, all our worries and hopes – everything will pass and disappear one day. Nothing lasts forever.

When my youngest daughter was about three years old, she would sometimes wake me up around three o'clock in the morning drumming on my head and declaring, 'Daddy, I'm bored!' Those days are gone. Today my daughter is a charming woman in her late 20s with two daughters – my granddaughters. They too get bored in the wee hours of the night. But that three-year-old girl, for whom I pine and who thought the night was too long and too boring, now exists only in my photo album and in the image bank of my memories.

So what conclusion can we draw from the fact that everything passes? How should we apply this understanding to our lives? Just as Zhuang Zhou teaches us, this insight is cause for neither joy nor despair. It's a reason to widen and deepen our attentiveness to our present moments and approach them with full awareness. The important lesson here is that the present moment is all we have.

CHAPTER 4

The Arithmetic
of Life and Death

Up to this point we have met Zhuang Zhou, my favourite Chinese philosopher. Let me introduce to you another Chinese philosopher whom I also admire greatly, although almost nothing remains of his writings. His name is Yang Zhu. He probably lived in the 4th century BCE.

Fung Yu-Lan, the 20th-century Chinese philosopher and historian (a student of the American philosopher John Dewey), wrote in his book *A Short History of Chinese Philosophy* (1948) that Yang Zhu was a loner. He distanced himself from others so he could observe the world from a more correct perspective: it's hard to examine a picture when you're part of it. Fung Yu-Lan display s a great deal of respect for Yang Zhu in his book, reflecting the fact that ancient Daoist philosophy can be quite clearly divided (with some overlap) into three stages:

1) Yang Zhu and what we know from various sources
2) Laozi and the book *Tao Te Ching* (*The Book of the Way and of Virtue*)
3) Zhuang Zhuo, the man and the book

Fung Yu-Lan notes that in ancient Daoist philosophy there is not always a clear distinction between the man and his works. The way I see it, Yang Zhu was the founder of the 'amusing, endearing school of egoism'. This is an institution I invented this very moment. To justify my creation, here is what others considered Yang Zhu's epithet to be, a statement that summarizes his reputation:

> I would not consent to plucking even a single hair from my head to benefit humanity.

How nice! Isn't that amusing and endearing? It's clear to me – and there is, of course, a chance that I'm wrong – that this sentence was not uttered in all seriousness. After all, the philosopher did not say he refused to amputate an arm or a leg or donate a kidney to save humanity. He said he refused to pluck a hair.

Seriously? My thinking is that he was prophetically mocking all the bleeding-heart do-gooders of today who brag of their holier-than-thou morals and, of course, all his fellow philosophers who unceasingly, in their cloying way, advise everyone to love everything equally and live a moral and exemplary life – that is to say, all preachers of morality. Preaching morality is immoral, unnecessary, and tiresome.

Michel de Montaigne despised any pretensions that a person might have to transcend their own nature. Unlike many philosophers, he did not see such attempts as showing the glory of the human spirit. Rather, he saw them as a decline into beastliness. He believed that anyone who tried to deny their humanity was simply insane: 'Instead of changing their image and becoming angels, they look like beasts. They end up crashing instead of taking flight.' How I love this line – what a valiant, accurate sentiment!

Yang Zhu went on to say that, while he would not lift a finger, still less labour for anyone, he would also never hurt anyone, because just one hair on a person's head is priceless. Live and let live! Yang Zhu's premise was that if no one ever harms another in the slightest, then no one will ever have to sacrifice anything for anyone else or preach morality to others. *Focus on your own affairs: do not give anything to anyone and do not take anything from anyone.* This, in the Chinese sage's opinion, will be your great contribution to the well-being of humanity. It will even assure us all long lives.

You're welcome, of course, to agree or disagree with this view.

In my mind, I imagine Tolstoy applauding Yang Zhu's ideas (perhaps with only one hand). Tolstoy's short story 'Clouds' (taken from the long-forbidden book *The Circle of Reading*) suggests that when torrential rains are pouring into one's house, instead of trying to direct the movement of clouds, one should simply plug up the hole in the ceiling. At the end of the story, Tolstoy urges that instead of preaching morality to others, you should just be a good person: instead of trying to fix the world, fix yourself. This certainly corresponds with the ancient Daoist philosopher's beliefs. Lev Nikolayevich (that is to say, Tolstoy – I'm on first name terms with him) concludes his story by insisting that if there were enough good people, there'd be no more need for sermons preaching morality.

From Lev Tolstoy we now go to Fyodor Dostoevsky.

Consider the protagonist of *Notes from the Underground*. Like Yang Zhu, he preferred to drink his tea in peace while the world went to hell, considering this better than the reverse – that is, having worldwide happiness at the expense of his own personal suffering. However, with Dostoevsky's underground man, there doesn't seem to be any humour at play.

Yang Zhu believed that, for the most part, life was futile and filled with misery. There is no God and no life after death. When life ends, it's completely and utterly over. There are no rewards for the righteous and no penalties for the wicked. Everything is just a matter of chance, and pleasure is the only thing worth living for. There is no one less selfish than he – he's simply the only one who admits it.

In the ancient Daoist book *Leizi* there's a chapter devoted to Yang Zhu that describes his thoughts on the arithmetic of life and death: even someone blessed with a long life will not live more than a hundred years; and, in truth, only about one in a thousand will reach this prodigious age.

Let us suppose we have such a person before us. Infancy, childhood, and old age will consume much of their time. Nights asleep will account for about a quarter of their life. Periods of boredom – a kind of death within life – will also take their share. Pain and disease, sorrow and suffering, mourning deceased loved ones, worry and fear will account for almost half of what's left. Even then, even in the 10 (perhaps a few more) years that remain, there will not be many moments when this centenarian will be able to attest to being completely happy and at ease, and worry-free.

If all this is true, what is life for? Why does a person need this gift – accidental and superfluous – called 'life'?

I'll tell you why. For beauty, for music, and for love. That's all. However, it isn't always possible to satisfy one's yearning for beauty, and it isn't always possible to enjoy music and love.

As if actual problems were not enough for us, we also burden ourselves with *imaginary* problems. We seek praise while alive and glory after death. We cannot be free spirits for even a moment. Thus, we lose the limited possibilities we have left to experience true happiness.

However, beauty, music, and love are the keys that allow us to escape the many-walled jail in which we have incarcerated ourselves. How could I not adore someone who understands that these blessings are what gives life its meaning and taste?

Losses in life and profits in death

Let us turn now to Anton Chekhov (1860–1904). Here is an excerpt (my translation) from his marvellous story 'Rothschild's Violin' in which the protagonist, Yakov Ivanov, nicknamed 'Bronze', is comparing life to death.

The next morning Yakov had a hard time waking but finally got up and went to the hospital. An assistant doctor instructed Yakov to put cold compresses on his head and also handed him all sorts of lotions. From the doctor's expression and tone of voice, Yakov understood that the situation was bad – very bad – and that no lotion could save him now. On his way home, Yakov began to realize that, in fact, death might have its benefits – it allowed a person to experience great economy. He thought a bit and realized that he would no longer have to eat and drink or pay taxes. He then realized that he would never again offend people – that would all be done with. Then he realized that once a man has been lying in his grave for centuries, or thousands of years, or hundreds of thousands of years, the sum of these blessings would indeed be immense. Therefore, life may be considered a deficit, whereas death may be considered a benefit. His reasoning was without fault, but it was also depressing and disturbing. Who had arranged the world in such an odd way that a person's life, given to them only once, would pass by without yielding any overall gain?

Yakov did not feel that sorry that he was going to die. But when he arrived home and saw his violin, a strange ache crept into his heart and his soul became distraught. He suddenly realized that he would not be able to take his violin with him to the grave. His violin would become an orphan: its fate would be that of the birch grove or the pine forest. Every single thing in the world would be lost forever and ever, and remain forever lost.

Yakov sat on the doorstep of his hut and cradled his violin to his breast. He thought of his life, and its losses, its deficits, and began to play, the music flowing unconsciously from the depths of his heart, as tears streamed down his cheeks. The more he thought, the more sadly he played his violin.

If you choose to argue that Yakov came to this sad end because he was a rude, stingy, grumpy man, here's another lesson about the arithmetic of life, this time from one of the greatest poets of all time, Johann Wolfgang von Goethe (1749–1832), creator of *Faust*. This is a 'lesson' I found in one of the oldest books in my library, *Conversations with Goethe* (originally published by Walter Dunne, 1901), by poet Johann Peter Eckermann, who was Goethe's friend and his companion in his final years:

I have not a single remorse about how I spent my life, but in order not to lie to myself, I will have to admit that there was almost nothing in my life other than affliction and suffering. Out of the seventy-five years of my existence, it seems to me that I have enjoyed no more than four weeks of true joy. Life, to me, is like a huge stone rolling down a mountain slope and one must, without pause, make a tremendous effort to keep it from reaching the bottom.

So wrote one of the greatest men who ever lived, and one who, perhaps surprisingly, was even considered particularly optimistic.

* * *

And now for a little more time travel – back to antiquity. Leave your cell phones behind please.

Abd al-Rahman III (891–961) was the first caliph of the Umayyad dynasty in Córdova. During his reign, from 912 to his death, Muslim Spain reached its peak of glory, flourishing both culturally and economically.

Here's what al-Rahman III wrote in his twilight days:

I have ruled for almost 50 years. I have experienced glorious victories on the battlefield and presided over long interludes of peace and prosperity. I am adored by my subjects, feared by my enemies and greatly respected by all my allies. Wealth, power and pleasures have perpetually accompanied me and, typically, any and all of life's comforts were available always, just waiting for my demand. And lo, I have diligently counted the days of pure, unadulterated joy that have fallen my way and they amount to merely 14.

Oh people of my time! Do not place your trust in this world!

Was Goethe familiar with this declaration by the Emir who ruled Córdoba?

Let's observe what was happening in Jerusalem and Athens. In Judaism, a huge debate took place in antiquity between Beit Hillel and Beit Shammai[3] as to whether it's better for an individual to be born or never to exist. This debate of the sages lasted for two and a half years. Beit Hillel contended that it's better for a person to be born; Beit Shammai asserted that 'one who has never been created will be better off.' Surprisingly, Best Hillel ended up agreeing with Beit Shammai's position.

Nevertheless, in the Talmud[4] (Tractate Eruvin 13, toward the end of page B) we are enlightened to learn that the Prince of Denmark's question, 'To be to not or be', is irrelevant for everyone. We are already here and must scrutinize our actions.

'Best is not to be born at all; next best is to be born and die soon after.' So are Oedipus's words rendered by Sophocles, the great tragedian of ancient Greece, in his final play, *Oedipus at Colonus*.

The renowned Slovenian philosopher Slavoj Žižek (b. 1949) claims to agree with Sophocles that the greatest good fortune is not to have been born, but – as the joke goes – very few people attain this distinction.

Oedipus the King tells the story of Oedipus' fall from the heights of success, power, and wealth to the seven circles of hell. *Oedipus at Colonus* describes his ascent from the depths of suffering to a state of god-given grace. And yet Oedipus's last words in the play do not reconcile anything: 'Not to be born at all is best, far best that can befall.'

We'll end our discussion of life and death at this point. No doubt the debate will never end, even if some of its proponents will.

From ancient Greece to ancient China

Yang Zhu thought – and it seems Leo Tolstoy thought similarly – that one sign of wisdom is to neither be afraid of death nor desire it. This is the right balance. The Chinese philosopher believed that death is the absolute end. When someone is dead, it really doesn't matter to them if they are buried in a luxurious coffin in their most beautiful clothes or if their body is thrown into the Yellow River. They are dead. They will have no concern about whether their funeral is attended by hundreds of mourners or there is not even any funeral at all, only vultures and hyenas making acquaintance with their lifeless body. They are dead. The dead will not smell any flowers laid on their grave, nor hear the music of a sombre procession. Neither will it matter to them if anyone ever visits their grave. In Yang Zhu's opinion, only one thing is important, and that's whether you had a 'life before death'. That is to say, one should not 'die' before one's death. This wise Chinese sage knew that the fact that someone dies doesn't necessarily prove that they ever properly 'lived'.

Fung Yu-Lan wrote that Yang Zhu greatly influenced Zhuang Zhou (I trust you've been missing him). An example of this influence can be seen in Zhuang Zhou's story 'The Tree in the Mountains', about a tree that has attained an extreme age because it's always been devoid of any usefulness. The tree is enormous and has many ugly scars. Its branches are bare and look like twisted fingers. The tree gives no shade, it's too rotten and mouldy to provide wood for a campfire in winter, and it can't even supply any resin to heal wounds or relieve pain. In short, the tree could not be any more useless. Therefore, whenever a woodchopper came near, he'd turn away and choose another tree.

Zhuang Zhou points out that most people understand the usefulness of useful things, but only the very wise understand the usefulness of being useless. I like this phrase. It seems to me Yang Zhu would have loved Zhuang Zhou's outlook on the usefulness of being useless.

I sometimes imagine my two favourite Chinese philosophers relaxing together in the mountains, far from all the hustle and bustle, surrounded by birdsong, the rustle of leaves, and the gurgling of a brook. Suddenly they spy a tiny fish in the water and try to decide whether the fish is happy or not. What do you think?

CHAPTER 5

The Sound of Silence

I don't like noise. I imagine many people don't like noise, but I really, *really* don't like it.

In the poem the *Epic of Gilgamesh*, from ancient Mesopotamia, there's a description of a tremendous flood quite similar to the one in the book of Genesis. Both versions feature a divine decision to bring a deluge upon the world and eliminate every creature living on the face of the Earth except for one special person who is instructed to build an ark in order to be saved – he will also manage to save selected representatives of every species.

In the Biblical story, Noah was the special man whom God favoured. He was known as 'a righteous man who was humble in his ways'. His counterpart in the *Epic of Gilgamesh* was Utnapishtim. It comes as no surprise that Noah's flood received most of the publicity – Utnapishtim isn't a very catchy name. Not catchy perhaps, but meaningful. Utnapishtim means 'quest for life'.

Despite the similarities between the Mesopotamian myth and the Biblical tale, the reasons given for the flood are completely different. In the *Epic of Gilgamesh* the pair of gods, Elli and Ea, decide to bring a flood upon the Earth not because the inhabitants of the land are corrupt or immoral. The reason is less high-minded: the excessive population is making a colossal noise and disturbing the gods' rest! A flood as punishment for noise – amazing!

By the way, the gods bestow upon Utnapishtim the gift of eternal life – something not gifted to Noah. Perhaps this is his reward for employing artists in his ark to preserve his country's cultural assets. As you might guess, based on the motive for the flood, the Mesopotamian story ends with severe restrictions being imposed on human procreation and emergency regulations for preserving tranquillity. In contrast, the Biblical story ends with a directive from God to Noah and his family to 'be fruitful and multiply and fill the Earth'.

As one who is unusually sensitive to noise, I must admit my heart goes out to Enlil and Ea. There's so much noise in our lives: that deafening trance 'music' at weddings that penetrates your ribs and jolts your heart; those raucous conversations where everyone speaks (or should I say, shouts?) simultaneously, each fighting to make their voice heard till the decibel level goes off the scale; a baby in a restaurant bawling, spoiling what was supposed to be a romantic evening; the constant clamour of horns by drivers determined to deafen everyone within earshot; the cacophonous howls of cats in heat at night, robbing us all of sleep; the gardener who comes to work bright and early and immediately turns on that thunderous leaf blower:

jet planes roaring overhead … I could go on. Where's the Geneva Convention when you need it?

The unbearable silence of Chenonceau

Many, many years ago my wife Daniela and I toured the Loire Valley in France. We stayed in a small town called Chenonceau. Before the trip – this was our first trip to France – I decided to impress my partner and spent a few months learning French on the sly with the help of a French-Hebrew dictionary. When we arrived in the country, I discovered I was an expert in a new language I'll call 'Frebrew' (or perhaps 'Hebrench'). Unfortunately, the French are not fluent in Frebrew. For some reason, they prefer actual French. So no one understood a word of what I said.

Chenonceau's single claim to fame is the magnificent, awe-inspiring Château de Chenonceau – a castle. The travel guide (these were the days before TripAdvisor) pointed out that when the castle closes, the whole town more or less closes too, and then there's no special reason to stay. So we decided we *would* stay.

After visiting the castle, we discovered a little *auberge* (inn) that was quite nice. In conversation with the manager I learned that my wife and I were the only guests that night. As it happened, the woman who told us this was not only the concierge, she was also the establishment's owner. She handed us an enormous key attached to a burgundy-coloured pompom, as well as a tiny key. We discovered that, contrary to our expectations, the tiny key opened the enormous outer gate, while the huge key unlocked our room. This kind woman promised she'd be there to greet us in the morning.

Before we set off to explore this tourist-free town, she recommended a restaurant not a 15-minute-walk away, particularly endorsing the house special, namely butter-fried mushrooms. We ordered this dish and to this day I can recall their exquisite taste, texture, and fragrance. Marcel Proust might have had his madeleines, but we – my wife and I – have buttered mushrooms *à la Chenonceau* to release our memories of lost time.

In the evening we strolled around and witnessed how, one by one, all the residents disappeared into their homes. The street lights in the alleys had no one to shine on. The town was falling asleep. It was quiet. Too quiet! Later, even the street lights retired for the night. We took the hint and made our way back to the inn.

My wife fell asleep. I stood at the window, gazing at the field in front of the hotel. This field stretched far into the distance, but it was so dark I had to strain my eyes to see it. The silence was so absolute I might have thought I could hear the grass growing.

I went to bed. I pulled the sheet over me and, due to the perfect silence, this action seemed almost clamorous to my ears. I tried to fall asleep. I failed. *Absolute silence is the loudest sound.* I tried to remember if this was some Koan argument or merely a random thought hibernating in my brain. I began to hear my own heartbeat. At first the beats were almost imperceptible, but as time passed they quickly metamorphosed to thrumming and then to pounding.

The silence had become an unbearably oppressive tumult. My thoughts reverberated through my head with the power of machines in a textile factory. I realized there was no chance of falling asleep.

Judaism teaches that good things can cease to be good if they are not meted out in due portion. It's clear that Aristotle and the Buddha share this perspective too.

Chenonceau's quiet was too much for me. I longed for even a single cricket on duty. Perhaps a light breeze rustling through leaves? A purring cat? A tin can being kicked along the road? But there was nothing … I was holidaying in a black hole of silence.

It was only at dawn, when the birds started chirping, that I finally fell asleep.

Daniela woke me up for breakfast. I'm crazy for the French-style breakfast – a large bowl of fine coffee, a croissant with unsalted butter and homemade strawberry jam, a glass of fresh-squeezed orange juice. What more does a person need in the morning?

We thanked the owner of the pleasant inn and headed out toward the Château Royal d'Amboise, on the banks of the Loire river about 20 kilometres from Chenonceau castle. In 1516, King François I of France hired Leonardo da Vinci to be the 'King's artist' and housed him in Clos Lucé, an estate about a kilometre from the Amboise palace and connected to it by an underground tunnel.

On 2 May 1519 Leonardo da Vinci was laid to his final rest. It's said that in the last 10 years of his life, Leonardo did not part with his *Mona Lisa*: he took it everywhere he went. The world-famous painting was by his side even as he left this world of noise and bustle and entered the realm of cold, eternal silence.

CHAPTER 6

A Harvest of Regrets

One of the grandest books (literally) in my library is the English version of Giorgio Vasari's *The Lives of the Most Excellent Painters, Sculptors, and Architects*. Vasari (1511–1574) was a 16th-century painter and art historian (some contend he was the founding father of this discipline) and a friend of Michelangelo. One of his chapters is dedicated to Leonardo da Vinci (1452–1519).

Vasari extols the gentleman from Vinci: in his preface he declares that only rarely does a unique and blessed cosmic event happen that bestows such a heavenly clutch of superior talents directly onto one particular man. So great and many were Leonardo's virtues that no one can doubt they were granted him by God. Vasari wrote that not only was Leonardo endowed with a noble soul, a strong spirit, supreme courage, a handsome body, immense power, and infinite grace, but also he could effortlessly solve any problem he turned his attention to, leaving all commonplace human beings far behind.

Vasari also correctly guessed that Leonardo's fame would grow as the generations passed.

So much has been written about Leonardo that all I wish to convey here (prior to the final point I'm aiming to make) is a partial, albeit very well-known list of things he engaged in and excelled at: painting and sculpture, philosophy and geology, cartography and palaeontology, music and geometry (among other things, he came up with an ingenious proof for Pythagoras's theorem using only a simple illustration), anatomy and aviation, hydrodynamics and optics, civil engineering and military engineering, solar energy (he designed a solar tower), and the invention of a calculating machine. Some even credit Leonardo with devising prototypes for a submarine, a parachute, and a tank (he did actually design a kind of armoured war machine). I'll stop here. All this was generated by one single man whose longevity barely exceeded one half of the 120 years of life that is prayed for in Jewish tradition.

Why am I telling you all this? Well, it's to make an initial point about regret.

Take a note of these words which, according to Vasari, Leonardo di ser Piero da Vinci (to use his full name) uttered in his last moments in the arms of King François I, who was caressing him with the utmost love:

I regret that I have offended God and mankind because I did not accomplish enough and my work did not reach the quality it should have done.

Regrets of the dying

Leo Tolstoy's masterful novel *The Death of Ivan Ilyich* attempts, among other things, to build a sort of bridge between a person's inevitable death and the meaning of their life. The book is laden with profoundly important philosophical concepts. One thought-provoking line of reasoning is that, contrary to that well-worn saying, wisdom does not always come with the years. Sometimes it comes haltingly, if at all, right up to the end of a person's life. Sometimes it reveals itself in one blaze of understanding that accompanies the terrifying apparition of the Angel of Death.

In Tolstoy's view, before they die, every man and woman knows exactly how they should have lived their lives. The problem here is the timing. When life is already trickling out between one's fingers, what could be the point of belated self-knowledge?

There's no re-take for life, as there is for many kinds of exams. How unfair this is. Nor is there any kind of preparation. There are introductory classes for learning French and for anyone learning to swim or to draw. There are academic preparatory courses at most universities, and if a student happens to fail first time around, you can resit the exams. Computer games have different levels of difficulty and books for learning piano start off with easy compositions. Very often in love, our first heady romance functions as a starter course for the loving relationships that follow.

But life? We face our final exam and our senior prom without any preparation or study. Wouldn't it be more logical and fairer if we could live two or three times so we can practise, prepare, get better, and only then live life truly and properly?

That's never going to happen.

I would replace the expression 'Wisdom comes with years' with one that might not sound quite as uplifting but seems to me to be much more accurate: 'Regrets accumulate with the years.'

It's a rare person who doesn't feel any remorse when facing their last moments on this Earth. (Two of my friends who are senior psychiatrists tell me that only a psychopath does not feel remorse, neither during life and nor at its end.)

Quite a few people, just like Ivan Ilyich, discover that intense regrets besiege them from every direction. Why didn't I help that person? Why did I refuse to talk to my brother for so many years? (I can't even remember what we fought about.) Why wasn't I more generous? What will I do with my money now? Why didn't I spend more time with my family? Why did I waste so much time on jealousy and gossip? Why did I hurt so many people, including some I love?

Tolstoy suggested using our knowledge of inevitable death as a guide to living a life with fewer regrets. What did he mean by this? I'm not sure I perfectly understand what the great writer was getting at, but there was one recommendation he unequivocally expressed: whenever you meet anybody, the most important thing is to imagine this is the last time you'll see them. This way, you'll refrain from saying things that are harsh or callous, and you'll avoid unbecoming actions too.

In one of his YouTube videos, Benjamin Zander (b. 1939), conductor, pianist, cellist, and lecturer extraordinaire, tells about a woman he knew who, as a girl, was bundled with her little brother onto a train whose destination was Oś wię cim-Auschwitz. As soon as the door to the train closed, she noticed her brother hadn't put his shoes on properly. As a result, one shoe had fallen off on the way and his little foot was left bare. The young girl yelled at her little brother, scolding him multiple times. She survived Auschwitz but her brother did not. The thought that the last words her brother heard from her, her dear little brother whom she loved so much, were harsh and unpleasant haunted her grievously. Zander goes on to tell us she decided that, for the rest of her life, whenever she met anyone, she'd imagine this would be the last time she'd see that person. Her words would therefore be appropriately pleasant.

This is clearly a valuable strategy, but one that it's very difficult to adopt and turn into a habit.

Bronnie Ware is an Australian author and lecturer who gained worldwide fame for her 2019 book, *Top Five Regrets of the Dying*.[5] The book is based on her many years' experience as a palliative care home-hospice nurse, whose aim has been to improve quality of life for terminally ill patients and their families. Bronnie was there with at least half of her patients in the last weeks of their lives.

In her book she relates some of emotional times she shared with them. In support of Tolstoy's theory, she also notes that people tend to transform considerably when facing the end of life, and with some the transformation is astonishing. All her patients, she says, experienced the full range of familiar emotions described in the literature: denial, fear, anger, remorse, and then again denial, and again fear … Finally, they accept the verdict. Before their death, Bronnie tells us, each patient – each and every one of them – ended up finding their peace.

She would ask these people on the verge of death what they regretted in their lives or what they would have done differently. (Remember, according to Tolstoy, people facing their end are most definitely aware of where they did right and where they went wrong.) She discovered there were five sentiments that were repeated over and over again. These are the top five regrets of the dying.

Before you continue reading, stop for a moment and think. If this were the last day of your life, what is it you would especially regret? What would you like to have done but didn't? Have you thought about this?

Before I list the five regrets, I will draw out the suspense a little longer. In my book *The Wisdom of Solomon*[6] I wrote that it's better to navigate our lives so that in our last days we'll regret things we have done and not things we haven't done – because remorse for things not done is infinite. I believe there's truth in this statement.

My dear friend Tal Ben-Shahar, one of the great experts on happiness,[7] read my book and sent me a fascinating article on how we experience these two types of regrets.[8]

Here follows my brief summary of the article. Authors Thomas Gilovich and Victoria Husted Medvec distinguish between remorse of commission (action) and remorse of omission (inaction). It turns out that the remorse we feel over something we did is greater in the short term, but its intensity decreases sharply over time and often disappears altogether. However, remorse over not doing something (that we should have done) grows over time and stays with us in one form or another throughout life.

And here's the crux of their psychological explanation. The pain we endure as a result of errors of commission diminishes because we start to forget them, we rectify matters, or else our mind is very good at consoling ourselves and justifying our actions ('Yes, perhaps it's true that my husband was the Sicilian mafia's head assassin, but he spoke such beautiful Italian. He also taught me how to throw knives at a target and to shoot two guns at once.') However, regrets over things we avoided or omitted do not provide the brain with any raw material to give us encouragement or comfort. Our suffering only increases as we repeatedly ask ourselves, what would have happened if … ?[9]

I once attended a conference on happiness where one of the lecturers reported that women in their 30s who said they had not wanted children were happier than those who'd had them. On the whole, the anti-natalism movement is quite popular in northwestern Europe. But as usual we must be careful in establishing our positions, because it turns out that women in their 50s sometimes feel deep remorse for having decided not to have a child, and this ends up being a millstone on their hearts, as an error of omission – the regret of inaction.

But finally – drumroll, please! – here they are: the top five regrets of the dying, in reverse order of … popularity.

5) I wish that I'd let myself be happier
4) I wish I'd stayed in touch with my friends
3) I wish I'd had the courage to express my feelings
2) I wish I hadn't worked so hard
1) I wish I'd had the courage to live a life true to myself, and not the life others expected of me

Let's review these one by one. I'll give you my comments and you can add your own (feel free to write in this book).

5) I wish I'd let myself be happier

Bronnie Ware says that this regret is surprisingly common. In her opinion, many people don't realize that joy is a matter of choice until the end of their lives.

I'm not sure I agree with her. It seems to me that, to a great extent, one's ability to be happy is determined by the cards our genes have dealt us, and all we can do is play the hand we've been given as best as we can. Mark Manson, in his book with the wonderful title *The Subtle Art of Not Giving a F*ck* (2016), explains that the desire to be constantly happy and emotionally buoyant can actually lead to very negative experiences. For many, getting up every morning with a smile is impossible – and also unnecessary. There's no one who isn't sad at times. Emotions that are unjustly called negative – take sadness, for example – can greatly enrich the rainbow of the human psyche. Eeyore the donkey, the insightful philosopher of the Hundred Acre Wood, does not wake up with a smile, does not jump in the air with joy, and is not at all sure that there won't be an earthquake tomorrow. Nevertheless, he lives a good and satisfying life in the gloomiest corner of the forest – which, by the way, he loves very much.

I do agree with Bronnie that introducing a little lightness into one's life – learning not to fear change, not getting stuck in a too-comfortably-familiar routine and, most importantly, not being afraid to engage in a little foolishness once in a while – is a great idea. A wise man once said: 'Avoiding foolishness in life is the greatest foolishness of all.' People who believe themselves to be so dignified and important that they take pains to avoid any type of lightheartedness are really, *really*, not as clever as they may think they are. The therapeutic power of healthy laughter has been explored very seriously (no pun intended) in medical schools.

Bronnie notes that precisely when a person is on their deathbed – when they aren't concerned about what others think, and when they don't care one way or another whether what they are doing is right or wrong – precisely then, they experience a miraculous release from carrying all the weight of the world, and they smile.

4) I wish I'd stayed in touch with my friends

This is a regret that's already brooding in my heart. I have not kept in touch with my friends. What a mistake!

There's not much I can do about it either. Philosopher and writer Alain de Botton (b. 1969) is correct when he says that finding a true friend in the later decades of one's life is so rare that it should be worthy of a headline in the *New York Times*. When he says 'friend', he doesn't mean a buddy to play bridge with – such people are not that hard to find. He means a true friend.

Most researchers about happiness insist that the true friends a person accumulates over the course of a lifetime have a very important role in making life better. The Bible states that 'two are better off than the one' (Ecclesiastes, 4:8) and everyone has learned at some point that 'it is not good for a human to be alone' (Genesis, 2:18).

However, the most common advice given in all those simplistic guides to happiness – to try and develop an extensive network of friends – is problematic at best and hopeless at worst. Perhaps it's sage advice, but actual execution ranges between difficult and virtually impossible. Even Forrest Gump knew this. Remember? 'Bubba was my best good friend. And even I know that ain't something you can find just around the corner.'

Bronnie Ware writes that people are often unaware of the immense benefit of the true friendship of old friends, people to whom you can express yourself and who really listen to you.

When someone asks me how I am and I answer 'Okay', there's at least one lie here. The questioner is usually not really interested in how I am, and how I am is not always okay. One day I was feeling slightly roguish, and I decided to answer the 'How are you?' question with abysmal seriousness. I started by divulging the results of some recent blood tests. I have yet to decide on the degree to which my answer was surprising or embarrassing – and to whom it was more embarrassing: me or the inquirer. For my part, I'm inclined to ask only people whose well-being truly interests me 'How are you?' Mostly I just greet people with, 'Hope you're having a good day.'

Have there been other intellectuals on Eeyore the donkey's level who have attempted to define friendship? In recent years, many articles have been published on the subject.[10] Preeminent philosophers who have dealt this notion include Plato, Aristotle, and Michel de Montaigne.

Aristotle defined true friendship as 'a single soul dwelling in two bodies'. He classified friendships into three types: for pleasure, for benefit, and true friendships. One test of a true friend is the 'in-time-of-trouble' test: for Aristotle, a true friend is someone who sticks by your side when everyone else is abandoning you. I certainly don't underestimate the value of 'a friend in need', but I would add the equally marvellous facility of rejoicing in a friend's joy. In fact, Nietzsche suggested that the ability to share joy was an attribute even loftier than being willing to help in times of need, and I heartily (though cautiously) corroborate his opinion.

American writer Gore Vidal also stated that the ability to share joy is not one that's self-evident. He came up with a disturbing if rather amusing quip: 'Every time a friend succeeds, I die a little.'

But back to Aristotle. This legendary Greek invested a lot of thought in all that concerns friendship. I present to you two insights from his *Nicomachean Ethics*:

Without friends, no one would choose to live, even if they had all other goods.

Those who wish for good things for their friend's sake are friends most of all.

The movie *Good Will Hunting* (starring Ben Affleck and Matt Damon) offers a lovely illustration of Aristotle's second insight.

Let us return now to the Australian nurse. She points out that many people become so distracted by their busy, stressful lives that they fail to notice when precious friendships are slipping away. She adds that everyone, in her experience, longed for their friends when they found themselves close to death.

I believe the magic of true friendship is the blessed comfort we get from being able to lay aside the pretences that have to be maintained in social gatherings. Chinese philosopher and translator Lin Yutang (1895–1976), whose English translations of classical Chinese literature (yes! he also translated Zhuang Zhou) became bestsellers in the West, made an interesting point in a lecture he gave in China in 1933. He said there's no such thing as true freedom of speech because no one would dare tell their neighbours or acquaintances what they really think of them. No lecturer standing on a podium really says everything they think: if they announced that they were going to share with their listeners all that was in their heart, many in the audience would probably get extremely concerned. We cannot manage in real life, says Lin Yutang, without a certain modicum of white lies. In fact, Frederick Nietzsche, many years earlier, wrote that lying is a condition of human existence; and before him fellow German Immanuel Kant (1724–1804), one of the most important philosophers of all time, expressed the view that one of life's great blessings is that no one knows what someone else is thinking.

I totally agree with both of them. I maintain that it's only with a true friend that one can appear in one's own version of the truth and say what one really wants to say without censoring one's thoughts. *Just as a pinnacle of erotic love is two naked bodies, a pinnacle of true friendship is two naked souls.*

Muhammad Ali (1942–2016), the world heavyweight boxing champion, said that we are not taught how to be a friend at school, nor at university, but whoever has not learned what friendship is has learned nothing in their life.

My good friend the late Assaf Adar, who passed away at the age of 47, once asked me a question and, to this day, I have no good answer: 'If you were someone else, would you want yourself as a friend?'

3) I wish I'd had the courage to express my feelings

A few years ago I watched an Israeli TV programme dedicated to Uri Avnery (1923–2018), an Israeli writer and politician. At one point he shared with the interviewer –boldly, I might add – his great remorse: he never told his wife, whom he loved very much and to whom he'd been married for ages, that he loved her. The moment she passed away, he wanted to say the words, but by then it was too late.

This is heart-rending. If you love someone – tell them; if you feel grateful – say it; if you want to hug a child or grandchild – do it. Love is the emotion that surpasses all others.

But what about expressing less exalted emotions? Bronnie Ware writes that many who suppressed free expression of their feelings ultimately developed diseases related to the resentment and anger they'd stowed away in their hearts for many years. If Sigmund Freud could read this, he wouldn't be at all surprised.

2) I wish I hadn't worked so hard

Bronnie reports that this regret was cited by *all* the men she treated. Amazing! A perfect consensus of regret attributed to the male sex. Do you realize what this means? It means that if you're a male reading this book, present company included, you'll regret that you worked too hard. By the way, some women also expressed this remorse, but in much lower percentages – perhaps because most of the female patients Bronnie treated were not the breadwinners in the family (this was a different generation).

Men who worship their work often miss their children's or grandchildren's childhoods and sometimes also the companionship of their spouses. Their admission ticket to the career race costs a fortune. I'm absolutely positive that no one on their deathbed ever said, 'How unfortunate that I didn't put in more hours at my job.'

In Japan workaholism is a severe social problem. The Japanese have even coined a special word for the most damaging result of this phenomenon: *karōshi*, which literally means 'death from overwork' – that is, sudden occupation-related death. There will be no remorse in such cases. Another serious consequence is *karōjisatsu*: suicide from overwork. I suppose that if special words have been created, these phenomena are not rare.

Nevertheless, I feel a strong need to play the devil's advocate and hereby list several ideas in favour of work:

1) Some people really have to work hard, and sometimes very hard, at least during a certain period of their lives, to support those dear to them. There's no room for remorse here either.

2) Sigmund Freud, Wilhelm Reich, and many other notable thinkers were convinced that work, love, and appreciation are the three cornerstones of every human being's psychic foundation.

3) Dr Jonas Salk (1914–1995), the American virologist who developed the first effective vaccine for polio,

stated that the real reward for work is the opportunity to keep working.

4) There are people for whom their work is their essence, their great love. Here too, in my opinion, there's no room for remorse. Thomas Edison, Bill Gates – even Mozart – worked a lot and worked hard. Mozart worked tirelessly in his last days to compose the *Requiem* and passed away writing the first bars of *Lacrimosa*. Many, many people's worlds would be different – much sadder – had it not been for this wonderful creation.

5) Tolstoy found a simple recipe for misery: idleness. As is written in Ecclesiastes (5:11): 'A worker's sleep is sweet, whether he has much or little to eat; but the rich man's abundance doesn't let him sleep (translation courtesy of Sefaria: A Living Library of Torah). Idleness is also, however, the gateway to asking existential questions: Who am I? What is my purpose here? What is all this for?

We have now arrived at the number one regret at the top of the regret parade:

1) I wish I'd had the courage to live a life true to myself, not the life others expected of me

Bronnie Ware points out that this was the most common regret of all the ones she found. It relates to our dreams, our aspirations. As we reach the end of our lives, we see that health and fitness, when we had them, gave us chances we never took. Being healthy allows us to accomplish things. Being healthy allows us to try to follow our dreams.

Bronnie noted that when people realize their life is nearing its end, and they take a penetrating look at what they've done, they understand that most of their dreams are unfulfilled. Even more painfully, they are approaching death in the knowledge that such unfulfillment results from life choices they did – or didn't – make. As the ancient Hebrew sages said, 'There is no one who leaves this world who has accomplished even half of their aspirations' (Kohelet Rabbah, Parasha, 1:13).

The idea that health and freedom of choice are connected is remarkably accurate, but with regard to abandoned dreams I have reservations – comforting and calming ones, at least in my opinion.

I think there's an 'if only' illusion here. It would not be sensible to think, 'Oh, if only I'd invested more in my studies I could have won the Nobel Prize in Physics or the Fields Medal in Mathematics'; or 'If only I'd had more courage, I could have been a test pilot or aerobatics champion'; or 'If only I'd approached the most beautiful girl in high school, I could have ended up happily married to her.' I exaggerate intentionally. To me, these are old wives' tales. Our fantasies that we could have become someone else are completely – in most cases – wrong and pointless.

As I accumulate more and more days, I have a growing belief that our freedom is pitifully limited. When I was a young man, I believed that I was a free person and my choices were indeed *my* choices only. I believed that if I tried hard enough I could navigate my life along almost any path I chose and fulfil almost any dream. Today I realize how wrong I was. We are complex beings in a complex world and it's pretty obvious that not everything is within our control. Although I agree with Dostoevsky, who said that people are not merely piano keys on a mechanical piano upon which the laws of nature play, it would be arrogant to think we have complete control over our emotions, our thoughts, our choices, and – most importantly – our actions. Does a person choose to want what they want? Can a person think what they want to think? (Of course, I'm not talking here about the infinite and wonderful power of imagination, which enables us to sail anywhere we wish.)

These thoughts do not really sadden me; actually, they are very comforting. Why? Because I understand that perhaps our choices are not mistakes. They are a part of who we are. Maybe the big mistake is to feel sorrow and remorse about the dreams we didn't realize and about the choices we made and those we didn't make.

* * *

We have looked at regrets – pretty thoroughly, I believe. Now it's time, in the next chapter, to look at their executive aspect: complaints.

CHAPTER 7

Tender Complaints

French composer and musicologist Jean-Philippe (1683–1764) wrote a charming piece for harpsichord (though today it's played on the piano) and gave it the wonderful name, *Les Tendres Plaintes*, meaning 'tender complaints'. This is a tranquil, seemingly very simple work, but the first time I heard it I realized I would have to find a place for it in my heart among the many residents already there.[11] I told myself that if I were ever to write an autobiography, 'Tender Complaints' would be a pretty accurate title. Then it dawned on me that this title would be appropriate for countless biographies or autobiographies. Then, a few seconds later, I realized I'd *never* write an autobiography, so I decided to adopt this as the title for my new chapter.

(If you're in the mood at this point for a musical interlude, why not try some Rameau pieces for piano? In my endnotes I offer a list of my favourite pieces, as well as my favourite performances.[12] As I write these lines, all are available on YouTube. Did you listen? Did you enjoy? Excellent!)

A pyramid of complaints

When I think of complaints as a hierarchy, the one that tops the pyramid is about life itself. This is a complaint that ripples through all generations and all peoples, starting way back in Mesopotamian literature. The author of Ecclesiastes claimed that all is vanity and the day of a person's death is preferable to the day they were born; and the Buddha saw human suffering as the salient feature of existence. The tradition continues with the wonderful Russian poet (for Russian speakers) Alexander Pushkin (1799–1837), who called life an 'accidental and unnecessary gift'. Like the 'father of pessimism', Arthur Schopenhauer, Pushkin believed that if humans had compassion in their hearts and common sense in their minds, they would never bring children into this world. Another complainant is Romanian philosopher Emil Cioran (1911–1995), who wrote books with such titles as *Heights of Despair* and *The Trouble with Being Born*. By the way, Cioran's pessimism is so extreme that reading his books sometimes gets me laughing out loud.

On the second level of the pyramid are those complaints that are not about our very existence, but are woven as negative threads into the fabric of life. Suffering, injustice, and mortality are the three most prevalent complaints in this category. The first two, of course, prompt ideas for improving our situation; death too can be pushed back by lifestyle changes or advances in medical science.

Portuguese poet and writer Fernando Pessoa (1888–1935) cannot compete with Cioran when it comes to pessimism, but holds a place among those whose depressing writing sometimes really cheers me up.

There are many ports in the world and countless ships, but no ship ever sails to a place empty of human suffering.

Fernando Pessoa, *The Book of Disquiet*

From here, as we move down our pyramid, the situation gets totally muddled. People start complaining about almost everything: our failing memories, boring work, elevator music, rebellious family members, the tax authority, cymbals in the orchestra, government too weak or too harsh, dirty rivers, the lazy maths teacher, airplane food, slow Internet speeds, the neighbours, the weather, hair loss, TV commercials, Israeli football, traffic jams, idiots all around us … the list doesn't end.

It seems to me there's only one thing that almost no one complains about – their own intelligence. Even people who cannot find satisfaction in anything else tend to be entirely satisfied with how bright they are (which isn't the same as how well-educated they are).

Is intelligence really distributed to us all so generously? Or are we satisfied with our intelligence simply because our judgment is made within the medium of our intelligence – our own minds? Since when did we start thinking that referees are part of the game? By the way, our brains are also responsible for our thinking that the brain is the most remarkable organ in the human body. Oops!

Also, the brain is responsible for what I've just written here in the last paragraph. Go figure.

You'll find many lists on the Internet of the type of complaint that focuses on 'First-World Problems' – that is, complaints made by people in the developed world.

It's important to note – better a little late than never – that people struggling in the war for survival have no time to complain. Complaining is a privilege in itself.

Here is my modest contribution to the litany of absurd complaints. I devote it with great affection (and a wink) to some of my friends, as it consists almost entirely of actual complaints they once made to me.

Problems of people who have no problems

'I was in Arezzo, Tuscany, during the truffle festival. In the evening we ate pasta at a restaurant that in general wasn't all that bad, but boy did they ever exaggerate those truffles! I had heartburn all night. It was a disaster.'

'My new home is so big that many things just get lost – I can't find them. I also had to install routers on every level, and also near the pool, otherwise the Internet is just awful. … In the wine cellar and garage the reception is still really weak.'

'I flew to the USA first class, as usual, but they didn't give me my own storage compartment. It drove me nuts the whole flight.'

'One morning, I decided to try almond milk in my cappuccino – this was truly one of the worst decisions of my life.'

'Restaurant choice is critical but I couldn't get a reservation for Noma. I'm in utter despair.'

'I finished watching every decent drama series on Netflix. All that's left is some creepy horror stuff. What am I supposed to do now?'

I could go on and on, but it would be more fun if you made your own list of complaints you've heard. Arrange them in a pyramid maybe.

And to all my bellyaching acquaintances, as the Yiddish saying goes, *'Ken dos zeyn di ergst frablemen vos ir hot alts'* ('May these be the worst problems you ever have'). Unfortunately, I rather doubt this blessing will come to fruition.

You've already read my complaint that we're not allowed to have a couple of trial periods before we 'subscribe' to real life. But, of course, this isn't my only beef. Here's a tiny and rather random selection. I'm very aware that some of these complaints belong to the 'First-World Problems' category. But I've thrown in some existential ones too to even the balance.

Let me sleep

I hate alarm clocks. A person should only wake up naturally. At times when I *have* to set an alarm clock, usually I can't fall asleep at all. There are some cultures that believe one should never wake another person up, because the soul leaves the body during sleep, and if someone is woken suddenly, their soul may not have had the time to return. In fact, observant Jews bless the Almighty each morning for 'restoring my soul to me'. Next time you're thinking about waking someone up, think about the risk involved. Is it really worth it?

The wonders of memory

How is it that people who can remember every little thing that happened to them on their last trip to Spitsbergen or Kamchatka are unable to recall they've told this story before once or twice or 77 times? How am I supposed – once again – to show enthusiasm for a story that bored me to the point of yawning even during its premier performance?

Unreliable sayings

It seems to me that the saying, 'No one is irreplaceable', is particularly stupid. I believe there is no one who *can* be replaced, and this is doubly true for people dear to our hearts. Also, I'm not particular enthusiastic about the saying, 'Time heals all wounds'. It seems to me that time heals only superficial wounds: deep wounds never heal.

The theory of special relativity

Happiness tends to be painfully brief, while anguish tends to arrive early and insist on staying until the late hours of our lives. This is a big problem for me and others. But who on Earth (or elsewhere) should I complain to?

Death's stinginess

We are all death's customers. Regardless of how many summers under the sun we've been granted, we will spend infinite time in the land of absolute darkness. Given this ratio, it isn't clear to me why death insists on allocating us a pitifully small number of years. What's 80, 90, or 100 years compared with endless empty infinite time? Less than a minuscule speck. Even if we lived 200, 1,000, or a million years, the weighting would still be in death's favour. Why so stingy?

A fixed boxing match

Life is a boxing match that has been fixed beforehand. The fight to the death may be long, or we may lose it in the very first round. We may get beaten up in every round, or we may keep the lead for most of the fight. The crowd may cheer us on or boo us. The referee may be scrupulous or corrupt. We may find large portions of this fight – perhaps most of it – enjoyable, sometimes immensely so. But in the end, nothing matters. Every round brings our defeat closer, and at some point, that knockout happens. The match is fixed … and this is quite a scandal.

The fall of Icarus

Modern art experts disagree on whether the painting *Landscape with the Fall of Icarus* is the work of Pieter Bruegel the Elder or a copy of the original by some other painter. I'm not an expert on art, so it doesn't really matter to me one way or the other. However, every time I look at this painting it instils in me a kind of sadness that borders on anger.

I imagine most readers are familiar with the story of Icarus, but I'll offer the gist of it here. Icarus was the son of Daedalus, best known as the architect of the Minotaur's labyrinth created for King Minos of Crete. (In his dialogue entitled *Meno*, Plato mentions Daedalus as the creator of marvellous sculptures.) King Minos refused to allow Daedalus and Icarus to leave the island, so to escape their captivity Daedalus fashioned wings for them both and attached them to their bodies with beeswax. With paternal concern, he instructed his son not to get too close to the sea, for the water would wet the wings, and not to fly too high, because the sun would melt the wax and the wings would fall away. Icarus, like many young people his age, was stubborn, and flew too close to the sun. The wax melted, and Icarus tumbled into the sea and drowned.

If we give the painting only a cursory glance (please look it up online), we may not grasp the meaning of the title. Where is Icarus in this broad view of coastal scenery?

But now look at the lower right-hand corner of the painting. Do you see the legs sticking out of the water? A boy has fallen out of the sky to his death, and nobody seems in the least perturbed. Some say this painting is Brueghel's representation of the Flemish proverb, 'And the farmer continued to plough' – an allusion to people's general indifference to the suffering of others.

Icarus is drowning, but ships continue to sail. The fisherman, who may have heard the splash, doesn't even glance up: he continues gathering his net. The farmer 'continues to plough' his field. The shepherd, with his back to the sea, leans on his staff, pondering something. The sun is slinking away, perhaps ashamed of itself for melting Icarus' wings. The tides continue to ebb and flow, and the sky remains adamantly silent. A person has died and the world is indifferent.

The most terrifying thing about death is its utter loneliness – we are completely alone as we meet our final destiny.

There's a version of this painting by one of Brueghel's students in which Daedalus, in flight, appears to be watching what is happening to his son. But in Brueghel's painting it seems nobody cares.

If we study the painting even more closely, it seems that in the left corner, near the tree trunk, there's another person who has died. A dead farmer or a dead Icarus, it doesn't really matter: the world will continue as usual without them. Or maybe the dead man lying in the bushes is actually Icarus after being pulled up onto land and the legs protruding from the sea belong to some boy frolicking in the water? Maybe … but probably not. In any case, it would hardly change anything.

Before we leave the complaints department, here's one final one: our body betrays us over the years. Whether we nurture or neglect our bodies, sooner or later they let us down. Czesław Miłosz (1911–2004), a Polish-American poet and winner of the 1980 Nobel Prize for Literature, claimed that every disease is the body's confession. Well, I say that the role of priest taking confession doesn't suit me at all – let the body keep its confessions to itself.

* * *

That's it. Enough complaining. It's far better to look at life from a completely opposite point of view, and therefore we'll turn our attention, in the next chapter, to one of the greatest experts on peace of mind. On the way, we'll meet another Chinese sage, whom I also like very much.

CHAPTER 8

Dudeism and Daoism

Many things amazed the eminent 17th-century French philosopher and mathematician Blaise Pascal (1623–1662). One was the fact that humans are unable to sit quietly at home, rock back and forth in their armchair (or rocking chair), flip through a book, look out the window ... and do nothing more. Not only did this amaze him, he also believed it was the source of almost all humanity's troubles.

Humans are creatures that get bored very easily, and boredom is a source of both suffering and trouble.

Let us now meet someone who is capable not only of not doing anything, but also of pursuing total inaction for a long period of time.

In 1998, following the success of *The Big Lebowski* – that strange and brilliant film by the brothers Ethan and Joel Cohen – and inspired by film's protagonist, Jeffrey Lebowski, known as The Dude (wonderfully played by Jeff Bridges), a religion/movement/philosophy/lifestyle called Dudeism was established (worldwide, but mainly in the

United States). This movement was a kind of mishmash of the ancient Chinese philosophy of Daoism, various concepts from the thinker Epicurus, the hippie lifestyle, and Winnie-the-Pooh's philosophy of life.

The character of Lebowski, The Dude, is based on an actual person named Jeff Dowd, whom the Cohen brothers met in 1984 while filming their debut film *Blood Simple*. Jeff Lebowski is an ageing hippie who is always sloppily dressed – he has a decided preference for bathrobes. He is lazy, sleepy, capable of writing a check for $0.69 at the grocery store, and as calm as the Buddha. His main interests are smoking pot, drinking white Russians, and ten-pin bowling. The Dude has no desire to succeed in anything, nor to impress anyone. Like Winnie the Poolosopher, he's also completely aware that just doing nothing is a wonderful adventure. In his opinion, there's nothing more important in the world than hanging out with friends.

As befits any self-respecting religion, Dudeism has a High Priest – Lama Oliver Benjamin – and festivals are celebrated by its followers: the Lebowski Fest in America and The Dude Abides Fest in London. By the way, the phrase 'The Dude abides' means 'The Dude takes it easy'.

I'm a big fan of The Dude, although apparently the only thing I share with him is his love for white Russians.

Many years ago, about a decade before *The Big Lebowski* graced the silver screen, I discovered something that saddened me a bit: it's really easy for me to do nothing; what's really difficult is for me to do nothing without feeling guilty about it. I tried to explain to myself that if I was enjoying the time I was wasting, it wasn't really a waste of time. Anyway, it was time that was wasting me, not me it.

Winnie-the-Pooh is right in saying it's okay to do nothing and nibble on a little something. I know this, but my dutiful Lithuanian genes tend to override such platitudes.

It's clear to me that, like any founder of a religion, Jeff Lebowski is an inimitable case who cannot be duplicated. Nevertheless, now and then, I'd be happy to be like him a little. I'd like to stop thinking too much; take a break, even a brief one, from the rat race of the city; spend a whole day bowling with friends (I bet this is the only sport in the world where you can drink white Russians without compromising your skills); take a sabbatical in a small village in Tuscany or a beach in Thailand while leaving my smartphone behind. By the way, the high priest of Dudeism, Oliver Benjamin the First, lives most of the year in Chiang Mai, in mountainous northern Thailand.

I believe Jeffrey Lebowski's philosophy adds a significant contribution to Arthur Schopenhauer's opinions on this subject. Schopenhauer believed that boredom is a form of suffering. This idea may surprise us – after all, the modern world offers so many options for occupying ourselves that it's really hard to imagine getting bored. We have entertainment options galore. Should boredom, then, be removed from the list of things that may cause us to suffer? Actually, the truth is otherwise. In an era so full of distractions in every shape and form, we tend to get stressed not only by boredom but also by the idea of being lonely. Perhaps such anxieties are the reason an entire generation of seemingly normal people have become addicted to smartphones and social networks? True, social networks with all those fake friends and virtual followers may give a person the impression they aren't alone in this world, but this is just an illusion. They *are* alone. If we believe the psychologists, people today are lonelier than ever. (By the way, Tolstoy claimed that boredom was the 'desire to have desires'.)

Arthur Schopenhauer believed that all states of mind, like the seasons, are transitory, although they lack the exemplary order of nature. He described a kind of vicious circle. We crave something and then we may successfully attain it, or not. If not, our yearning, and all the suffering that brings, continue. If we do attain our object of desire, then – according to Schopenhauer – we enjoy a not-very-long period of pleasure and joy until boredom descends again, prompting further craving. In the opinion of this German philosopher, our states of mind are driven by continual dissatisfaction and the relentless pursuit of its opposite. In his entertaining book *Afterthoughts*, American-born British author Logan Pearsall Smith (1865–1946) offered a remarkably accurate insight: 'There are two things to aim at in life: first to get what you want, and after that to enjoy it. Only the wisest of mankind has achieved the second.'

Schopenhauer claimed that the anguish of boredom is in due course replaced by a longing for something new – that is, a new agony. This may be followed by, again, a brief moment of pleasure, followed once more by boredom. This vicious cycle repeats: craving, attainment, brief pleasure, new craving … over and over. According to Schopenhauer, the cycle of unquenchable longing holds more pain than pleasure (which he defines as the absence of pain).

Unfortunately, said Schopenhauer, unlike the seasons, no one knows how long this or that state of mind will last. It may end up being a never-ending winter; or, switching to a shorter metaphorical time frame, a particularly dark night that no morning seems ever to displace.

If the great philosopher of suffering and grief hasn't depressed you yet (for some reason he always seems to cheer me up), then let me add this: he also believed that human beings, by thinking so often of what is to come, increase their suffering even more. Schopenhauer was aware that animals feel suffering – he was actually one of the first animal rights activists. However, he believed that a bear, for example, never worries about future suffering or dying in agony. Perhaps this is why it can enjoy a long, satisfying hibernation when winter arrives.

So ... after all this, the time has come for the humble contribution of Jeff Lebowski, indolent philosopher *par excellence*. The Dude proved that, in practice, there's a quality that Schopenhauer somehow missed, namely 'peace of mind'. This is a mind-state that's free of both suffering and desire; and it doesn't have to end in a flash. The condition can be precisely labelled: equanimity. The great Jeff may be lazy – 'quite possibly the laziest in Los Angeles County, which would place him high in the runnin' for laziest worldwide' – but he doesn't get bored, and certainly doesn't complain about being bored. Lebowski feels no particular desire for anything because he knows desire undermines peace of mind. Also, since he doesn't spend time thinking about the future, he has no particular anxieties.

Pre-Dude idleness

In 1932 British mathematician and philosopher Bertrand Russell, the 3rd Earl Russell (1872–1970), wrote an article with the provocative title *In Praise of Idleness*. In its opening sentence Russell wrote that, like most of his contemporaries, he'd been brought up on the proverb, 'Idle hands are the devil's workshop.' As a dutiful child, Bertrand wholeheartedly complied with this maxim. However, at the time he wrote the article he was no longer a child, and it was reasonable to point out the immense damage caused by how much the modern world overvalues the concept of work. Russell would surely have admired the Russian proverb, 'Work is not a wolf: it won't run away to the forest.' (On the other hand, all work and no play makes Jack a dull boy.) Thus, Russell believed that the key to individual well-being and happiness would be, first and foremost, an organized reduction of working hours and an increase in leisure hours. But then, this wise British nobleman suggested, comes the most difficult challenge of all: to convert leisure time into quality time.

By the way, do you remember that 'I wish I hadn't worked so hard' is second on the list of regrets uttered by the dying? (In this context, I think a good general foundation for a happy life would be to keep that list of regrets thoughtfully in mind.)

Russell begins his article by telling a story about a man who travelled to Naples, where he saw twelve beggars lying in complete repose in the sun. The traveller announced he'd present a gold coin to the laziest. Immediately, eleven of them jumped up from where they were lying, each claiming to be the one who deserved the coin. Naturally, the traveller gave the coin to the twelfth man: the one who took no action. Jeffrey Lebowski really liked this story, observing that he could really identify with the title of Russell's article but hadn't bothered to read the text, as he was too lazy.

Laozi: a Chinese riddle

I'll come out now with a confession. The most important and influential book about Daoist philosophy, the *Tao Te Ching*, did not overly impress me. The book comprises 81 brief sections, most of which I couldn't quite relate to. However, if Laozi had sold his wares separately, I would have happily bought a few wonderful sections.

There are some legends regarding the history of this book. One claims that when Laozi discovered that the Emperor favoured Confucius for the position of legislator (or perhaps court philosopher) over himself, he decided to retire from public life and embark on a journey toward the Tibetan border and the Himalayan mountains. Another says that the reason Laozi decided to leave the Emperor and all his citizens and seclude himself in the Himalayas was that he was so severely disappointed by the stupidity and wickedness of the people. Be that as it may, when Laozi reached the border, the border guard recognised him and said he'd grant him permission to continue only if Laozi would write down his most precious gems of wisdom and leave them for the posterity of the Kingdom of China. Again, there's no consensus about what happened next. Some say Laozi wrote his entire book in one day – but this is a bit unbelievable as it comprises about 5,000 Chinese characters. Another version claims the task took several months, during which time he taught the border guard some of the secrets of his teachings.

The *Tao Te Ching* has been translated into many languages. If you compare different translations in the same language, you'll find that there are places where they are so very different from one another it's hard to believe they originated from the same text. I researched the subject, and it turned out that the original *Tao Te Ching* was, in fact, a *poetic* text, offering a kind of riddle book of Chinese characters, captivating in their beauty (even Pablo Picasso admired Chinese calligraphy). Each character could have more than one interpretation, depending on the characters standing alongside it. Sometimes an entire principle was represented by one specific character: for example, the combination 無為 symbolizes the main principle of behaviour in Daoist philosophy, *wu wei*. Sometimes this is translated as 'non-intervention', sometimes as 'inaction', sometimes as 'effortless action', and sometimes as 'action without action'. Winnie-the-Pooh is considered an expert on this type of philosophy.

It isn't really surprising that different people offer different solutions to Laozi's riddles. As a mathematician, I love brain teasers, and so I'll present below my own interpretations of my favourite sections of the *Tao Te Ching*. Of course, Chinese is 'all Greek' to me, so alongside engaging with the characters (an occupation that gave me first-class aesthetic pleasure) I was assisted by dozens of Chinese-English translations (one of them by our old acquaintance, philosopher and Chinese translator Lin Yutang). I also read two Chinese-Russian translations. Thus I set out on my mission. Its goal was to compose my own personal version of the book based not only on the many translations I read but also on everything I'd ever learned about Daoist thought.

I made an effort to make my version as beautiful and interesting as I possibly could. The helping of artistic license I gave to my interpretations was especially generous in this case – it's always substantial.

Inspired by Jeff Lebowski, I hereby present my favourite sections – to be more precise, usually *portions* of sections. It's no coincidence that there's a large overlap between my choices and those that influenced Dudeism.

Section 1

The Eternal Dao is the source of all that is,
Words cannot describe the eternal Dao,
No name can come close to the essence of the Dao,
The Dao that you are able to explain is not the actual Dao,
The moment of creation cannot be comprehended by the mind,
Everything you imagine is incorrect,
The Dao is a secret within a secret within a secret.

In most translations the term *Dao* or *Tao* is not translated. However, where it *is* translated, the most common versions are 'the Way' or 'the way of the world'. I've also seen 'the law of heaven and earth', 'nature', 'truth', 'the wisdom of the world' and even 'infinity'.

Pre-Socratic philosopher Anaximander (*c.*610–*c.*546 BCE) believed that everything that is, or was, or will be was created from the *apeiron* – something so eternal and infinite that it's impossible to talk about its essence. Everything also reverts back to this mysterious abstract entity. He proposed a theory, that what he calls the *apeiron* is the source of the universe. This was in direct response to the theory put forth by Thales, his teacher and the first philosopher of ancient Greece. Thales, much more pragmatically, suggested that water was the primordial substance and the source of everything in the universe. Aristotle quotes Anaximander in *The Physics*: 'The *apeiron* is unlike all the elemental materials, but they all are a product of it.'

Anaximander's *apeiron* is sort of a Greek version of the Dao, an infinite, indefinite thing that has always been and will always be and that defies literal description. By the way, according to knowledgeable sources, Anaximander had two famous students: Anaximenes and Pythagoras. Pythagoras, though not the first philosopher, was the one who coined the term 'philosophy' and the first to be *identified* as a philosopher.

Pythagoras believed that relations between numbers are at the heart of all natural phenomena: 'number is the ruler of forms and ideas and the cause of gods and demons.'[13] In his book *Metaphysics* Aristotle noted that the Pythagoreans were the first scholars of mathematics; and they were the ones who decided that mathematical principles formed the basis of everything that exists.

Here is what Albert Einstein said about numbers/ mathematics: 'As far as the laws of mathematics refer to reality, they are not certain; and as far as they are certain, they do not refer to reality.' This is practically a Daoist statement. (By the way, the quote comes from a lecture Einstein gave to the members of the Prussian Academy of Sciences in 1921, entitled 'Geometry and Experience'. The text of the lecture may be found in its entirety online.)

In his lecture the distinguished scientist also asked a stimulating question about the correspondence between mathematics (a product of human thought unrelated to actual experience) and reality: why is it that numbers are able to describe reality so exquisitely? Martin Gardner

(1914–2010), legendary editor of the mathematics section of *Scientific American*, asked an even better question (in my opinion, of course): which scientific law proves the necessary existence of scientific laws?

It isn't difficult to imagine a situation without scientific laws. Let's try it together. Imagine that an apple detaching from a tree sometimes falls directly to the ground, but sometimes falls in spectacular spirals, or rises into the sky and disappears completely, or perhaps breaks up into 17 pieces, each of which dances chaotically around the tree. Stanisław Lem, in his book *Solaris* (I've already mentioned this wonderful book: see page 28), describes a group of scientists in a space station orbiting the planet Solaris, where the laws of science have no validity. Identical experiments that the scientists conduct give different and unexpected results each time.

I'll stop here. We'll bid our farewells to Einstein and Pythagoras and make our way now to the holy land of Israel.

In his book *The Thirteen Petalled Rose* (1980), the great scholar Rabbi Adin Even-Israel Steinsaltz (1937–2020) explains that in Judaism the essence of God is called *ha'Einsoff Baruch Hu* – 'The Infinite Blessed Be He.' The sobriquet names something that cannot be named, and this attempt to label the divine essence implies, simultaneously, a vast, indeed infinite distance and a wonderful, blessed closeness. Like Dao, *ha'Einsoff Baruch Hu* is simply an epithet for the divine essence, which is infinitely far from being understood.

In Hebrew, the sacred language, the word *kadosh,* usually translated as 'holy', actually means 'completely separated'. In other words, God (in Hebrew, *Elohim,* or *haKadosh Baruch*

Hu) defies any mortal description, whether by affirmation or by contradiction. Thales, who, you may remember, was Anaximander's teacher, said: 'What is holy? Something that has no beginning nor end.'

We cannot know anything, not even an inkling, about God. We cannot assign Him any appellation or image. It is not by chance that Judaism has a strict prohibition on creating a statue or image of God, an entity so absolutely and infinitely different from ourselves.

God is transcendent.

To eliminate any doubt, not only is it impossible to describe God in the terms we use to describe humanity, it's also meaningless to resort to terms we use to describe what makes him different from humanity. In other words, not only can He not be described as jealous, loving, or merciful, He can also not be said to be good, all-knowing, or perfect. God is outside humanity's experience and grasp.

May I dare now to suggest this idea: the divine essence is so remote from our comprehension that we cannot even say 'God exists' or 'God doesn't exist'. God is beyond existence or non-existence. I've no idea what you might think of this suggestion, but I'm almost sure that both Laozi and Zhuang Zhou would have gone along with it.

Let's move on to the moment of the Creation. Re-read, if you will, the beginning of this book about that moment: the point which, on the one hand, was so infinitesimal it did not exist at all; and, on the other hand, comprised the entirety of infinity. Where did it come from? When?

Immanuel Kant's famous antinomy (contradiction) from the *Critique of Pure Reason* attempts to imagine the moment of creation – that is, the beginning of time. Kant expounds that it doesn't matter whether we assume there was a point at which time started or whether there was not. Either way, we reach a dead end and bump into impossibility.

If we assume that time has no beginning, that means an infinite period of time must pass before any particular event occurs – whether negligible or important. But infinite time cannot pass. If you don't want to meet someone, but worry about hurting their feelings, just tell them, politely and gently, 'See you in an infinite number of minutes,' then part as friends forever. I repeat: no event could possibly have occurred if we assume that time has no beginning.

This has become complicated, wouldn't you agree?

Alternatively, if we assume that time did have a beginning, the situation would not be any simpler. Many questions will immediately arise. Who created time? Why and for what purpose was it created? Where was time before the beginning of time? If there was no time previously, can the word 'before' hold any meaning? Is time finite or infinite? Can time disappear? Why is there anything at all? How is it possible to create 'something out of nothing'? What did God do before He created time? And so on, and so on, and so on …

Maybe we'll never know for sure how the world was created and why.

Who knows whence this creation had its origin?
He, whether He fashioned it or whether He did not,
He, who surveys it all from the highest heaven,
He knows – or maybe even He does not know.
Rig Veda, Mandala 10, 129 (translation Ralph T. Griffith, 1896)

Turning again to the last line in the first section of the *Tao Te Ching,* 'The Dao is a secret within a secret within a secret,' I should like to mention that sometimes the idea passes through my mind that everything we think about the world and reality may not be true. Obviously our worldview is much more accurate now than it was for the ancient Chinese or ancient Greeks. Even I know more about prime numbers than Euclid knew – even though his proof that there are infinite prime numbers is one of the most beautiful proofs in the history of mathematics. I also know that the world isn't flat and doesn't rest on three giant turtles. Knowledge grows and improves over time. But I can really identify with the approach of British scientist J.B.S. Haldane, who wrote: 'Now, my own suspicion is that the universe is not only queerer than we suppose, but queerer than we can suppose. ... I suspect that there are more things in heaven and earth that are dreamed of, or can be dreamed of, in any philosophy.' (The second part of Haldane's quote corresponds, of course, with Shakespeare's famous line from *Hamlet* (Act I, Scene 5), 'There are more things in Heaven and Earth, Horatio, than are dreamt of in your philosophy.'

In the introduction to *The Thirteen Petalled Rose,* a wonderfully thought-provoking sentence appears: 'A true secret is a secret even when it is visible to all.' I don't know what Rabbi Adin Steinsaltz meant, but it seems to me that our universe, visible to all and open to all inquiry, is a true secret and will remain so.

The mystical is not how the world is, but that it is.
LudwigWittgenstein,*TractatusLogico-Philosophicus*,6.44

Dao is impossible to talk about. It is mystical.
Laozi

American author Ursula K. Le Guin (1929–2018) is among those who have translated Laozi's work. She wrote that the first section, which she entitles 'Taoing', does not lend itself to translation at all. It reminds her, she says, of Jorge Luis Borges' story 'The Aleph'. In Borges' story, the Aleph represents a point in time that includes all other points. Anyone who looks at this point can, at one and the same time, see the whole universe at all moments in time and from every possible angle.

By the way, Ursula K. Le Guin's writing was influenced quite a bit by Daoist philosophy, so it seems no coincidence that she decided to translate the *Tao Te Ching* into English. Her philosophical short story 'The Ones Who Walk Away from Omelas' has always been on my list of favourites.

Section 2

When everyone is aware of beauty, ugliness arises,
To say of the beautiful that it is beautiful is ugly.
When everyone is aware of good, evil develops skin and
    tendons.
To say of the good that it is good is bad.

Non-existence seeps into existence,
And the nothingness that exists is everywhere.
The light and the heavy gauge each other,
The height and depth depend on each other,
The 'after' awakens after the 'before',
Sounds and silence give birth to harmony,

> *The Dao does nothing, everything is done according*
> *to its word.*
> *And the wise man does everything without doing anything.*

The first four lines of this section of the *Tao Te Ching* comprise an aesthetic assertion and the ethical assertion that follows in its wake. Each is worthy of a course in the Department of Philosophy. Even before he published the *Tractatus*, Wittgenstein wrote in his journal that ethics and aesthetics were one and the same. In a number of online forums, lively discussions about the meaning of this statement are conducted. Feel free to join (simply search 'ethics and aesthetics are one'), but take into account that you'll need to be familiar with Immanuel Kant's and Ludwig Wittgenstein's philosophies.

A warning about the dichotomy of good and evil can also be found in the Biblical sources. For example: '… but as for the tree of knowledge of good and evil, you must not eat of it; for as soon as you eat of it, you shall die' (Genesis, 2:17).

Our old acquaintance Anaximander held the opinion that his *apeiron* was responsible for creating the opposites good-bad, cold-hot, life-death, and so on.

We will remain with the pre-Socratics. Here's my rendering of Heraclitus the Obscure's version of the continuation of our Daoist passage discussing opposites:

> *Nothing will survive if its opposite disappears.*
> *We recognize what is good because evil exists. We*
> *feel healthy because there are sick among us. We feel*
> *satiated because we have known hunger, and blessed*
> *rest exists only thanks to fatigue. Wet things dry out*

*and what has dried may get wet. Furthermore, do
not forget that the same way that leads up also leads
down and that the beginning of the circle is also its end.
The whole is made up of many things and many things
may emerge from the whole. To live is to die; those who
are mortal are immortal and those who are immortal
are mortal. To be awake is to sleep, to be young is to be
old – one flows into the other. So, how is it possible that
the great poet Hesiod, the wisest of teachers, did not
comprehend that night and day are but one?*

(Note that there seems to be hardly any substantial difference of meaning between the Greek and Chinese versions. It's difficult to decide which might be the source, because almost nothing is known about Laozi's life. We don't know when was he born, and indeed his whole historical existence is shrouded in fog. And yet all the stories about this Chinese philosopher's last days are similar: one day he was seen a long distance away riding on the back of a water buffalo, and then he disappeared forever.)

The German philosopher Georg Wilhelm Friedrich Hegel (1770–1831) held Heraclitus in great esteem. He claimed that Heraclitus introduced concepts central to philosophy and credited him with inventing the dialectic method. Others who, like Hegel, held Heraclitus in esteem included Friedrich Nietzsche and Friedrich Engels. In my opinion the biggest compliment to Heraclitus occurs in Raphael's painting *The School of Athens*, which depicts many philosophers and mathematicians from ancient Greece. Why do I think so? Because Raphael chose as his model for the portrait of Heraclitus none other than … Michelangelo.

I'm pretty sure that while reading what I've written above about opposites, many of you will have thought about *yin yang*, the opposing and complementary forces at work in the universe. The *yin* and the *yang* exist within each other as well as parallel with each other. Just in case you aren't aware of it, the concept of *yin yang* originated in ancient Chinese philosophy, particular Daoism.

☯

Carl Gustav Jung invented a long and especially sonorous word, *enantiodromia*, which means 'opposites flowing into each other'. Jung gave Heraclitus the credit for this word or concept, remarking that the notion is present in all spheres of life – from the most trivial to the most fundamental.

Solon (d. 560 BCE), an Athenian statesman, lawmaker, and poet, is considered one of the seven sages of ancient Greece. He suggested there's no difference between existence and non-existence or between life and death. When asked why he didn't commit suicide, his reply was precisely this: that it wouldn't make any difference.

It's also told that Solon cried bitterly after his son died. His friends were astonished by this and asked him if he didn't know that crying wouldn't help? 'Of course, I know nothing will help,' Solon replied. 'This is exactly why I'm crying.'

Section 3

When people are not praised for their virtues,
Competition is averted.

If you do not overvalue things that are hard to attain,
There will be no desire to steal.

If we do not display objects that arouse passion,
People's hearts will not be bewildered and they will feel
  no embarrassment.

People who do not know much and do not compare
  things
Do not need many things, and their hearts are at peace.

In the modern Western world, it isn't all that customary to praise people. There's a graduated division between people who are famous and those who aren't: the graduations occur with people sinking or rising in esteem. The scale has very little to do with real merit. Any correlation between virtuous attributes and degree of fame, if it exists at all, is very weak.

Out of curiosity I decided to search the Internet for the 'most famous people in the world'.

The first site that came up was entitled 'Top 20 Famous Persons in the World 2021'. Who do you think topped the list? A scientist who invented a vaccine for coronavirus and perhaps saved the world from catastrophe? Maybe someone who came up with a vaccine for some other terrible disease? The winner of the 2021 Nobel Peace prize? A world-famous philosopher? A multi-billionaire who donated money to help people leading miserable lives? Yazidi and Kurdish fighters who bravely fought against ISIS? Nadia Murad? A world leader who did nothing but good for his nation and the world?

I'm not sure what you're thinking and whom you're betting on, but I wasn't even close to correct!

Are you holding your breath? Here's the result:

Dwayne Douglas Johnson, also known as 'The Rock', a well-known actor who starred in many films, most notably the *Fast and Furious* series. But the Rock is a philanthropist who, among other things, founded a foundation for at-risk and terminally ill children. Apparently, I'm not really up-to-date with things, but Dwayne Johnson topped charts on other websites as well.

As soon as I typed the full stop of the preceding sentence, I remembered that Plato also dealt with the affairs of celebrities and was outraged at the excess amount (in his opinion) of fame accorded to some wrestler or boxer named Cretan or Charitone (my memory is sometimes a bit foggy). In any case, Plato, who in his youth was a wrestler himself, emphasized the significance of this choice, since those selected unquestionably provide an example both to the younger generation and to adults, who will identify with them and learn what values are worthy (again, 'worthy' according to Plato's opinion, of course).

Actually, the Athens Academy's founder seems to have dealt with almost every subject. In his *Process and Reality* philosopher and mathematician Alfred North Whitehead comes up with one of the most famous and most quoted lines in the history of thought in suggesting that the best general definition of European philosophy is that it's a series of footnotes to Plato's writings. Nick Romeo, in an article entitled 'Platonically Irrational', published in 2017 in *AEON* (an online journal of philosophy for the general public), claimed that Plato knew 'pretty much everything' about behavioural economics and cognitive biases 2,500 years before Daniel Kahneman's and Amos Tversky's breakthrough studies.

Well, I've digressed slightly. But anyway, a few years ago I witnessed something pretty disheartening when I was invited to deliver a lecture to a class of gifted Israeli high school students and discovered that some of them didn't know who Janusz Korczak was. (He was a well-known doctor and author who ran a Jewish orphanage in Warsaw from 1911 to 1942. He met his death after refusing sanctuary and staying with his orphans after the institution's entire population was sent to Treblinka extermination camp.) I have a pretty strong feeling that had I asked them who 'The Rock was and in what movies he'd acted, they would have been able to rattle off the answers without hesitation.

Back to the list of 20 famous people. I sorted the 20 personalities on this list into fields of endeavour, with the number of figures in each field, and here's the result:

Classification	Incidence
Presidents of the United States	3
Vice Presidents of the United States	1
Filthy-rich multi-billionaires	2
Golfers	1
Actor-wrestlers	1
Female singers	3
Singer-actresses	2
Football players	1
Rappers	1
TV hosts	1
Kardashian family	2
Hollywood actors	1
Teen idols (singers)	1

Obviously, I could have just posted the list of names, but I thought it would be more interesting for you to guess at the people hiding behind those statistics. Think of this as a quiz if you like (and if you can time-travel back to 2021).

I noticed that, although this table didn't go viral, it was nonetheless re-posted on quite a few sites that simply 'copy-and-pasted' it. As a result, the table itself became 'almost famous'.

I have no idea how the list was compiled but can guess why it was the first to pop up in my search. Many sites use this technique: optimizing visibility according the number of 'likes' received.

So here's my list of my 10 favourite *Dialogues* by Plato:

1) Republic
2) Symposium
3) Phaedrus
4) Meno
5) Phaedo
6) Apology
7) Crito
8) Theaetetus
9) Euthyphro
10) Protagoras

Feel free to 'like' this. Delve into the books. Rank them according to your own preference.

Further on, I'll expand on some other thoughts that came to mind when I was reading my version of Laozi's Section 3, but I'll mention here (it's a key point) that one of the basic concepts of capitalist economics is to exhibit everything that's attractive and, more importantly, arouse in people a desire for things they don't really need. For example, one way to convince us that we absolutely must buy the latest, state-of-the-art smartphone is that, besides the 18 cameras installed in the device, it can play Bob Dylan songs in Yiddish and iron socks. The idea is to arouse our envy by pointing out to us that this amazing gizmo is already in the possession of others. The desire-comparison syndrome, as foretold by Laozi, is a blight on our souls.

Section 5

Heaven and earth are not 'human'
And there is neither anger nor pity within them.

All creatures are equal in Nature's eyes,
Straw dogs are lavishly decorated and ready for sacrificial worship.

Wise rulers are also not 'human',
They do not favour anyone, because there is no difference between people.

Confucius's philosophy speaks volumes about humanity and morality and is essentially anthropocentric. Laozi's doctrine is much more universal – the Dao supersedes all humanity, all anger and pity, all our demands for special treatment. The Dao may be indifferent, but the Dao is not cruel. Schopenhauer believed that if we can understand that we're all brothers and sisters in misery, and that there's no real difference between one person and the next, then maybe we'll feel compassion for each other and for all creatures.

Ursula K. Le Guin sums up the idea of this section wonderfully: 'You can't be indifferent if you are not different.'

Death bestows complete equality on all. Everything returns to dust and oblivion. Wise men and fools, the arrogant and the humble, those at peace with the world and those quick to anger, the righteous and the wicked, the destitute and the rich – all hurtle toward sameness. As Marcus Aurelius wrote in his journal, in the end the exact same thing happened to Alexander the Great and his mule driver. Nothing will save any one of us from death. Mother Earth/Nature/The Dao/Infinity – all will gather us into their bosom.

Section 12

The five colours
Blind our eyes.
The five sounds
Deafen our ears.
The five flavours
Dull our sense of taste.
Chases and competitions
Drive people crazy.
Anyone who strives to be rich
Is entrapped by greed.
The wise man's eyes observe the world,
But he only trusts his heart.

The wise man allows things
To come and go,
He concentrates on his needs
And not on his desires.

'Five' at the beginning of the quote can be replaced with 'too many'. Make this adjustment and read the opening lines once more.

In the intimate and endearing Italian film *Caos Calmo* (*Quiet Chaos,* 2008), directed by Antonello Grimaldi, there's a wonderful scene where the protagonist, played by brilliant actor, screenwriter, and director Nanni Moretti, goes into a diner and orders a portion of artichoke. The dish arrives at the table but after a few minutes the guest summons the owner. 'Why did you serve the artichoke with pecorino cheese? Were you not confident that it was good enough? It's excellent. The pecorino is good too, but absolutely superfluous.'

As far as I can understand, this story expresses one of the cornerstones of the philosophy of Italian cuisine – as already formulated by Laozi: *Too many flavours dull our sense of taste.* If you have fine porcini mushrooms, all you have to do is fry them in fine butter. That's it. It will be amazing. There's no need to add eggplant and zucchini and gorgonzola cheese and dwarf pineapple and peanut butter and peeled tomatoes wrapped in strings of halva.

It's been said that the marvellous Romanian pianist Radu Lupu once claimed that if he could hold a concert in which he performed only the slow, *adagio* movements of the concerti for piano and orchestra, he'd be very happy.

Can I refrain from putting together a programme for such a concert? Absolutely not! I've chosen Mozart as the core of the programme:

1) *Wolfgang Amadeus Mozart*: Adagio, Piano Concerto No. 23
2) *Ludwig van Beethoven:* Largo, Piano Concerto No. 3
3) *Maurice Ravel:* Adagio Asai, the Piano Concerto in G
4) *Wolfgang Amadeus Mozart:* Largo, Piano Concerto No. 24
5) *Sergei Rachmaninoff*: Adagio, Piano Concerto No. 2
6) *Wolfgang Amadeus Mozart:* Largo, Piano Concerto No. 27
7) *Dmitry Shostakovich*: Andante, Piano Concerto No. 2
8) *Wolfgang Amadeus Mozart:* Andante, Piano Concerto No. 17

That's it. We've reached the end of a wonderfully tranquil evening.

And yet, for all the immense love I feel for music, no less pleasant are the soothing sounds of the waves in the sea or the wonderful *pianissimo* of trees in the forest when the wind caresses them.

* * *

I'll end these thoughts with a few words regarding the last verse of Section 12 of the *Tao Te Ching* and the difference between need and desire.

A need is directed at an object that satisfies that need: if I'm cold, a coat will satisfy my need to raise my body temperature. Desire is directed toward an object that arouses desire – a beautiful woman, the incomparable music of Bach, an all-absorbing work of fiction or philosophy. Someone who has been lucky in life can usually satisfy most of their needs, but our passions almost always go unsatisfied. I don't think

I'll ever say I've had my fill of looking at beautiful women or listening to beautiful music, that I've read enough books, or that I've seen enough sublime landscapes. Slavoj Žižek pointed out that the *raison d'être* of desire is not satisfaction, but the continued replication of itself. Israeli songwriter Naomi Shemer (1930–2004) provided a compelling argument for the notion that love is a desire. These are her words: 'I have not yet loved enough.' Had love been a need, she would have written, 'I have loved. Enough.'

Section 17

Great leaders
Are almost unknown by their subjects.
Then come leaders
That people know and cherish;
After them, are those who are feared;
And after them, those who are despised.

Today, TV and social networks have made democracy unbearable and perhaps even impossible. There can be no great leader today: according to Laozi, a great leader must be humble and reticent and 'almost unknown by their subjects'. Nowadays anyone with these qualities will not even be elected to their apartment house committee, never mind how talented they may be. We live in an era of repulsive populism and cheap demagoguery. Decades ago, Austrian-Jewish writer and journalist Karl Kraus (1874–1936) figured out the best-kept secret of demagoguery. Here it is: 'The secret of the demagogue is to make himself as stupid as his audience so they will believe they are clever as he.' And I'll just add that there are quite a few demagogues who don't have to put a lot of effort into making themselves as stupid as their followers.

Section 23

Nature does not deliver long speeches,
And a person also should not talk too much.
A whirlwind does not last all morning,
And a cloudburst soon ceases.

What causes wind and rain?
Heaven and earth.
As the heavens and the earth will not last forever,
A person, of course, does not need to either.

After the Beatles disbanded, George Harrison released a solo album called *All Things Must Pass*. The title song is really an interpretation of this section of the *Tao Te Ching*. I don't know if Harrison made the reference consciously or not. I would happily quote Harrison's version, but 70 years have not yet passed since his death and there's a matter of copyright. So just listen to this great song on YouTube.

The last two lines of this section by Laozi have many versions. One of the most beautiful was expressed by King David: 'Man is like a puff of air; his days are like a passing shadow' (Psalms, 144:4). This was re-expressed by the Bard of Avon as 'Life is but a walking shadow' (*Macbeth*, Act V, Scene 5).

Section 24

It is impossible to stand on tiptoe all the time,
This is not a stable stance.

It is impossible to walk while jumping high,
It is fatiguing and one will not go far.

Man need not praise nor glorify himself,
It is ridiculous and embarrassing.
People who are proud of themselves are not helpful to
*   anyone,*
And those who are constantly trying to sell themselves
Have erred in their way and will not be enlightened.

Such things are vile,
Followers of the way [Dao] will avoid them.

People who take pride in themselves are a pretty strange phenomenon to me.

In my opinion, it's much easier to value and respect other people than yourself. This may be because, usually, we visit others in their living rooms, where what we see is, almost exclusively, what they wish to present to us. We know ourselves much more deeply, because not only do we visit each and every room of our house, we quite often go down into the basement. It isn't that we're unaware that other people have basements. We know they do, but as long as someone else's basement is hidden from the visitor's eye, its contents remain unknown and therefore we may imagine that they comprise mainly items of good quality. But how can you imagine yourself in a more positive light than the truth when you've known yourself for so many years, in a deep and daily acquaintance?

So what about self-love? Self-love is a necessary condition for loving others. The commandment, 'Love others as you love yourself,' would have no significance if we didn't love ourselves. African-American poet and writer Maya Angelou (1928–2014) wrote that she didn't trust people who told her 'I love you' but didn't love themselves. The situation reminded her of the African proverb, 'Beware when a naked man offers you a shirt.'

The marvellous Jane Austen provided us with a wonderful perception about the different kinds of pride. In *Pride and Prejudice* she wrote the following:

Vanity and pride are different things, though the words are often used synonymously. A person may be proud without being vain. Pride relates more to our opinion of ourselves, vanity to what we would have others think of us.

I rather doubt that Laozi would have liked people who gravitated to modesty. After all, if we think a little about the psychology of modesty, we'll see an interesting dynamic. Why would someone be modest? Perhaps because they believe that if they say what they really think of themselves, we, their listeners, will be infected by an overdose of admiration? Rest assured, we'll manage.

By the way, Winnie-the-Pooh was once overcome by modesty when he found out he had no brain at all: he didn't want to brag about that fact.

I'll end my thoughts about Section 24 of the *Tao Te Ching* with a short story my mother told me. Konstantin Stanislavsky (1863–1938) was a seminal Soviet Russian theatre actor and director – there's an acting method named after him. Solomon Mikhoels (1890–1948) was a Latvian-born Yiddish theatre actor who was murdered on Stalin's orders. The two men once had an argument on the question of how a bird begins its flight.

'It spreads its wings,' said Mikhoels.

'No,' said Stanislavsky. 'It becomes proud.'

Section 33

Knowing others is clever,
Knowing yourself is wisdom.
Overcoming others requires strength,
Overcoming yourself is heroism.
True wealth is contentment.

Living until the day you die,
This is a long enough life.

It's clear that this verse is equivalent to both *ΓΝΩΘΙ ΣΕΑΥΤΟΝ*, the made-in-Greece 'Know thyself', and the famous verse from the Talmud, Tractate Avot (4a):

Ben Zoma said: 'Who is wise? He who learns from every man, as it is said: "From all who taught me have I gained understanding" (Psalms, 119:99). Who is mighty? He who subdues his [evil] inclination, as it is said: "He that is slow to anger is better than the mighty; and he that rules his spirit than he that takes a city" (Proverbs, 16:32). Who is rich? He who rejoices in his lot, as it is said: "You shall enjoy the fruit of your labours, you shall be happy and you shall prosper" (Psalms, 128:2).

I've already discussed 'Know thyself' at length, and therefore I'll add here only a small note. Where does it come from, this inflated, strange confidence that it's easier to get to know other people than to get to know yourself? If it's so hard for me to understand myself, how can I suggest I could become a great expert about other people's secrets?

It should come as no surprise that the word 'person' evolved from the Latin, *persona*, which means 'mask' or 'role'. There's so much depth in the etymology of this word. Indeed, we all wear a mask and embody some role or other. We pretend. Furthermore, if we know we're wearing a mask when we encounter others, how can we not believe that we're all simply part of some ongoing masked ball?

By the way, in French, the meaning of *personne* is both 'nobody' and 'anybody', depending on the context. The French seem to be a little more profound than we are.

Now, with regard to the last two lines of Section 33 about death, it seems to me that Laozi's meaning closely approaches that of our old acquaintance, Yang Zhu. I'll allow myself to blend the two ancient Daoists:

Only one thing matters:
whether you had a life before death.
The fact that someone dies
does not necessarily prove they ever lived.
Do not let moments of death
intrude into your life.
One must not die before death.
If you have lived each day until the day of your death,
then you have lived a long enough life.

Section 48 of the *Tao Te Ching* section features the great creative lazy philosopher Jeffrey Lebowski's favourite line. It *is* only one line, this section. In a translation by Lin Yutang (1895–1976) it sounds like this:

Section 48
When nothing is done, nothing is left undone.

Amazing!

Section 56
He who knows
Does not speak.
He who speaks
Does not know.

If you are not controlled by love
Or by rejection,
If you are not controlled by profit
Or by loss,
If you are not controlled by praise
Or by humiliation,
If you are not controlled by health
Or by sickness,
Then you have found the way.

There are many Biblical passages that parallel the opening lines of Section 56. Here are three of them:

A fence to wisdom is silence.
Mishna Avot, 3:13

> Where there is much talking, there is no lack of transgressing, But he who curbs his tongue shows sense.
> **Proverbs, 10:19**

> … therefore let your words be few.
> **Ecclesiastes, 5:1**

The English proverb, 'Speech is silver, silence is golden,' originated in Arabic culture in the 9th century, although it is usually attributed to Scottish historian and philosopher Thomas Carlyle (1795–1881). The second part of the saying, 'Silence is golden,' was borrowed as the title of a song recorded in 1964 by the American band the Four Seasons (a famous cover version was recorded in 1967 by the English group the Tremeloes.)

The second part of Laozi's section predates Aristotle's idea of 'autarky happiness', which centres on self-sufficiency, and also echoes one of the central ideas in philosophy of Epictetus (*c*.55–135), which I discuss later.

Section 67

I have three treasures.
I guard them carefully.
The first, compassion,
The second, moderation,
The third, humility.

This section summarizes the ethics of Daoism.

Section 81

Real words are not beautiful,
Beautiful words are not real.

Good people are not contentious,
Contentious people are not good.

People who know are not scholars,
Scholarly people do not know.

The best interpretation of this verse would be the absence of any interpretation.

Il dolce far niente

To conclude our discussion about Daoism and Dudeism, here are two stories from Italy. Nobody can appreciate the art of blessed idleness like the Italians.

More than a quarter of a century ago, I attended a conference on the overt and covert connections between science and art. It took place in the picturesque city of Siena in the region of Tuscany. The conference was multi-topic and multi-participant, and dozens of lectures were held simultaneously in different venues in the city. In those days, few tourists came to Siena and there were no pedlars' stalls in its famous Piazza del Campo and no flags or umbrellas of organized and less organized guides in all the colours of the rainbow. It was my first visit to Siena, and although I had sincere intentions to attend the prestigious lectures, I simply couldn't manage it – the city streets worked their magic on me.

To relieve myself of the guilt of skipping the lectures, I excused myself as follows: 'This is a huge conference!

This afternoon there are 17 lectures and discussions taking place at the same time. This means that no matter what, I'm doomed to missing at least 16 lectures this afternoon. Well, is there such a big difference between 16 and 17? Moreover, if I miss them all, I can sit in the square, drink *vino santo*, munch on *cantuccini* biscuits, discuss the overt and covert connections between art and science with Daniella, and enjoy this wonderful day under the Tuscan sky.'

This led me to ponder on the innumerable lectures that were taking place at this very moment in Italy, Israel, Russia, China, and everywhere else in the world that I had no way of attending, which made my absence from the lecture I'd originally planned to attend and my idleness and relish of the wonderful day ahead even more satisfying and enjoyable.

Thus, I devoted myself to *il dolce far niente*, the 'sweet art of idleness'.

Italian for beginners

Many years ago I was a guest at Castello di Proceno in the Lazio region in Italy. The town that bears the name of the castle was very small and very quiet. My wife, myself, and our two daughters comprised the total complement of tourists in the town. One morning I went to the grocery store to buy provisions for the dinner my wife had decided to prepare for us all. The evening was planned to entail many hours of dining and chatting by the light of candles (which were featured on my shopping list). I was careful to procure every item on the list and then went to stand in line to pay. The cashier was the owner and sole employee of the grocery store. Even though there only a few customers, the queue crawled at a snail's pace because of the long conversations the cashier had to have with everyone. In front of me stood a rather elderly woman with whom the cashier had a discussion about all sorts of issues that bother only residents of small towns in Italy. I waited very patiently – when in Proceno one must do as the Procenesi do.

After a few minutes of conversation, the cashier informed all those waiting (at first I hoped I might not have understood the Italian properly) that they'd have to wait while he helped this lady carry her baskets home, but there was nothing to worry about because her home was near by – at most a five- or six-minute walk. I figured he was directing this information mainly at me, because the locals probably knew where she lived. He took three baskets in his right hand, two in his left, and set off. No one at the grocery store, except me, seemed at all perturbed. The Procenesi know that there's no point in rushing about … just like the great Lebowski.

CHAPTER 9

Aristotle's Blog on *Eudaimonia*

In his 1950 article *On Being Modern-Minded* Bertrand Russell describes an almost irresistible illusion regarding our view of world history and intellectual progress over the years. Because the people living in any particular age tend to exaggerate its uniqueness and imagine it to be the pinnacle of progress, they tend to ignore the continuity of preceding periods of history. New words we've invented often hide from us the thoughts and feelings of great intellectuals from ancient times, despite their being only slightly different, in essence, from our own.

Who is the greatest philosopher of all time? There are three names that invariably appear at the top of any list of the prime philosophers: Plato, Aristotle, and Kant.

Aristotle was one of the founding fathers of Western philosophy. He dealt with science and also with the border between philosophy and science. His interests included physics and metaphysics, economics and politics, biology and zoology, geography and meteorology, ethics and aesthetics, theatre and poetry, music and rhetoric, mathematics and psychology. Just as Plato was Socrates' most famous student, Aristotle was Plato's most famous student. He taught at the Athens Academy and also served as private tutor to Alexander the Great. At the age of 50, Aristotle founded his own institution of learning – the Lyceum. Aristotle and his teachings greatly influenced the three monotheistic religions.

In the Middle Ages he was revered by both Muslim scholars, who called him the 'first teacher', and Christians. The most important philosopher in the Christian world in the 13th century, Thomas Aquinas (1225–1274), an Italian Dominican friar and priest, addressed him simply as 'The Philosopher', and Maimonides, in his *Guide to the Perplexed,* engaged in conversation, back and forth, with Aristotle's ideas. I'll add that in the 14th century the poet Dante called Aristotle the 'Master of Those Who Know' in *The Divine Comedy*.

Aristotle was born 384 years before the advent of the Christian calendar. He's considered the pioneer of the logical system of biology and also of the inductive-deductive scientific method. And the list goes on. Aristotle presents the greatest example of the human spirit of all times and of all peoples.

It seems to me that Aristotle can also be viewed as the founding father of the 'science of happiness', a subject he discusses in great detail in his work *Nicomachean Ethics.* (Philosophers who preceded him had also dealt with the subject, but no one as systematically and extensively as he.) In line with Russell's observation, the more modern words and concepts that have developed in the interim have produced a semantic fog around Aristotle's archaic technical language. They obscure the fact that this Greek philosopher's views about happiness are only slightly different from ours.

However, before we buy Aristotle's book as an up-to-date guide to happiness or install his image as our screensaver, it's worth noting that *Nicomachean Ethics* is quite complicated and, unlike Plato's letters, is almost entirely devoid of any literary beauty. And if that's not enough, then I'll tell you that when Aristotle writes about happiness, he doesn't really mean the feeling you'll get from a retreat in an Indian ashram or a cruise among the Greek islands. His concept is something completely different: more abstract and difficult to achieve.

Nicomachean Ethics comprises 10 books. In Book 1, Chapter 2, Aristotle focuses on a very specific type of happiness he calls *eudaimonia*, a word that implies 'supreme human goodness' (in Greek, *eu* means 'good' and *daimōn* means spirit). Aristotle tries to uncover exactly what 'supreme goodness' entails – in other words, how we should best conduct our lives to give it meaning.

So what is *eudaimonia*?

Until only a few years ago the term *eudaimonia* was almost always rendered in Western languages as 'happiness'. However, I've recently come to notice fewer and fewer translations using 'happiness' and more that use terms relating to self-fulfilment or prosperity – for example, 'flourishing', 'well-being', or 'living well'. For Aristotle *eudaimonia* is, first and foremost, the correct way to conduct one's life, which doesn't necessarily guarantee 'happiness' in the modern sense of the word. He claimed that *eudaimonia* is a rational behaviour aiming to seek out all that's worthy in life.

Eudaimonia, according to Aristotle, means 'to live well and do good' (*Nicomachean Ethics*, Book 1, Chapter 4). (Later we shall meet other schools of Greek philosophy that interpreted the term completely differently.) A person is most likely to attain the eudaimonic state if they (take a pause for breath now) comprehend what sets them apart as an individual, engage in philosophical contemplation and profound self-observation, strive to be worthy of everything that happens to them in this life (for better or worse), understand that *being* good is no less important, and perhaps even more important, than *feeling* good, strive to contribute as citizen to their city and country, foster the aptitudes they have acquired as an intelligent being in order to realize their full potential, and be loyal to the best possible version of themselves. However, all of the above is merely a *necessary* requirement for *eudaimonia*: it isn't a *sufficient* requirement. *Eudaimonia* requires fulfilling all these conditions *and also* having health, family, wealth, luck, and friends during the whole of one's life.

Eudaimonia is an intrinsic purpose in itself and the purpose of human existence. (Note that, from now on, I'll sometimes employ the term 'happiness' to refer to *eudaimonia* – it's good to ring the changes.)

When Aristotle declares that happiness is an intrinsic purpose in itself, he means – as far as I understand it – that happiness has no external purpose: it isn't a means to achieve something else, nor is it subject to any purpose higher than itself. We don't strive for happiness in order to achieve other things. The purpose of happiness, says Aristotle, is happiness.

I'll try to explain this further.

It will probably come as no surprise if I say that certain objectives we set in our lives depend on other objectives, which in turn depend on others. Let's examine some examples.

Why do we study? Is it because we believe this is the way to integrate better into society? Is it to help us find an interesting and rewarding job? Or perhaps it's simply because accumulating knowledge gives us pleasure and satisfaction? In other words, studying is a means of attaining other goals and not an end in itself. What is the purpose of work? Work can provide self-esteem, satisfaction, and enjoyment, but for most of us work is also, and perhaps mainly, a source of income. In other words, work is also subject to other goals: satisfaction or money.

And what about money? Is it a goal in itself or is it for another purpose? Arthur Schopenhauer contended that for many people accumulating money becomes *the* purpose, *the* ultimate goal. However, he continued, such people are confused about what they are doing, simply because they don't bother to question what happiness is. When money stops being a means and becomes the ultimate goal, it turns into a kind of 'abstract happiness' – which isn't truly fulfilling. Like Aristotle, Schopenhauer believed that wise people consider money to be a means and not an end in itself. He adds that, for many, money is like sea water – the more you drink, the thirstier you get.

Schopenhauer fully agrees here with Aristotle, who articulated this idea in Book 1, Chapter 5 of *Nicomachean Ethics*. Aristotle wrote that a life devoted to making money arises from a barely controllable impulse, yet wealth, important as it may be, isn't the ultimate goal some might imagine: it's just a useful means to achieving another, loftier purpose.

This sequence, whereby one goal becomes subordinate to another, can continue on and on, but at the end of the hierarchy lies one ultimate goal that serves as the *underlying* motivating factor, instilling value into all intermediate goals. This epitome of goals is 'happiness', even though it isn't at all clear that happiness can ever be truly – or even approximately – achieved.

And why does a person want to be happy? Because, argues Aristotle, this is the culmination of all our questions, all our striving: *people want to be happy simply because people want to be happy*.

So what does Aristotle mean when he says that happiness is the point of human existence?

In his wonderful book *The Varieties of Religious Experience* American philosopher and psychologist William James (1842–1910) echoed Aristotle:

How to gain, how to keep, how to recover happiness, is in fact for most men at all times the secret motive of all they do.

We all know, of course, the famous combination embodied in the American Declaration of Independence: 'Life, Liberty, and the pursuit of Happiness'.

I should like to draw your attention to the fact that Thomas Jefferson, author of this declaration, placed happiness on the same level as freedom and life itself. However, it's also worth noting that 'happiness' appears at the end of the list, as a last detail, implying that there's no point in talking about happiness if you aren't already living as a free person. In the interests of of proper disclosure, I must point out that Aristotle was never hungry for bread and was always a free man.

We often speak of *pursuing* happiness, as if it were some elusive creature of the hunt. However, could it be that this 'pursuit' is the greatest *obstacle* to happiness? By the way, the word 'pursuit' has another meaning. This is one of its definitions in the *Cambridge Dictionary*: 'Pursuit: An activity that you spend time and energy doing.'

All this seems to have made Thomas Jefferson's simple reference more complicated than first appeared. In any event, perhaps instead of chasing after happiness more and more, it would be better to stop for a moment and just … be happy? Is this possible?

Here is Michel de Montaigne's supposition: 'In actuality, the lives of thousands of ordinary women in their villages have been more gentle, equable and constant than [Cicero's].' Cicero, Aristotle, and many other philosophers who were popular in Montaigne's day seemed to imply that treading the path to happiness required exerting one's powers of reason; and that anyone not endowed with wisdom would lack the ability to be properly happy. The exalted place these philosophers gave to reason greatly angered Montaigne. Schopenhauer shared this anger. The German philosopher (who admired Montaigne) believed that despite the arrogant yet prevalent belief that our bodies are meant to serve our souls, the opposite is true: our souls serves our bodies. In his opinion, there's a force that precedes all reason, all thinking, all common sense. He called this force the 'desire for life' and argued that it could distort all plans and choices born out of reason, even among philosophers.

I believe that both Aristotle/Cicero and Montaigne/Schopenhauer are correct, despite the fact that their claims seem to be almost the exact opposite of each other.

How can this be possible? I summon American national poet Walt Whitman (1819–1892) to my defence:

> Do I contradict myself?
> Very well then I contradict myself …
> **Walt Whitman, 'Song of Myself'**

And here's some further assistance. I present to you the opinion of physicist and Nobel Prize winner Niels Bohr:

> There are trivial truths and there are great truths.
> The opposite of a trivial truth is plainly false. The opposite of a great truth is also true.

Thousands of years ago, the author of the marvellous book of Ecclesiastes offered numerous examples of Bohr's principle. Here are two quotations relevant to our discussion. They can even serve as an interim summary of the advantages and disadvantages of reason:

> For as wisdom grows, vexation grows;
> To increase learning is to increase heartache.
> **Ecclesiastes, 1:18**

A wise man has his eyes in his head,
Whereas a fool walks in darkness.
Ecclesiastes, 2:14

The first passage expresses the problem with wisdom; the second, the advantage a wise man has over a fool, like the advantage light has over darkness. I identify with both.

Furthermore, let us now revisit the concept of 'Wittgenstein's box' (see page 22). Aristotle, Cicero, Michel de Montaigne, Arthur Schopenhauer, William James, Thomas Jefferson, the writer of these very lines, and the reader of these lines – all are aware of a thing called 'happiness'. But let's not get confused: there's hardly any resemblance between the contents of all these separate boxes where the concept resides.

It's worth, at this point, delving a little deeper into Aristotle's *eudaimonia*. To understand why *eudaimonia* is so difficult to attain, I want to address another of Aristotle's postulations. He claimed that one way to test if a person has achieved happiness is to ask whether they feel they are no longer in need of anything. However, I must immediately point out that he doesn't recommend asceticism – it's incumbent on a person to live a full life, to be an active citizen, to have superior moral standards, and, of course (I hope you recall this), to make friends.

Anyway, if I were a psychoanalyst, I'd say that it seems Aristotle claims that happiness is a betrayal of one's passion or, perhaps better, that passion is a betrayal of one's happiness.

The following insight is found in the Hebrew sources: 'Who is rich? He who rejoices in his lot' (Mishna Avot, 4:1). To this I'd add the variation, 'Who is happy? He who rejoices in his lot.' Aristotle called this particular attribute of happiness *αὐτάρκεια*, or 'autarky'. It refers to a kind of self-sufficiency. Today the word 'autarky' is used mainly by economists – an autarkic economy is one that doesn't conduct foreign trade and tries to satisfy all its needs on its own. (In these days of the coronavirus pandemic, the idea of an autarkic economy sounds less strange than before.)

Eudaimonia, according to Aristotle (and according to Stoic philosophy, which I'll expand upon later), is, in economic terms, autarky happiness. That is, it can thrive independently and doesn't depend on anything external to it. The Stoics (who were influenced by Aristotle) believed that a person in a state of *eudaimonia* is usually not dependent on events taking place in the outside world, nor influenced by the actions and thoughts of others. Clearly, this is a mental state that only a few can achieve: the air at the summit is thin and not suitable for those who have not properly trained their body and mind.

> *Regarding happiness … Well, after all, desires torment us, don't they? And it is clear as day that a person is happy when they have no more desires, not one … What a mistake, what a ridiculous, old-fashioned prejudice to always mark happiness with a plus sign. Absolute happiness should, of course, carry a minus sign – the divine minus.*[14]

These are the words of Russian author Yevgeny Zamyatin in his dystopian novel *We*. The book was written in 1920–21 but for censorship reasons was published in Russia only in

1988. George Orwell suggested that Aldous Huxley's *Brave New World* was greatly inspired by *We*. Did Zamyatin try to validate Aristotle's concept of autarky happiness in those lines? Absolutely not – read the book (there are a number of translations available in English). I shall return to what Aldous Huxley took from *We* a little later.

* * *

If a person has reached a state where they do not desire anything and are not moved by anything, attaining autarky happiness (and I'll state this again because it's important: autarky happiness is not the happiness of a solitary person but of someone with family, friends, and community), then, states Aristotle, this individual has reached the degree of *perfection*. The word 'perfection' is not too grand to describe this situation. However, it's reasonable to ask if this situation is at all possible. Think about what it means: you've achieved everything that's worth achieving and now you don't yearn for anything, don't want for anything, don't need anything, aren't affected by anything. All is perfect and sublime. You're fulfilled and all is good in the world. (As I ended this previous sentence, I imagined Lebowski and his friends bowling …) For mortals like me, I believe such a situation can be possible only for brief and rather rare periods of time.

Loyal readers of my books may remember that my wife defines such times as 'moments when a person feels nostalgia for the present'. How beautiful! But Aristotle isn't talking about moments: he has in mind a situation where things don't change but remain as they are until the end of the happy person's days.

To not want a thing? It seems that this almost contradicts human nature. Perhaps you remember Logan Smith saying, 'There are two things to aim at in life: first, to get what you want; and after that, to enjoy it. Only the *wisest of mankind* achieve the second.'

As if that weren't exacting enough, Aristotle also believed one should speak of someone's happiness/ *eudaimonia* only toward the end of their life, as a kind of wrap-up of everything they've accomplished under the sun. Anyone who hears in this an echo of the famous saying by Solon (considered to be one of the seven sages of Greece), 'Count no man happy until the end is known', has excellent literary/philosophical perception.

Here's what Aristotle wrote in the first book of *Nicomachean Ethics*:

Just as one swallow or a single sunny day does not herald the coming of spring, so good days or even a blessed year are no guarantee of a person's happiness.

Aristotle wouldn't have liked the phrase 'a *moment* of happiness' or 'a *moment* of *eudaimonia*'. According to him, and also many other scholarly minds, if you experience a moment of 'happiness' that suddenly disappears, it doesn't deserve to be called happiness. Call it a moment of joy, an hour of bliss, a day of pure pleasure, or a year of satisfaction … anything will do. Just not happiness! *True happiness, for Aristotle, cannot disappear.*

The happiest man in the world

Anton Chekhov has a short story that beautifully illustrates this point. The story, 'A Happy Man', is not that well known.

Here's a summary of the plot. In the very first sentence we meet the protagonist, Ivan Alexyevitch, who is entering the carriage of a train that's slowly and decisively embarking on its journey. It's obvious that Ivan is in a particularly good mood, and also a bit intoxicated. Our hero is surprised to bump into his long-time friend, Pyotr Petrovitch.

'How are you, Pyotr?'

'I'm fine. You know… life. You get good days and bad days. And how about you, Ivan?'

'Listen,' says Ivan, breathless with excitement. 'You see before you the happiest man … Yes, just like that, the happiest person in the world. Everything is so wonderful that I'm even a little embarrassed. I'm on the first day of my honeymoon. Just on my way to the carriage where my wife is waiting … She is the most beautiful of women … blonde, sweet little nose … and her eyes! … And what legs! Slim and shapely. And how wonderful she is to me. I've absolutely no idea how to deal with all this happiness. I never knew that a human being, and certainly not a fool like me, could be so happy. I never imagined such happiness was even possible …'

Ivan was unstoppable. He ponders his happiness from all angles, and then, a touch philosophically, adds, 'But the truth is that anyone can be as happy as I. It's a matter of choice. Want to be happy? *Be* happy. Want to suffer? Suffer. We only live once, so why suffer, eh? All those philosophers with their stupid analyses don't understand a thing. We're meant to be happy and marriage is the most important thing for a person's happiness … Life is so beautiful …'

The ticket collector enters. Ivan tells him his ticket is in his wallet, which is with his wife, in car number 219, to which the ticket collector responds that there *is* no car number 219. The last car on this train to Moscow is number 209.

'Moscow?' exclaims the surprised Ivan. 'But isn't this the express train to St Petersburg?'

'The train is indeed an express, but its destination is Moscow,' answers the ticket collector.

Slowly the meaning of the ticket collector's words dawns on Ivan. He realizes that the worst has happened: apparently, at the last stop, after he got down from the train for a smoke and a glass of cognac, he accidentally got on board another train heading in the opposite direction. After a few seconds of utter astonishment, Ivan Alexyevitch holds his head in his hands and begins pacing back and forth in large, striding steps. All the passengers in the car pity him. The first day of his honeymoon, and this!

'What an idiot I am! My poor wife is now alone and has no idea what to think. She's probably crying … Oh, what a disaster this is! … Oh, oh!' Ivan starts to sob. 'I'm the most miserable of people … In this entire world, you won't find anyone more wretched. It's awful … It's awful and terrible … I don't believe it … What a disaster'!

Pyotr tries to comfort his friend and suggests sending a telegram at the very next stop and changing trains.

'Where will I send the telegram to? Also, I don't have money for a ticket. My wallet is with my wife … I'm an unbearable person. I'm an idiot. Finished … What will I do? What?'

Ivan Alexyevitch's spirit is shattered. The hearts of the car's occupants go out to the unfortunate man, and they all pass a hat round to collect money for a ticket to St Petersburg.

At this point, while writing this summary, I paused and came to the conclusion that perhaps the story Chekhov is trying to tell us is more serious than I'd thought prior to starting my translation.

Most people easily move back and forth from states of joy to states of sadness. What will happen when Ivan meets his wife again? Will he become the happiest man once more? What if his new wife, choking in her tears, tells him that while he was riding the wrong train, she, in the correct train, met a wonderful man and then, although she doesn't quite understand how it happened, during their short conversation their hearts became entwined, and now she's uncertain what to do? Will be Ivan again become 'the most wretched person in the universe?'

This fictional addition I've concocted for Chekhov's story describes a quite dramatic event, but even trivial things can cloud our spirits, just as trivial things can be comforting. A ray of sunshine in the morning can bring jubilation; a sniffle that just won't go away can depress a person to the depths of their soul. As someone once said, there aren't many (if any) philosophers who, despite all the sublime theories they've come up with, are able to quietly endure the pain of an infected wisdom tooth.

But *eudaimonia*, according to Aristotle's model, is as stable as a rock. Even a raging hurricane, never mind a light breeze, couldn't possibly budge it!

I imagine that, for most of us, a stable state of happiness seems an excessive and perhaps even impossible demand, but I still think we should stop in our tracks for a moment to think about Aristotle's ideas. Happiness shouldn't vanish into thin air just because you get into a muddle on a train. To

Aristotle, ping-ponging (of course, he didn't use this term) between sublime happiness and abysmal misery, between joy and gloom, seems to be rather ridiculous.

Aristotle raised an important point, but we must remember this is not an exact science, and we're under no obligation to agree.

Can we define 'happiness'?

In Book 1, Chapter 3 of *Nicomachean Ethics* Aristotle writes that one sign of an educated person is that they strive to arrive at a level of accuracy appropriate to the subject under discussion. One would never accept a mathematical conjecture without indisputable proof, but it would be foolish to demand scientific reasoning from someone talking about rhetoric. Ethics, by its nature, is neither precise nor absolute, and it wouldn't make sense to expect explicit demonstrations that are overwhelmingly rigorous.[15]

> The happiness we have built for you is flawless mathematically. If you happen to refuse to accept it, we will be forced to compel you to be happy.
> **Yevgeny Zamyatin, *We*, List Number 1**

Actually, the ping-ponging that seems trivial to Aristotle seems to me to be human … very human indeed.

Now, let's ask this question: do any of us, consciously or unconsciously, agree with Aristotle that happiness is the purpose of human existence and that we indeed want to be happy? In my opinion, most people will answer 'yes', and this often includes, paradoxically, even those who claim to have loftier goals in life. I have no idea how any particular individual views their own happiness. It doesn't seem to me that many will actually pursue Aristotle-style *eudaimonia*, but I believe most of us want to be happy, each in our own way.

After all, I can think of no one who is likely to say, 'I don't want to be happy, I prefer to be miserable.'

Albert Einstein said that happiness really doesn't interest him, and that happiness is the 'ideal of a pigsty': he prefers to solve complicated equations and discover the secrets of the universe. However, I'll allow myself to disagree with the great physicist on this matter. Later in life he'll disagree with himself: Einstein, too, wanted to be happy. But for him happiness took on particular characteristics: it involved, among other things, an attempt to glimpse the secrets of creation.

Russian philosopher Nikolai Berdyaev (1874–1948) argued that the burning hatred followers of Nietzsche's Zoroastrianism felt toward those seeking happiness was a sacred abhorrence of humanism's insulting lie. Berdyaev's belief that Zoroastrianism preaches creation rather than the search for happiness isn't quite right. Zoroastrianism calls for a person to climb steep and dangerous mountains and not prefer the serenity of the plains. Some might say this requires passion to be privileged above happiness. But I disagree. If someone likes to climb steep and dangerous mountains – whether real or metaphorical – that doesn't mean that person doesn't want to be happy.

There are some philosophers, Slavoj Žižek among them, who look at the topic of happiness quite contemptuously and claim that what really matters is the *meaning* a person gives to their life. I don't agree with them at all. 'Meaning', in my opinion, is an important part of the equation of happiness.

It was Tal Ben-Shahar, the American-Israeli teacher and writer (b. 1970) (we met him on page 56), who suggested a basic equation for happiness:

Happiness = pleasure + **meaning**

Note that the purpose of this *equation* for happiness is to present the matter with an element of descriptive algebra: this isn't a *formula* that tells us exactly what to do to be happy.

Also, it isn't an error that one half of the equation – the word 'meaning' – is typographically emboldened to give it greater weight. Despite the value we may assign to pleasure, the importance of giving our lives meaning easily surpasses pleasure's importance. No one at the end of their life will say, 'That truffle pie I ate at Robuchon's restaurant was sublime – I had a good life,' or 'I so enjoyed that eight-hand massage in Macau, I'm so glad I was born.' It's more likely that their measure of a good life will be their loving relationships with their children, their partner, true friendships, as well as worthy things they have done and are proud of.

Heraclitus claimed that for him happiness was composed solely of bodily pleasures. Taking this line, we might say that the peak of possible happiness would be experiencing something like a bull that, after eating a hearty meal of herbs and vegetables, mates with a few cows.

I've stated that I believe that most people want to be happy. I didn't claim *all* people want to be happy, simply because the concept of 'all' is, as usual, complicated.

Aristotle's claim that happiness is the purpose of human existence is probably true to one degree or another for most of Western culture. However, what about other cultures? There's no doubt that different cultures vary in their attitudes to happiness. But are there any cultures in which a desire for personal happiness doesn't even exist?

It transpires that, yes, there are some. There are quite a few articles on this fascinating topic (for those who wish to delve deeper, I cite in the endnotes an article that presents an excellent introduction to the subject – it can even be found online.[16]) Quite aside from a number of secular exceptions, what about religions? The pursuit of happiness that focuses primarily on 'I' is not supported by most religions I'm familiar with. For example, in Sikhism there's the concept of *haumai*, which was introduced by Guru Nanak (1469–1539), the faith's founder. It means 'here I am', signifying self-centredness. The term may be understood to refer to unrestricted egoism. Nanak taught that *haumai* is the source of the five cardinal 'thieves' (vices) that lead to worldwide suffering: lust, greed, wrath, attachment, and ego (excessive pride).

Immanuel Kant believed that happiness was unattainable. He was convinced it was merely the 'ideal of imagination' – in other words, that the happiness we strive for exists only in the realm of our own minds. After all, a person will always want more: to be richer and/or smarter and/or more beautiful and/or braver and/or better and/or healthier (or, at least, wanting future health) and/or more appreciated and/or more loved, and so on.

Kant even claimed that we're unable to put into words all that we long for. I think he was absolutely correct.

Can one happiness fit all?

Given our individual peculiarities, theories regarding happiness, as Aristotle stated, cannot at all be compared with mathematical theorems, which are true for all. These things are personal. In the same way that most people love music but we each have our own playlist, we all want to be happy but the 'playlist' of what will make us happy differs from one person to another.

American philosopher Robert Nozick (1938–2002), among other things, served as president of the American Philosophical Association and taught for many years at Harvard. In his book *Anarchy, State, and Utopia* (1974) he offered a long list of different people from all periods and all walks of life[17] and asked if anyone could seriously believe that one way of life could suit all these individuals.

Inspired by Nozick's list – how could I possibly resist? – I compiled a list for you that doesn't include any baseball players and, in general, is less biased toward the United States. You can decide if it's possible to speak (or write a book) about happiness or the proper way of life or the meaning of life that could apply to all these people at once. My list:

Aristotle, Helen Keller, Ludwig Wittgenstein, Anwar El Sadat, Kim Kardashian, Caitlin (formerly Bruce) Jenner, Bruce Lee, Diogenes, Elizabeth Taylor, Alan Ginsberg, The Buddha, Albert Einstein, Thich Nhat Hanh, Rebbe of Lubavitch, Pablo Picasso, Ayaan Hirsi Ali, Muhammad Ali, Bill Gates, Billie Eilish, Hugh Hefner, Sigmund Freud, Usain Bolt, Socrates, Vladimir Putin, The Dalai Lama, Ted Bundy, Lady Gaga, Golda Meir, Meir Lansky, Ayn

Rand, Mahatma Gandhi, Indirha Gandhi, the Baron Rothschild, Aishwarya Rai Bachchan, Moses, Bobby Fischer, Mike Tyson, Marie Kondo, Leo Tolstoy, Marie Curie, Donald Trump, Chimamanda Ngozi Adichie, Greta Thunberg, Greta Garbo, Gregory Perlman, Emma Goldman, Frida Kahlo, Franz Kafka, LeBron James, a poor woman who toils all day in rice fields in a remote region of Myanmar, Zhuang Zhou, Glenn Gould, Maradona, Madonna, Elizabeth Báthory, Leonardo da Vinci, Leonardo DiCaprio, Leonardo Fibonacci, my next-door neighbours, and prisoners all over the world with life sentences.

What can the Rebbe of Lubavitch, Marie Curie, and *Playboy* founder Hugh Hefner possibly have in common?

Obviously my list names mostly celebrities: it doesn't at all represent a cross-section of the average population. However, I've noticed that reading it out during my lectures does help to internalize the idea that *not only are there no organized tours to the realm of happiness, there are probably no shuttles that go anywhere in its vicinity.* We all need to discover our own path and pave it as best we can, according to our own design.

One of the problems (and there are many!) that affect both simplistic how-to guides to happiness and scientific studies on the subject is that, while they may offer concepts or conclusions that are true for many, they will not necessarily be true for everyone.

The great Aristotle perhaps didn't pay enough attention to the differences between one individual and another, but he did identify (in *Nicomachean Ethics,* Book 1, Chapter 5) three different kinds of happiness based on the different worldviews people may have. At the lowest level is a perception of happiness derived from mere pleasure: this applies, in Aristotle's opinion, and to his sorrow, to most people. At the next level is a concept of happiness that's based on some matter of honour – for example, someone who becomes a politician to contribute to the well-being and good of others (in Aristotle's day such a concept wasn't so far-fetched). At the highest level is the scrupulous study of philosophy, with whose aid one can strive to reach the realm of *eudaimonia*.

Friends, wisdom, and the pursuit of happiness

A widely accepted notion in contemporary studies on the subject is that having friends contributes greatly to one's happiness (which is what Aristotle believed). However, when another variable – IQ – was introduced into the study, it turned out that those with way above-average IQs actually enjoyed being on their own more than being with others: it's preferable, it seems, for a wise person to keep their own company, or if with friends, they should be few in number and of high quality.[18] I know several people for whom Sartre's saying, '*L'enfer, best les autres*' ('Hell is other people') applies perfectly, and I couldn't attest whether their IQ level is above or below average. On the other hand, I also know some people with a very high IQ who are most certainly very sociable.

What's clear to me is that there's nothing special about IQ, and there will always be other variables that would skew the results differently.

As a mathematician, I find another problem posed by the research on how happiness and sociability are connected. As I've stated, I agree that people with many friends are happier than those with only a few or none at all. But perhaps this is an issue of – as it's called in the language of statistics – 'reverse causality'? Does having multiple friends make a person happier or do happier people tend to develop more friendships? Psychologists are aware that when people with bipolar disorder are at the nadir of depression, they tend to avoid others and descend into the blues, but when they shift to the opposite pole, when they feel elated, they tend to do what happy people do – get involved in social relations.

This convinces me that happiness win us friends, more than friends win us happiness.

(My mention of winning reminds me that sometimes I have heretical thoughts: perhaps what we win in our genetic lottery is responsible for our happiness much more than it's customary to think.)

Reverse causality might apply not only in connection with studies of friendships but also with other inquiries into what makes people happy. For example, does making donations contribute to a person's happiness or is a happy person more likely to donate? Does a good night's sleep contribute to a person's happiness or do happier people tend to fall asleep more easily and enjoy a better quality of slumber?

Similar complexities arise when we consider the significance of wisdom in this respect.

Ernest Hemingway (1899–1961) concluded – apparently based on his own life experience – that happiness is the rarest thing in the world for smart people. I'm not at all sure he's correct. The criteria for who can be counted a 'smart person' are by no means exact: this is a vague subject area. I'd also argue that the verse previously cited, '… for as wisdom grows, vexation grows' (Ecclesiastes, 1:18), might not be so accurate. In fact, I'd suggest this alternative: 'As wisdom grows, so do wonder and comfort.'

I wouldn't dare guess their distribution in percentages, but it's quite clear to me that there are four groups of people: smart and happy, smart and miserable, stupid and happy, and stupid and miserable. Not to mention the gamut of intermediate shades between smart and stupid, and happy and unhappy.

More than two decades ago I was in Singapore teaching maths and statistics to graduate business administration students. Most of the students were quite mature and already held senior positions in the Singaporean economy. During breaks, they wanted to talk to me about politics, while I preferred to discuss Chinese philosophy and Buddhism. To my delight, during one break, the conversation took the turn I was hoping for. One of the students told me that, in Mandarin, the word that comes closest to 'happiness' has multiple meanings that range from 'having a worthy life' (Aristotle would have loved that) to 'having a good death'. A worthy life and a good death – it seems to me that speakers of Mandarin know what they're talking about.

Now, let's consider again the *pursuit* of happiness.

In recent years there has been an increase in the number of voices – including some belonging to my friends – arguing that forsaking the pursuit of happiness is a necessary (and sometimes sufficient) requirement for attaining a happy life. Of course, many studies have investigated this proposal, and as usual I'll select one example. In 2018 a study published in the journal *Emotion* showed that excessive thinking about happiness can lead people to become obsessed with any negative emotions, which then start to strike them as a sign of failure. When such failures happen – as they inevitably will – people often fall into a state of anxiety and depression.[19]

There's a quote circulating on the Internet (sometimes attributed to Nathaniel Hawthorne, sometimes to Henry David Thoreau) that goes like this: 'Happiness is like a butterfly. The more you chase it, the more it will elude you. But if you turn your attention to other things, it will come and alight softly on your shoulder.' Apparently, neither of the aforementioned luminaries is responsible for this sentiment, but that doesn't make it any less correct.

Let us now revisit our longtime friend, Chinese sage Zhuang Zhou, who tells of a man who pursued his own shadow. The faster he ran, the faster his shadow ran. Only when at last he became totally exhausted and sat down did he discover his shadow sitting alongside him.

I think we need to try to find the balance between obsessive pursuit of happiness and complete disregard for it. English philosopher John Stuart Mill (1806–1873), one of the founding fathers of Utilitarianism and a militant feminist, wrote that whoever thinks solely of their own personal happiness will never be happy. I agree with Mill's sentiment, but I doubt, by contrast, whether someone who thinks solely of *other people's* happiness will be happy either.

CHAPTER 10

The Secrets of the Virtues: Aristotle's Art of Finding Balance

Aristotle tried to answer the question of what makes a person worthy and what attributes are necessary for them to approach *eudaimonia*. With this question in mind, he assembled a collection of 12 virtues. Here they are: courage, temperance, liberality (generosity), magnificence, friendliness, proper ambition, magnanimity (greatness of soul), wit, equanimity (patience, even temper), credibility (sincerity and truthfulness), shame, and justice.

There are some who think this list is quite strange. I'm not of their opinion, however: the list might seem less strange if we consider that Aristotle composed it not for us in the modern world but for the men of ancient Athens. I believe Aristotle's list of virtues holds a considerable benefit for many even today – men and women alike. I refer to it often. In any case, no one will stop you from compiling your own list of good or bad attributes, and clearly there's no need to produce 12 of them. The truth is that Aristotle didn't actually compile a 'list' of virtues: rather, he scattered their descriptions throughout *Nicomachean Ethics* and left the job of assembly to his readers. (In his book *Rhetoric*, by the way, he does list nine virtues.) Some scholarly interpretations have yielded shorter or longer lists. I'll stick with the classic version.

Aristotle believed that each virtue lies on a scale between two extreme behaviours. Courage, for example, lies somewhere between recklessness and cowardice. This is, of course, *the middle way*. At this point, though, it's imperative for me to point out that the optimum isn't 'exactly' between the two undesirable extremes (in truth, we don't know where this middle is located), but *somewhere* between them. (Today we speak of the 'golden mean', but Aristotle didn't use this expression.) Sometimes the best point may be very close to one end of the scale or the other.

As far as I'm concerned, this list of Aristotle's is not a directive to be followed blindly: instead, it's a starting point for individual navigation.

Basically, Aristotle presents to us the boundaries of the attribute in question. Each of us needs to find our own appropriate point, and this may well be different from person to person.

Incidentally, the concept of the middle way appears in early Buddhist texts. For example, it's referred to in the second paragraph of the *Dhammacakkappavattana Sutta*, which according to tradition describes the first sermon delivered by the Buddha. It was also suggested by Confucius and also – do you remember? – it's cited in the inscription engraved on the gate of the Temple of Apollo at Delphi ('Do not exaggerate'). We may also find echoes of the idea of restraint and control in the ancient Hindu *Bhagavad Gita* scripture, as well as in the poetry of Cleobulus of Lindos, one of the Seven Sages of Greece, who wrote that 'moderation is the best choice of all'. Maimonides attributed the concept of a 'middle way' to the Hebrew sages, and I also found mention of the importance of self-restraint in a passage in Ecclesiastes that warns against zealous excess: 'Do not overdo goodness' (Ecclesiastes, 7:16). I trust there's no need to add that the idea of moderation also appears in Plato's writings.

If wise people from different times and diverse cultures extolled the middle way, can we ignore it?

So now let's consider the concept of the *middle way* in action. Let us discuss each of the virtues listed. As usual, my rendering will be quite personal, very associative, and more contemporary than that of the wise Greek thinker.

I'll develop my analysis of the first virtue – courage – quite extensively, both to understand how the whole business works and also because, in my opinion, courage might be considered a prerequisite for all the other virtues. Perhaps even for proper conduct. I don't consider myself a particularly brave person, hence the special interest I have in this issue.

Courage

Man's happiness is based on having freedom, and having freedom rests on the degree of courage in his heart.
Thucydides, *The History of the Peloponnesian War*

> *Courage is rightly esteemed the first of human qualities,*
> *because, as has been said, it is the quality which*
> *guarantees all others.*

Sir Winston Churchill, *Collier's* magazine, 1931

Courage (*ανδρεια, andreia*), according to Aristotle, lies on the scale between cowardice and recklessness. One may very prudently say that it's located closer to recklessness. Clearly, a person who fears his own shadow can't be considered brave, but on the other hand someone who ignores any dangers and plunges into reckless action is also not being courageous.

Performing an Olympic-style double vault while bungee jumping without a harness into the crater of an active volcano wouldn't be considered courageous: on the contrary, it's a fine example of recklessness and stupidity.

It's also important to point out that only someone who is able to show fear can be considered brave. Aristotle stressed that courage isn't possible in the absence of fear. He even adds that a brave person may sometimes fear things that not everyone tends to fear – however, they know how to overcome their fear and deal with it rationally.

Have you seen the TV series *Game of Thrones*? In one of the episodes (it may also occur in the source book, *A Song of Ice and Fire,* by American author George R.R. Martin) there's a brief dialogue I really liked in which Bran asks his father if someone who is afraid could be brave at the same time, and his father replies that the *only time* a person can be brave is when he also feels fear.

I hope you're convinced. If not, I shall tell you that even the great heavyweight boxer Muhammad Ali (Cassius Clay) claims in his fascinating book *The Soul of a Butterfly* (his autobiography, written in collaboration with his daughter Hannah Jasmine Ali; 2003) that there's no heroism without fear. This revelation has been voiced by many and has become a kind of cliché, but its credibility depends on who's saying it – it doesn't only matter what's said, but also how and by whom.

True courage, in my opinion, should be defined as some kind of function that takes into account the gap between the genetic/evolutionary fear inherent at different levels in each of us and our ability to overcome that fear. Fear is natural for everybody, but if we don't know how to overcome it, life will become a kind of slow death. Living in the shadow of fear is death before death. American writer John Augustus Shedd (1859–1928) coined the saying, 'A ship in harbor is safe, but that is not what ships are built for' (sometimes the saying is mistakenly attributed to Albert Einstein). Indeed, a desire for complete security is a form of mental disorder and also impossible. I would add to Shedd's adage that ships that remain in harbour for an extended period of time end up rusty and useless.

The decision to not take any risk is often the most dangerous decision of all.

According to Nietzsche, fear is one of the three most serious afflictions that can befall an individual (the others are hypocrisy and apathy). He lists the many anxieties that accompany us: fear for our health and the health of loved ones; fear for our economic welfare; fear of the judgment of others; fear of loneliness; fear of old age; and fear that at any moment we might die.

Nietzsche believed that behaviour fuelled by anxiety is an affliction. However, I'm not in complete agreement with this, and think it would be prudent to call for Aristotle's 'middle way' to clarify things. The key is not to stop being afraid or worrying or feeling anxious: the absence of all fear is not human! Who *doesn't* worry about the health of their children? Who *isn't* concerned about growing old? The trick is to avoid extremes and not let the fear control us.

A person who is ruled by fear instead of ruling fear needs help. Anyone who isn't afraid of being alone, and doesn't care about the health of their loved ones, and isn't afraid of old age or the collapse of all the ideals they once believed in, and isn't anxious about their mental well-being, nor afraid of their impending death – this person also needs help!

Many will disagree with this last statement.

Benjamin Disraeli, for example, believed – rather like Nietzsche – that one of the strangest things in life is the vast and unnecessary accumulation of anxieties that almost all human beings suffer from. My grandmother, the late Rosa Itzikovich, felt that most of a person's anxieties are for things that will never happen and therefore are totally unfounded.

Imagine I'm flying to a vacation in Thailand or the Maldives or wherever suits your fancy. All kinds of imagined scenarios are likely to cross my mind as I sit there. What if the plane crashes? What if a tsunami comes and turns our hotel into a floating guest house? What if there's a breakout of a new strain of coronavirus in our hotel? What if half my body goes numb from too many massages? What if I contract diverticulitis? What if I get fired from my job while on vacation? What if my daughter runs away from home with a Jeffery Lebowski look-alike who works as a full-time dog-food taster?

My grandmother believed such anxieties are useless, and an unfortunate waste of time and energy, and here's one reason why. If the captain suddenly announces the plane is about to crash, we'll be very sorry we wasted precious time worrying about a tsunami. And if we survive the crash but then get caught up in the biggest tsunami ever, would we care at all about being fired?

Think about another scenario, and the chances of it happening. It's the middle of the flight. The captain announces the plane is about to crash, and not just crash, but straight into the middle of a tremendous tsunami. We're going to end up right in the heart of that tsunami wave. At that moment, our heart starts pounding so hard that it becomes an SVT (supraventricular tachycardia) event. Then, contrary to the medical literature, this transforms into a heart attack. We clutch our hands to our chest and our thumb encounters a strange lump near our armpit which we immediately diagnose as a malignant tumour. At that very moment, still shocked by what's happening, we get a call from our boss announcing that we're fired. But we switch him to call-waiting because, at the same time, our daughter is calling to say she's decided to elope with a homeless bow-and-arrow maker and spend the rest of her life in a portable yurt. … And then a terrorist emerges from the cockpit!

Mostly when we worry, we're aren't in a position to take any action to address our anxieties in a practical way – for example, by reducing a risk we've identified. We simply let imaginary bad scenarios eat into our peace of mind.

On the other hand, the idea that one should stop worrying (entirely) is so much *bubba maiseh* – the Yiddish term for an 'old wive's tale'. My grandmother's personality allowed her to apply her own advice to her life, but for most of us this will scarcely be possible.

Jordan Peterson (b. 1962), Canadian psychologist, philosopher, and author (of *12 Rules for Life: An Antidote to Chaos*, 2018), believes – somewhat contrary to Disraeli and my grandmother Rosa – that at any given moment each of us has excellent reasons for being anxious. I tend to agree with him. However, I discovered that Piglet, Winnie the Poolosopher's friend, preceded Peterson by many years when he quipped that it was hard to be brave if you're a 'Very Small Animal'. And are we not all Very Small Animals?

French-born American diarist Anaïs Nin (1903–1977) was a very brave, wise woman. She wrote in her diary that life expands or shrinks depending on how much courage a person has.

Sometimes a person needs considerable courage simply to push back the duvet, extricate themselves from between the sheets, get out of bed, open the shutters, and take a small step into the big world.

It's been a while since I offered you, my readers, a list, so here's a list of things for which courage is a prerequisite:

Saying 'I love you', bringing children into the world, believing that life has meaning, believing in an ideal, being true to one's values, subjecting one values to critical scrutiny, expressing an unpopular opinion, trying to change the status quo, coping with illness, keeping one's moral fortitude even when facing tremendous fear or a burning desire, making difficult decisions in a forest of doubts, publishing a book, resisting a destructive passion, saying 'I was wrong', saying I'm sorry', not losing one's temper in the heat of battle, stopping lying to oneself, lying for a worthy purpose (I don't advocate telling the truth at all costs), straying out of your comfort zone, forgiving someone who hurt us (the more we were hurt, the more courage we require to forgive), doing what is right and not what is easy, initiating a conversation with strangers, asking for help, swimming against the stream …

Feel free to add to the list or delete anything you take issue with. I'll add that Immanuel Kant wrote in his article 'Answering the Question: What is Enlightenment?' (1874) that it takes courage to think for yourself and not rely too much on the opinions of others. I believe he was right in this.

Ask yourself, have you ever thought a real thought of your own? Fyodor Dostoevsky believed the vast majority of humans have never had the courage to think for themselves. Bertrand Russell in *The ABC of Relativity* (1925) adds his support to the Russian author's sentiment: 'Most people would die sooner than think.'

One of Plato's earlier dialogues is called *Laches (Λάχης)*, after the Greek general and statesman. Also participating in the dialogue (along with Laches) are another general, a general's son, and a general's grandson. The discussion is conducted under the guidance of Socrates, a citizen-soldier known as a brave warrior with high mental resilience. The purpose of the dialogue was to answer the question, 'What is courage?' The participants focus on *military* courage, but they also attempt to expand the definition of courage to all areas of life. In any case, the discussion ends in an *aporia* (ἀπορίᾱ), which in philosophy means a state of impasse: a kind of unsolvable paradox.[20] If you try to define courage, you will realize that it isn't at all easy.

For example, one can start, as Plato does, from a military standpoint. Where exactly should the line be drawn between courage and devotion to purpose on the one hand, and criminal recklessness and blatant irresponsibility on the other? When can refusing an order be considered courageous and when is it cowardice, and betrayal of one's comrades? (I'll refrain from giving specific examples.)

At the Battle of Thermopylae in 480 BCE, Leonidas I, 300 Spartans and 700 Thespians faced a massive Persian army of at least 120,000 men. To research the proportions of courage, cowardice, compulsion, commitment, fear, and other emotions among the combatants would be fascinating … but there's a good chance you'd end up without a definitive conclusion.

I'll add two further remarks. First, based on life experience, I've decided that it's wiser to say, 'here, this person showed courage,' than 'this was a courageous person.' I've seen quite a few people who have demonstrated courage in one situation and behaved in a cowardly or reckless way in another. Nevertheless, it's clear that some people are more likely than others to show courage in the face of danger.

My second point, which I'll put more briefly, is that no one knows how they'll act until they are put to the test.

Let's delve a little deeper into what Aristotle has to say on the matter. (If you want to follow along, open up *Nicomachean Ethics*, Book 3, Chapters 6 to 9.)

As already stated, according to Aristotle true courage lies somewhere between cowardice and recklessness/overconfidence. In his opinion, someone who fears what there's no reason to be afraid of (he counts 'noble death' and poverty among such things) is a coward. On the other hand, those who don't fear what deserves to be feared or who are never afraid of *anything* (Aristotle gives the Kelts, or Celts as they came to be known, as an example of such people) are insane. It's important to note that Aristotle thought it was logical and even desirable to fear really bad things, including disgrace, and danger to one's wife and children.

I might express the matter this way: courage means knowing what to fear and what not to fear. I'll refine this definition later.

Aristotle's main touchstones in his explorations of courage had to do with death and battle. He declared there are many evils that we fear with good reason – for example, humiliation or serious illness. Death is the evil of all evils, but in Aristotle's opinion a noble death in battle is a particularly fitting way to end one's life, so not only is there no reason to fear this prospect, but indeed one could even consider it dignified and desirable. I suppose you already appreciate that honour plays an important role in this Greek philosopher's teachings. Heraclitus taught that it's only in war that one can discover who has the soul of a slave and who of a free man, as he put it, and there's no doubt that Aristotle's opinion did not veer very far from that of Heraclitus, the philosopher who pontificated about flux and the unity of opposites.

Plato was convinced that fearing death implied believing oneself wiser than one possibly could be – as usual he puts words into Socrates' mouth. In other words, fearing death could be considered a sin of pride. Everyone is afraid of death, and some see it as the ultimate insult, but no one really *knows* death. Might it not be possible that death is the greatest of blessings?

> Cowards die many times before their deaths;
> The valiant never taste of death but once.
> **William Shakespeare, *Julius Caesar*, Act II, Scene 2**

Aristotle goes on to say that suicide to escape illness or poverty, or because of unrequited love, isn't a suitable action for the courageous. They should face life's difficulties, not run away from them. I once talked with my father about suicide. He told me, 'You really don't need courage to commit suicide. It's a natural choice when life is more frightening than death.'

In the *Apology of Socrates*, the dialogue by Plato, Socrates speaks to his fellow men just before he swallows the poison he has been sentenced to drink as a result of his trial. He tells them that he faces death while they will continue living, and only the gods know whose fate is better.

If we believe Plato, his devoted disciple Socrates went to his death with complete peace of mind. Socrates even managed to explain to his students that there are two possibilities: either there's nothing after death or else there's life after death. In the first case, death may be compared to a very deep, dreamless, eternal sleep – what bliss! Eight hours of uninterrupted, tranquil sleep is such a blessed thing, so how much better would be an *infinite* length of absolute, flawless sleep? The second possibility also heartened Socrates: if it transpires that there's life after death, he'd be able to migrate to a higher plane of existence where he could meet Homer and Hesiod and Heraclitus and many other wise and fascinating people with whom he'd dearly wish to exchange a word or two.

Epicurus (341–270 BCE) – we'll soon get to know the principles of his philosophy – explained it thus: as long as we are here, death is not; when death is here, we are no longer. In other words, we never actually meet death so how can there be anything to fear from it? Epicurus' views are encouraging to many, but in my opinion they're a bit deceptive. He refrains from saying anything about *how* one makes one's way into the world that some believe is the better of the two. My father exhibited supreme heroism facing a number of serious ailments, but even he was deadly afraid – not of death, but of the loss of human dignity and the thought of becoming a burden. How happy I'd be to learn that Dignitas was opening a branch in Israel and that everyone could have ownership over their own life (why should it be otherwise?) and could end a life when they can no longer bear it. In my (exaggerated) opinion, the burning of witches in the dark days of Europe's Middle Ages was a crime that pales into insignificance compared with the sin of prolonging the lives of people who are suffering excruciating pain and have no wish to go on.

Michel de Montaigne said that those who fear suffering are already suffering from the fear. Then he added that fear is what scares him most of all.

Aristotle lists five types of behaviours that seem brave but, in his view, are not – that is to say, he points out that there's a difference between true courage and fake courage, and his list focuses on fake courage. Do you even think that there's a minuscule chance I won't present the list to you? Here it is (though I'm sneaking it in as ordinary text this time):

First, a soldier who bravely faces danger because he fears that otherwise his colleagues will despise him and he wants to win their appreciation. He exhibits behaviour that, in Aristotle's opinion, is not worthy of being called 'brave'. This strikes me as unfair. A soldier displaying heroism – charging the enemy – because they are afraid to disobey a command is another matter: that would be uncourageous. In the first case, the motive is noble (in Israel we call it army camaraderie); while in the second, the motive is fear of punishment, and there's nothing like nobility involved.

Second, the 'courage' of an experienced professional mercenary. Such a person is familiar with the dangers of war, and anyone who sees them as brave is being somewhat naïve. In any case, when danger comes close, professional soldiers may turn cowardly, fearing death more than they fear disgrace.

Third, someone who behaves recklessly, without hesitation, sometimes for wrong or inappropriate reasons, and without being aware of the lurking peril. Aristotle doesn't consider such a person brave according to his criteria. He explains that someone with 'correct' courage acts unhesitatingly, but to qualify as courageous he must do so for a worthy, honourable purpose and will be well aware of the dangers.

Fourth, someone who is overconfident owing to drink. Aristotle warns that if things don't turn out the way they expect, or if they sober up and start behaving differently, these are not people you'd want to trust.

Fifth, someone who is simply not aware of the danger ahead. Those who are better informed and aware of the peril may see such a person as brave, though they are less likely to do so if they know that the pseudo-courageous person has missed some important factor in the situation.

Just one thought from me now as a coda to this list: sometimes, you might need courage to be afraid.

By all means add your own categories to these five of Aristotle's.

This seems the right moment to tell you that one of my favourite English poets, Lord Byron (1788–1824), author of the epic *Don Juan*, wrote as follows to his publisher John Murray:

> *French courage proceeds from vanity, the German from phlegm, the Turkish from fanaticism & opium, the Spanish from pride, the English from coolness, the Dutch from obstinacy, the Russian from insensibility, but the Italian from anger.*

Politically correct this is not. Political correctness wouldn't have bothered Aristotle at all, but if he had read the above, he certainly would have explained to Byron that everything he'd written has nothing to do with real courage. Can you see why?

What, then, is true courage? In contrast to what he wrote in *Laches*, Aristotle might have said this:

> *Courage means doing what is right when you need it and only when you need it, and doing it for the right reason and for a worthy purpose and in the correct way while being aware of what danger is involved and overcoming that danger.*

(Don't look for this in *Nicomachean Ethics* – I put it together myself, based on my own understanding of Aristotle's ideas.)

I'll end this section on courage with a reminder: death is always so close to us that it's really silly to be afraid of life. And there's no life without courage.

Temperance (*σωφροσύνη, sōphrosýnē*)

Temperance – that is to say, moderation – pertains to engagement in bodily and mental pleasures. Aristotle discusses this virtue in *Nicomachean Ethics*, Book 3, Chapters 10 to 12, immediately after delving into courage. Moderation sits somewhere between overindulgence (hedonism) and celibacy/inability to feel pleasure. Aristotle, I'm sure, would not have been fond of people who drink to the point of total inebriation or habitually in solitude. However, he also wouldn't have admired people who insist on never indulging in a glass of fine wine at a party with friends. Moderation is the guiding principle for almost any type of pleasure: abstinence and addiction sit at opposite ends of the scale, and the right measure is found, as usual, at some hard-to-define point between them.

In *Paradise Lost* 17th-century English poet and scholar John Milton gives his definition of temperance: 'the rule of not too much'. He even maintains that those who follow this rule will live a long life.

Mental pleasures, too, should be enjoyed with a degree of moderation. Blaise Pascal and Arthur Schopenhauer both advised that due measure should be applied even to the act of reading. Pascal recommends not reading too fast; Schopenhauer warns us not to read too much, or as he puts it, 'not to read oneself to stupidity'.

Aristotle informs us that someone who follows the virtue of temperance will, as a result, suffer neither shortage nor pain. Conversely, someone who does *not* exercise moderation will end up suffering pain even in his pleasures: his excessive longing will work against him. My good friend the wise Professor Yoram Yovell expressed the idea to me like this:

> *There is one, and only one, thing on which all the great philosophers and all the sages of the world agree: the road to happiness does not pass through any route that includes addiction to pleasure. Whoever tries to maximize his pleasures in life to the limit will never be happy. Finally realizing that pleasure and happiness are two different things led me to happiness.*

I emphasize that Professor Yovell doesn't advocate all abstinence from pleasure but, rather, advises one must maintain the *right degree of pleasure*.

The idea of abstinence is foreign to Jewish thought. I would not reject outright the notion that God inflicted his punishment on Adam and Eve, not so much not for the sin of eating from the tree of knowledge but more because they didn't taste all they could from the abundance of trees he'd planted in the Garden of Eden. In the Jerusalem Talmud there's a commentary that goes: 'In the name of Rev: In the future, a person will give a judgment and accounting over everything that his eye saw and what he did not eat' (Jerusalem Talmud, Kiddushin, 4:12, 3).

Let me organize things a bit. I see a huge difference between the obsessive pursuit of pleasure that makes it the *sole purpose of life* and making pleasures, large and small, one of many of our everyday goals. No one I know would want to give up those pleasures any particular day may allow: snuggling inside a duvet when it's cold and wet outside, playing football with friends, feeding a stray cat, listening to music. I will not – at this point – compile a list, because I've done so already, in *1,000 Ways to Be Happy* (just read it again). (Having had this thought, I've just hit upon the idea that my use of the word 'happy' in my title would have upset Aristotle: he would have preferred *1,000 Small, Important Pleasures.*)

To paraphrase Nietzsche, I'd say that if not for these small pleasures, life might be deemed a mistake. And speaking of pleasures, let me tell you now about a fascinating thought-experiment.

The ultimate pleasure machine

Our friend from several pages ago, philosopher Robert Nozick, conceived a thought-experiment he named the 'experience machine' or 'pleasure machine'. Let's call it the 'pleasure machine'. Nozick wrote several times about this experiment, and I think the presentation is to be found in *The Examined Life: How We Lose and Find Ourselves* (2013) (I shall expand upon this book in Chapter[11]).

The experiment goes like this. Imagine a machine that can give you any experience, and even any sequence of experiences, you might desire. Connected to this pleasure machine, you can write a great poem, win a marathon race, rule the world and bring all nations together in peace, or love someone and be loved in return. You'll experience the pleasures of these wonderful things viscerally. And here's another bonus: you can program all the pleasures you'll experience for the rest of your life; and if by chance your imagination is a bit meagre, there's a compendium of suggestions gleaned from the biographies of fascinating people, improved upon by top writers and psychologists. You'll be able to experience all your most beautiful dreams. As soon as you enter into the machine, you will not remember doing so, so your experience of pleasure won't be spoiled by understanding that it isn't real. So the question is: would you want to be connected to this pleasure machine *for the rest of your life*?

Imagine you're offered the choice between this ultimate pleasure machine and real life, over which you have little control and during which it's likely you'll have to endure some suffering. What do you say? 'Open the door to a world of pleasure'? Or are you still undecided? Perhaps you know immediately that this miraculous machine isn't for you?

Nozick didn't agree with the hedonistic philosophers, who believed that people would always choose pleasure over the absence of pleasure and possible accompanying distress. These thinkers thought most human beings would find a reason to hook up to a 'pleasure machine' that would give them only enjoyable, positive feelings. In Nozick's opinion, though, this wouldn't be the case.

It's worth remembering that 'suffering' is not always the opposite of happiness, and that not every pleasure necessarily contributes to happiness. A friend of mine, a heroin addict, once told me that heroin, more than anything else imaginable, leads to pleasure that actually *prevents* one from achieving happiness. Heroin, he said, is as far from pleasure as London is from the star Antares.

Pleasure, in certain circumstances, can quite easily be unmasked as a fraud. I believe the pleasure machine falls into this category, and I wouldn't connect to it even if you paid me a small fortune.

I've described this thought-experiment several times in my lectures, and each time I did so 70 to 80 percent of my audience responded that they would *not* want to connect to this machine. So my decision isn't an unusual one. Real life, with its authentic range of feelings and emotions, is generally preferred to false pleasures.

Truth and meaning, including the truthful experience of a wide range of emotions, are essential components, perhaps even the cornerstones, for building happiness. Had this not been the case, humanity would have invested much more of its energy in developing hallucinogenic drugs and foraging for psychedelic mushrooms.

In his *Critique of Practical Reason*, Kant wrote that the primary function of morality isn't to teach people to be happy, but to teach them to be *worthy* of happiness. Do the results of this thought-experiment confirm Kant's insight in this respect?

Nozick conceived the experiment as a way of contradicting the basic assumption of hedonism, which is that everything humans do is motivated by a desire to experience pleasure and avoid suffering.

I'm sure you would have expected that Plato has something to say on this topic. Indeed, in his *Philebus Dialogue,* there's an argument between Philebus and Socrates. Philebus claims the purpose of life is to attain joy (χαίρειν) and pleasure (ἡδονὴ); Socrates claims there are more important things than pleasure, and that quite a few pleasures can lead to harm and even misery in the long run.

We know the unbridled pursuit of pleasure may lead to addiction, because it's in the nature of pleasure to seek an increase in its dosage and diversity. One can get addicted to sex or heroin, alcohol or gambling, eating or weight-training, social networks or pornography. Additions like these are, in fact, almost contradictory to happiness.

Does Nozick's experiment succeed in refuting the claim of the hedonists? You be the judge. A lively debate exists among philosophers, with arguments on both sides.[21]

Literary scholars like to compare George Orwell's novel *1984* (1949) with Aldous Huxley's *Brave New World* (1931), noting that the former is a scathing critique of communist totalitarianism, the latter an equally scathing critique of capitalist totalitarianism. In *1984,* the masses are controlled by surveillance and torture; in Huxley's book, they are controlled by generating sexual pleasure, among other things, via a drug called SOMA, which fabricates happiness. However, it's a happiness that has no connection with truth or reality. *Brave New World* explores the interplay between pleasure, truth, and freedom.

Writer and mass communication researcher Neil Postman (1931–2003) was chairman of the Department of Communication Arts at New York University and founder of its Media Ecology Program. He wrote more than 20 books. In one, *Amusing Ourselves to Death: Public Discourse in the Age of Show Business* (2005), he puts forward the view that modern TV fills the place of Huxley's SOMA. For him – and I'm in total agreement – TV has become a drug for the masses who voluntarily submit to it and just want more and more entertainment. It seems that Huxley's gloomy vision is developing real skin and bones. That's not to say there aren't some great programmes on TV: there's more than enough quality viewing. However, such programmes don't often get the ratings they deserve. They aren't pure 'entertainment', to which a great proportion of the population is addicted.

Something amazing happens in both Orwell's and Huxley's dystopias in the context of sex and sexuality. At first glance, it seems that each book approaches the subject from completely opposite perspectives. With Orwell, sex is assigned and permitted only for the continued existence of humankind. With Huxley, sex is no longer used for procreation: it's for pleasure only, with a recommendation to engage in it as often as possible with as many people as possible and from the youngest possible age – 'like a gay butterfly from flower to flower through a sunlit world' (Huxley's words). Yet here is what's amazing. Despite the contrasting treatments, both schools of thought come to the same conclusion: sex ends up losing all its magic and value and turns into something entirely trivial.

To me, as to Aldous Huxley, it's pretty clear that happiness is much more than a series of delights, enjoyable as they may be. Nevertheless, I accept this isn't going to be true for everyone all the time. I have a friend who's an expert in Virtual Reality. He claims my conclusion is flawed because it stems entirely from my scepticism toward VR technology, from my excessive sense of responsibility, and from my 'not very young' age. During one of our discussions he presented an argument he hoped would persuade me to connect to the 'pleasure machine'. 'What if your entire family and all your friends,' he said, 'could also connect to this machine so that, in the virtual world, you'd be an exemplary family man? You'd all be leading a life of immense pleasure and no suffering inside the machine. Wouldn't you want to connect then? Is truth *that* important to you? Maybe, for all we know, we all exist in a fabricated world anyway, like that of *The Matrix* or *The Truman Show*? What if everyone in the world decides they want to connect to the machine? Would you want to be all by yourself in the real world? What if everyone else's ability to connect is conditional on *your* connecting? What if …' I stopped him mid-argument and told him he was inventing new thought-experiments nothing like Nozick's original one, about which we shall continue to disagree.

I must admit that any psychological experiment beginning with the question, 'What would you do if …,' leaves me very suspicious. The fact that people claim they *would behave* one way or another doesn't guarantee this is how they would *genuinely* behave, given the real situation (and that includes, of course, yours truly). So, while it's interesting to note that most of those who respond to my surveys during my lectures believe they wouldn't connect to the machine, it's just that: interesting. It doesn't prove a thing, since I've no way of knowing how they'd really behave in this situation.

Time to return to the list of virtues.

Liberality (generosity, *gennaiodoría*)

Liberality lies between extravagance and stinginess and is much closer to the former. Miserliness is a serious mental illness, and the only reason they don't hospitalize misers is their high prevalence in the population – which anyone who has ever been involved in fundraising knows about.

Here's a strange thing I've discovered over the course of my life: stinginess increases with age and wealth. This seems rather strange to me.

Aristotle deals with liberality in Book 4, Chapter 1 of *Nicomachean Ethics*. He offers, implictly, the following advice: if fate has smiled on you and your financial situation is solid (or at least reasonable), be generous to those who have been treated cruelly by fate and can't put their hands on everything they need. You don't have to be rich to be generous.

Money is just one aspect of generosity. I'm an avid reader of the writings of French philosopher Simone Weil (1909–1943). She believed that sincere, genuine attention – in other words, sharing our most precious resource, time, with someone – is the highest expression of generosity possible.

It's also important to remember you must offer people what *they* need, not what *you* would like to give them.

Magnificence (*megaloprepeia*)

The virtue of magnificence (Book 4, Chapter 2) may be considered an extension of liberality to a larger scale. There's a difference between *gennaiodoría*, translatable as 'liberality' (or 'generosity') and *megaloprepeia*. The Greek word combines *megalo*, meaning 'great', and *prepeia*, related to 'conspicuousness', and thus may be equated with 'magnificence', whose Latin origin is *magnum facere* – that is, to do something great, spectacular, or astonishing. Thus, this virtue involves doing things on an appropriately grand scale. It covers the expenditures we should make, gladly and lavishly, as we shape the unfolding of events.

Aristotle has a message intended for really rich people. He says there's no need to decide to give up all one's belongings, as Leo Tolstoy suggested would be desirable. However, Aristotle would have understood why Tolstoy, who by the way was a very wealthy man, often quoted this verse from the New Testament: 'It is easier for a camel to pass through the eye of a needle than for a rich man to enter the kingdom of God' (Matthew, 19:24). All those high flyers competing to see who has the highest bank balance and not using their money for the good will fail to find appreciation either from Aristotle or Tolstoy.

And what does Aristotle's famous friend and teacher think in this regard? In the fifth part of *Laws*, Plato wrote: 'Very rich people are not very good people.' A simple statement, and a harsh verdict. Plato made a clear point here, but it's very sweeping, and I'm not sure how correct he was.

Gabriel García Márquez (1927–2014), Colombian writer and Nobel Laureate (for Literature), taught that there's a huge difference between a rich man and a poor man with a great deal of money. Such a wonderful distinction! I've met a few individuals with rich hearts but poor pockets; and I also know quite a few people who are as wealthy as Croesus but poor of heart.

I once wrote a short article entitled 'Why a person who has $12 billion in the bank needs to have $14 billion.' Here's the gist of it: because they are suffering from a type of mental illness.

Anyone who is not satisfied with a little will not be satisfied with anything.

Wealth beyond what is natural is like pouring water into an overflowing container.

Epicurus

But as usual, nothing is simple.

Many a very rich and/or famous person has found their own path between Tolstoyan munificence and the behaviour of a huge number of stingy tycoons. Let me tell you about one of them who has very much weighted his actions toward generosity.

Charles (Chuck) Francis Feeney (b. 1931), an American businessman and philanthropist, is co-founder of the Hong Kong-based Duty Free Shoppers Group. In 1982 he created the Atlantic Philanthropies, one of the largest private charitable foundations in the world. It advocated 'giving while living'. Over the course of almost 40 years, Feeney gave away his fortune anonymously, until a business dispute resulted in his identity being revealed in 1997. He has given more than $8 billion to charity. Feeney closed down the Atlantic Philanthropies in 2020, after having accomplished its mission of giving away almost all of his money.

The Jewish sages claim that a person who donates anonymously is greater than Moses. Indeed, if it's important to someone that others notice their 'altruistic' actions, they aren't really so altruistic. Eventually Chuck Feeney went public with the information, but not by his own choosing. He is a co-signatory, by the way, of the Giving Pledge campaign. His actions greatly influenced both Bill Gates and Warren Buffett (also co-signatories), both of whom called Feeney their hero.

In the second part of his book *On Duties* (*De Officiis*), Marcus Tullius Cicero (106 BCE–43 BCE) explains that extremely wealthy people have been granted a great privilege – the opportunity to do good without harming their capital – and to exercise this faculty is their moral duty.

And while on the subject of duty and obligations, let me tell you that there's a distinction in the philosophy of ethics between deeds that are 'obligatory' (that is, it's our duty to perform them) and those that are 'supererogatory' (good, worthy deeds that aren't obligatory). It seems to me that the phrase *ex gratia* (applying to a voluntary action, done 'out of kindness or grace') is similar in meaning to 'supererogatory'. The Australian moral philosopher Peter Singer (b. 1946), famous as an activist for animal rights, wrote in an article entitled 'Famine, Affluence, and Morality'[22] that in his opinion buying extremely expensive clothes that don't fulfil any actual need is immoral: the money saved should be donated to those who need it.

By the way, fashion production makes up 10 percent of global humanity's carbon emissions – more than aviation and shipping combined.

When I think about people who have a collection of 72 Rolls Royces or cabinets overflowing with Tiffany trinkets or Fabergé eggs, it makes me wonder. Why? What need are they satisfying?

Peter Singer wrote his article after the shock of witnessing the famine, in 1972, in Bangladesh. But it's clear that the article – available online for anyone who wants to read it – is also relevant today. Singer argues that we aren't sacrificing anything important if we carry on wearing our old clothes (by the way, the fashion industry is also one of the most polluting activities in the world) and give our money to the needy. Wearing last year's clothes in good condition or even 'vintage' clothes, says this professor of ethics, is neither charity nor generosity, and can't be considered supererogatory. It's something that simply *must* be done.

I read Singer's article and agreed with him, but then felt completely confused. Am I supposed to sell my new car and replace it with the cheapest model available and donate the difference to charity? I don't think I'm going to do that. Also, if we all stop buying new clothes and fancy vehicles, this will affect the economy, and the livelihood of many people. So what does a person do?

I immediately turned to Aristotle for advice, and from there to the Jewish sources. In Judaism Aristotle's virtue has a clear quantitative expression. It is the 'tithe', the commandment that obligates Jews to set aside a tenth of their agricultural crop for the welfare of the Levite tribe. The Levites, unlike the other 11 tribes, did not receive any parcel of land when the Israelites entered Canaan after their 40-year sojourn in the desert. This was because the purpose of Levites (some of whom were priests) was to serve in the Temple and not to be landowners. Later, after the Jewish people were exiled from the land, the commandment was changed. Instead, more generally, one tenth of a person's income is supposed to be set aside for charity.

Of course, there are many ways to contribute and help – some donate money, some their time and energy. Some even donate organs.

On the topic of generosity and magnanimity, I want to say a few words about 'Effective Altruism'. This is a philosophical and social movement whose underlying concept is to use scientific evidence and philosophical reasoning to try to help as many people as possible within the constraints of a particular budget. Peter Singer is the movement's most famous supporter. Effective Altruism believes that the purpose of 'doing good' is not to make the contributor feel better but to determine what's best for the largest number of beneficiaries. Instead of doing a specific good deed, or what feels good or seems intuitively appealing, Effective Altruism aims to do the *best* possible good.

Suppose we're interested in donating a million dollars. Donating them to the King of England might be altruistic, but quite ineffective. It really wouldn't help anyone: even trained financial investigators would be hard pressed to notice the difference this would make to the Crown's bank account. Giving a million dollars to a homeless person would be more effective, but here we would have helped only one person – a pity. George Clooney gave a suitcase with a million dollars to each of 14 of his friends – very impressive and very nice, but I'd assume his friends were not among the poorest of the city, so this is not yet effective altruism. On the other hand, donating a million dollars to install a plumbing system in a developing country in Africa so that the children won't die by drinking contaminated water *would* be quite effective. There are, of course, many other objectives that may be considered effective altruism, such as building shelters for battered women, donating money to the Make-A-Wish Foundation or World Food Programme, contributing to scientific medical research dedicated to finding cures for incurable diseases, legal support for wrongfully convicted prisoners, and building animal shelters. There's no lack of worthy goals: the real difficulty is deciding which ones to donate to. These are exactly the questions Effective Altruism contends with, aided by philosophical deliberations and economic research.

In this connection, the Longtermism School argues that most of humanity's investments should focus on long-term survival at the expense of short-term well-being. Jewish-German writer Karl Ludwig Börne (1786–1837), were he alive today, would not join this movement. He claimed that living for the future was like constantly tuning one's instrument but never performing in a concert.

Story time

One day I was following an argument online about the amount of money a reasonable person requires in order to feel satisfied. Various numbers were suggested. The names of Daniel Kahneman and Angus Deaton were mentioned several times.[23] Suddenly a bomb dropped on the discussion group. A participant from India said that everyone was wrong big-time, and that the more capital and wealth a person has, the more blessed they are. 'If you thought in less selfish terms,' this contributor continued his rebuke, 'you'd understand what I mean. When a person thinks only of themselves, one can discuss how much money they need. But if that person is empathetic and understands that there are other people out there with needs, not only us, then the richer the person, the better – they'll be able to buy raincoats or build a shelter for the homeless, donate money to develop new drugs, build clinics in remote places … and so on.'

Cicero thought likewise almost 2,000 years ago.

Friendliness (akin to *philia*)

Aristotle discusses how much familiarity and warmth one should display toward others (*Nicomachean Ethics*, Book 4,

Chapter 6). Behaviours may range from abject grumpiness to outright grovelling, obsequiousness, and flattery. The philosopher's tone seems to be quite restrained but, in my opinion, he seems to be greatly bothered by any exhibition of subservience or flattery, especially if a subservient sycophant seems to be out to gain some personal benefit.

He does assign a place of honour to friendship, but here too there are pitfalls – it must be properly measured. Be friendly, he implies, but don't feel you need to offer friendship to people you barely know.

At this point, I should like to address an issue that's indirectly related to Aristotle's discussion. (I believe I'm allowed to, as it's part of my personal interpretation.)

This is my question: how many true friends can a person have?

In Ecclesiastes it's written that the two is better than the one, implying also that the three is better than the one. But it isn't ever said that seven or 14 or any other number higher than three is better than the one. I have a feeling the authors believed that true friendship is similar to true love in its classic and most common version: two.

Blaise Pascal believed that anyone who has a true friend is fortunate, because most people don't. Even more, anyone who thinks he has many true friends has no idea what a 'friend' really is.

Michel de Montaigne wrote that not only is true friendship rarer than true love but also, as in love, the human psyche simply doesn't have enough fortitude to be a true friend to more than one person.

In *The Little Prince* (1943) Antoine de Saint-Exupéry wrote that there's nothing sadder than losing a friend, because not every person has the luck of having one. Saint-Exupéry, like Montaigne and Pascal, was French. Why is this noteworthy? Simply because I once came across a study with a rather staggering piece of information: more than four million French people admitted in a survey that they didn't have a single friend. That's sad.

But, of course, it isn't only the French who suffer from loneliness. This problem seems to be epidemic in the Western world. Here's a trivia question: who is Tracey Crouch? In 2017 Crouch was appointed Minister for Sport, Civil Society and *Loneliness* in Theresa May's UK government. It seems loneliness was dishearteningly rife in the UK too.

In general, I have a feeling (and there are studies that support this) that in this age of social networking people have actually become less sociable and more lonely.

Personally, I identify with the opinion (not with the man himself) of the pragmatically philosophical boss of organized crime, Al (Alphonse) Capone. His words, 'Be careful who you call your friends. I'd rather have four quarters than 100 pennies.' I can practically see Aristotle applauding this sentiment, while at the same time condemning the man who conceived it.

Proper ambition versus pride

The virtue of proper ambition lies somewhere between the poles of an obsession to succeed at all costs and the absolute absence of such desire (*Nicomachean Ethics*, Book 4, Chapter 4).

For Aristotle the discussion tended to revolve around honour – a major issue for him. Accordingly, the right balance of this virtue involved sensibly pursuing acceptable forms of honour from worthy sources.

I shall focus, however, not on honour but on the ambition for success.

Several times now I've come across the following story on the Internet. It's generally attributed to motivational lecturer Eric D. Thomas and concerns a guru who found a secret to success that could work for anyone.

Here is the gist of the idea: if you believe that your need for success is just as vital as air you breathe, you'll succeed.

In the developed Western world there are not a few – this is probably an understatement – people who just want to succeed! Success and nothing else! At any cost.

Aristotle would probably immediately ask, 'What is the goal of this success? Will it serve a higher purpose? If so, which one?'

And I ask, What is success anyway? Who determines it?

I turned to the *Online Oxford Dictionary* and here's what I found: 'Success: The attainment of fame, wealth, or social status.'

This is success? Fame, money, or a high social status? I can clearly see Seneca, Epictetus, and Marcus Aurelius, whose doctrines we shall soon become acquainted with, shocked to the depths of their souls by this definition.

Are we supposed to strive energetically, even single-mindedly, to achieve these things? Social status? Exactly how does society determine our status? And why should we care about what society decides?

The way I look at it, what's important are the opinions of the people near and dear to us. But this is just my opinion. I'm well aware that for many, social status is extremely important. The number of likes they get on Instagram or shares on Facebook can raise or lower someone's mood.

In my book *The Most Beautiful Childhood Memory* (2017, in Hebrew) I offered my own definition of 'success'. Here it is:

1) being a good person
2) knowing how to love
3) being loved and appreciated by the people who know you and especially by the members of your family;
4) knowing how to be a friend
5) knowing how to accept all the bitterness in life without becoming bitter
6) being generous
7) being mostly in a good mood
8) being wise and modest
9) excelling in some field
10) having many people who will miss you when you leave this world.

The opposite of all these would be the definition of 'failure'.

Magnanimity (greatness of soul or *megalopsychia*; μεγαλοψυχία)

This subject is dealt with in *Nicomachean Ethics*, Book 4, Chapter 3. In Latin, *magna* means 'great' and *animus* is 'mind/spirit'. Magnanimity relates also to the Greek *megalo*, meaning 'great', and *psychia*, which has to do with mind and spirit. Thus, to my mind, this Greek term, *megapopsychia*, might be correctly interpreted as 'proper self-esteem' or 'honest self-esteem'.

Just as the virtues of 'liberality' and 'magnificence' differ only in scale (ordinary people versus really rich people), so do 'proper ambition' and 'magnanimity', the former referring to 'ordinary' people, the latter to those who are truly great in spirit and soul.

Schopenhauer believed that if an ordinary person exhibits modesty, that's worthy of praise, but that modesty in a great person is hypocritical.

Aristotle got there first. Proper self-esteem (self-confidence), according to the Aristotelian middle ground principle, lies somewhere on the scale between delusions of grandeur and the sin of arrogance at one end and underestimating oneself at the other.

Unlike Aristotle, Baruch Spinoza (1632–1677) did not distinguish between people of great spirit and those who lacked great spirit, but he did address the fault of arrogance, which he considered a form of excessive self-esteem and the result of exaggerated egocentricity. This great Jewish philosopher also believed that arrogance is a kind of madness.

I would add that arrogance is a judgmental mistake caused by an overdose of self-love. Sometimes this is expressed not in one's *over*estimation of oneself but in one's *under*estimation of others.

Spinoza also pointed out that arrogance based on self-love has no opposite: it's extremely difficult to find someone whose self-hatred causes them to value themselves less than they deserve. What's certain is that learning to love yourself with a non-narcissistic love and finding the right amount of self-esteem isn't at all an easy task.

Aristotle warns that most people who are proud of themselves have no real reason to be so: they are simply afflicted with *hubris* (excessive pride or harmful self-confidence).

If you're wondering what type of person Aristotle considers to be a 'great soul', here is what he said on the matter. People who are great souls may be characterized by the following: they'll never ask for help from others but willingly offer help to those who need it; they aren't impressed by rich people or those of high social status, but are kind to those whose fate didn't confer such status upon them; their hearts are an open book in both love and hate, for concealment implies an unworthy shyness; they don't gossip and are more concerned with the truth than what people think; they speak and act with candour (even when they despise someone, they will say so in complete honesty); they don't harbour resentment (for it isn't a sign of greatness of mind to recall injustices done to you that should be ignored); they live the life they have chosen for themselves and not the life others expect them to live.

Wit (*δικαιοσύνη*, **dikaiosýnē**)

The discussion of this virtue may be found in Book 4, Chapter 8 of *Nicomachean Ethics*. Aristotle believed that a correct and healthy degree of wit (you might call it 'charm') lies between unnecessary gravity and the craving to be a clown who tries to make everyone laugh all the time (also unnecessary).

Wit is important for spicing up a conversation or literary work. However, if it's excessive, it may be likened to a stew consisting *only* of spices. Even if the spices are of the finest quality, the result will not be palatable.

However, on a personal note, I'd just like to point out that people who are constantly taking themselves too seriously can amuse me to the point of tears.

Equanimity (patience, even temper; *praotēs*)

This virtue is covered in *Nicomachean Ethics*, Book 4, Chapter 5.

Ralph Waldo Emerson (1803–1882) noted that different people 'boil over' at different temperatures. There are those who are mostly steadfast in their serenity, and others who will turn to anger at just about anything, sometimes even before the reason behind their anger becomes clear.

If Aristotle were to run an anger management workshop, his first recommendation would probably be to foreground reason and intellect and push anger into the background. But anger is an emotion. How are we supposed to eliminate emotions and base our behaviour only on common sense?

It's a scientific fact that people who lose their temper tend to die earlier and their lives are of lower quality, so it's best to use anger only as a response to something that's likely to change. As the author of Ecclesiastes wisely said, anger transforms an outraged man into a fool. Indeed, it's common knowledge that fools, who are unable or have no desire to understand the other side of a situation, tend to anger quickly. Maimonides' advice is lovely: accustom yourself to always speak all your words calmly, to everyone and at every time. In doing so you'll prevent your anger from flaring up, which is a bad attribute for anybody, and may lead you into sin.

It isn't manly to be enraged. Rather, gentleness and civility are more human, and therefore manlier.
Marcus Aurelius

But does understanding the value of such wise advice help anyone to implement it? This is quite doubtful. In any case, to clarify one key point, Aristotle didn't think complete detachment was a worthy trait – indifference to certain things might be reprehensible, even downright disgraceful.

Aristotelian equanimity lies somewhere between utter indifference and constant irascibility.

This is what Aristotle wrote in *The Art of Rhetoric*: 'Anybody can become angry, that is easy; but to be angry with the right person, and to the right degree, and at the right time, and for the right purpose, and in the right way, that is not within everybody's power and is not at all easy.'

If it seems easy to you, just think again, with complete honesty, about how you've handled anger in the past.

Credibility (honesty about oneself; *alētheia*)

With respect to this virtue, Aristotle's focus was predominantly on how a person presents himself to others. The proper degree of honesty lies between excessive boastfulness and undue modesty (*Nicomachean Ethics*, Book 4, Chapter 7). Someone who brags and someone who is overly modest are both lying about themselves – and this isn't seemly. The line between modesty and humility is so thin that it's barely visible to the naked eye. 'Humility', ideally the opposite of arrogance, is sometimes actually used as a *disguise* for arrogance.

The subject of this discussion overlaps quite a lot with Aristotle's discussion about 'magnanimity' and therefore I shall tidy it away at this point and instead discuss the virtue of 'honesty', in the sense of telling the truth.

Truthfulness (versus lying)

Immanuel Kant considered being truthful to be a moral obligation of the first degree – a 'categorical decree'. I believe that, in most cases. telling the truth is the right and good thing to do, but I don't blindly follow the (to my mind foolish) idea of telling the truth, the whole truth, in every situation every time.

There are quite a few situations where not telling the truth might be the right moral choice. So as to not waste words and time, let's go straight to an extreme example. A Polish farmer hiding Jewish children in his cellar during the First World War ought to lie to German soldiers who came to look for them, right? I was quite surprised to find that not everybody thinks like me. I heard a YouTube lecture in which the speaker, a philosopher by profession, discussed this exact situation and claimed that Kant would have been in favour of telling the truth even in this extreme case. I'm not sure. It seems to me that in dramatic cases turning on life and death, even Kant would have adjusted his principles. But then again, maybe not.

In halls of justice in English-speaking countries, such as the UK, the United States, Canada, Australia, and India, there's what is known as the 'sworn oath'. This requires the witness to swear to tell 'the truth, the whole truth, and nothing but the truth'. Wow! To me this is quite an ask. Who knows what the truth is? This oath seems to be only suitable for

God if he/she/they/it is ever required to give testimony. For mortals like us, I think the right demand would be simply to say what we *believe* to be true. This isn't easy either.

Consider, too, how lucky we are that this oath doesn't apply to doctors, because otherwise, at the end of every consultation, the doctor would need to inform us of all kinds of harsh truths, perhaps even the fact that one day the end will come and we'll have to return our body and soul to their source.

> What is truth? said jesting Pilate, and would not stay for an answer.
> **Francis Bacon, *Of Truth*, 1597**

I believe that a 'white lie' here and there does not stand at the apex of the pyramid of absolute no-nos – I've already mentioned that sometimes a white lie is actually somewhat courageous. Moreover, a 'black truth' delivered with intent to offend is worse than any white lie. Of course, you must be careful that lying doesn't become a regular habit or, Heaven forbid, a way of life.

In the spirit of Aristotle's philosophy, let us place honesty (in the sense of telling the truth) between a chronic tendency to lie and absolute insistence on telling the truth indiscriminately and without regard to the damage it may cause others.

Shame

I need to point out straightaway that Aristotle doesn't really consider our ability to feel shame to be a virtue (some count only 11 virtues, since they don't include this in Aristotle's list).

Even so, it can be said that having the right measure of shame lies somewhere between total shamelessness (psychopaths don't feel ashamed) and a pathological sense of shame.

People may feel embarrassed by almost anything they do or think: their appearance, their income level, their social status, their parents' home, their strange accent. It would be much better to reserve feeling embarrassed for those times when we've made wrong choices, and exempting ourselves for life circumstances over which we have no control.

I'm sure we all sometimes have thoughts we're ashamed of. Conversely, I hope that many of my readers can recall deeds they are proud of. But I have no doubt that we all have a list, some longer, some shorter, of deeds we're much *less* proud of – there's no righteous person who doesn't sin. The key thing, according to Aristotle, is correct balance: that the reasons we feel proud are more numerous – by a large margin – than the reasons we feel ashamed.

Here's a pretty good thing, in my opinion, to feel ashamed about if it accurately describes your behaviour: preaching morals to other people while emphasizing that your own actions are, of course, flawless. I would suggest to such people that they shouldn't get too excited about their own moral attainments, as they may turn out to be the *only ones* who are at all impressed by them. I've noticed that many people who claim to be highly sensitive to others are actually mostly sensitive to themselves, and such 'lovers of humanity' are not and will not be among my friends.

As a concluding exercise, try to think about the difference between shame, blame, and guilt. This can be revealing, especially when you apply the terms to your own life circumstances.

Justice (δικαιοσύνη, *dikaiosýnē*)

Justice is such an important virtue for Aristotle that he dedicated the entirety of Book 5 to it. This is such a big topic that I'm going to surprise myself and refrain from expanding upon it. Maybe I'll tackle it in another book.

Developing the virtues

So we've reached the end of the list. After listing and describing the virtues, Aristotle continues by saying that they don't occur in us naturally: we must consciously embrace them. First, he says, proper behaviour, often resulting from the influence of worthy teachers, promotes the development of sound, decent habits. These, in turn, will foster a stable character, in which good habits have become a natural part of the individual's behaviour, which in turn will increase the chance of reaching the state of *eudaimonia*.

Can this sequence of self-development to acquire the virtues be followed by everyone? The answer is: no.

Not everything is done according to our will. Aristotle himself says that it's impossible to train a stone, which by nature falls downward, to ascend, even if you try to get it started by throwing it up in the air 10 thousand times. So too it's impossible to teach fire to move downward, and indeed if anything by nature behaves one way, then it's impossible to train it to behave another way.

It seems that in these matters Aristotle's explanations need improving upon, because his imagery isn't entirely clear. The problem is that he's comparing humans – living, conscious creatures – with stones and fire, which are objects without soul or awareness.

Is Aristotle confused and perhaps contradicting himself? I don't know. I do know that there are some who will never become brave or generous or charming or even-tempered even if they read all Aristotle's writings over and over again or take the time and effort to try to cultivate these virtues. On the other hand, there are people to whom such qualities come almost naturally and effortlessly – like a gift from the gods.

Resistance movement

Aristotle's ethics of virtues has been criticized by many, and you're free, of course, to come up with your own criticisms on whichever front you choose – he's used to it. On the other hand, you might opt instead to expand on his list or compile your own list.

I should like now to address two points arising from the many attacks levelled against this teacher of Alexander the Great.

First, many critics claim that Aristotle's epitome of human nature will actually be a dreary, boring creature – not really brave but not a craven coward either, not especially generous but also not stingy. In short, a run-of-the-mill, ho-hum person.

I really don't agree with this assessment. I think to be really brave and really generous and have real composure is indeed not easy: it requires supreme effort in a life-long endeavour. A person of virtues deserves appreciation: certainly this will not be a boring individual.

Secondly, Hugo Grotius, a 17th-century Dutch jurist, philosopher, and theologian, and one of the founders of international law, believed that Aristotle's greatest error was his emphasis on moderation, and that for some virtues – love of God, for example – there's no room for moderation: the correct degree is at an extreme point of the scale and not somewhere in between. I agree with Grotius that there may be situations in life where there's no room for moderation – a person who aspires to be a world chess champion, for example, cannot practise moderately. However, in my opinion, love of God without limits is really dangerous. And not only love of God. Being right at the end of the scale when it comes to romantic love can lead to depraved jealousy, immoderate possessiveness, loss of sanity, and other troubles that have nothing to do with true love. I know this sounds unromantic, but it's the truth.

These days, with the arrival of the coronavirus pandemic as a very unwanted guest in our homes, our country, and our world, I try my best to locate the perfect point between caution and recklessness. On the one hand, I have acquaintances who have decided to ignore the pandemic completely and have changed almost nothing in their lifestyles. In their opinion, if they ignore the pandemic, it will ignore them. I consider this to be a reckless and immoral stance. On the other hand, some of my acquaintances hardly left their homes for months. To me, this is insanity.

Extremes must always be subjected to critical scrutiny, whether we trust ourselves to find the Golden Mean or not. Aristotle's method of finding the middle way influences me in all kinds of ways, not least in not following any extreme political ideology – neither extreme left nor extreme right. All uncompromising worldviews seem unattractive to me. As W.B. Yeats said, 'All empty souls tend to extreme opinion.'

Clearly, there are many more examples of the 'middle way': finding the right balance between what one wants to do and what one must do, between family and career, between spoiling one's children and over-protecting them, between being a helicopter parent and total neglect … you'll no doubt wish to continue.

CHAPTER 11

The Appeal of Socrates: What Is Philosophy Supposed to Deal With?

Do you remember, I promised to go back to Socrates' statement, 'The unexamined life is not worth living'?

Now is the time. I'm reluctant to rule on this question definitively, but I do believe that this assertion by Athens' most famous citizen has a certain degree of truth: most people wouldn't want to live their lives without trying to understand what they are doing on this Earth and why they are here.

I'm surprised that relatively few modern philosophers have chosen to pick up Socrates' glove and respond to the challenge he posed. However, there are three who have: Robert Nozick, Bertrand Russell, and Frederic Lenoir.

Robert Nozick wrote that his book *The Examined Life* (1989) presents a modern and direct answer to Socrates' proposition. The book discusses happiness, love, faith, family, the sanctity of life, emotions, politics, sexuality, wisdom (there's a wonderful chapter entitled 'What Is Wisdom and Why Do Philosophers Love it So?') – all those subjects that philosophy once dealt with and which for some reason have fallen by the wayside these days.

Our acquaintance Bertrand Russell preceded Nozick by almost six decades. In 1930, about two years before he decided to praise idleness (see page 83), he published *The Conquest of Happiness*, in which he gave wise, perceptive advice on how to succeed in life without paying too high a price, on the sources of envy and how to conquer the emotion and, as mentioned, on the importance of leisure (a topic to which he also paid close attention in his article on idleness). As far as Russell was concerned, the ability to fill leisure hours wisely should be the cornerstone of a mature personality and the hallmark of a mature civilization, but few have arrived at this level. He wrote about enthusiasm and boredom, love and sympathy, and also about work (another topic covered in 'In Praise of Idleness'), his attitude being that anyone who thinks that their work is so important that allowing themselves a day off would lead to disaster is clearly on the edge of a breakdown. He also dealt with sources of unhappiness and declared that self-esteem is a necessary condition for a decent life. I could cite many more of his views from this book, but it isn't really necessary: the book is available online, free of charge, for anyone who wants to read it.

(Incidentally, Russell won the Nobel Prize for Literature in 1950.)

I'll just mention that I was particularly fascinated by the author's sincerity: in the very first chapter Russell tells us that in adolescence he frequently wanted to put an end to his life. What stopped him every time from doing so was – you'll never guess – the urge to learn more and more mathematics! By the way, in his own time, Russell was considered one of the most important philosophers in the Western world, but he himself believed his most significant achievement was his discovery of Ludwig Wittgenstein. He passed away at the age of 97 and ¾ (as a mathematician, Russell would have appreciated my accuracy).

To return to the matter in hand: there's a chance we may be on the brink of a change in philosophers' attitudes toward the question of what kind of life is worth living. In his excellent short book *Du Bonheur: Un Voyage Philosophique (Happiness: A Philosopher's Guide)* (2013) French philosopher Frédéric Lenoir (b. 1962) wrote that more and more serious philosophers – even in France! – understand that, with all due respect to Deconstruction and Post-structuralism, the time has come to engage in life itself.

The three books I just mentioned – Russell's, Nozick's, and Lenoir's – are a good starting point to read from a philosophical perspective about happiness, the meaning of life, and all that matters. After all, even a completely ordinary person whose life floats on still waters, and whose script for tomorrow will play out not much differently from the way it played out yesterday, may one day ask themselves what they have been up to for so many years. We can try to ignore questions about happiness or meaning, but it's doubtful whether they'll ignore us.

I must immediately qualify the above by saying that I don't really believe anyone has a key to the secret door of the Garden of Happiness – perhaps because such a place doesn't exist. Some claim to have found the magic recipe, to have cracked the code, but this, I fear, is either self-delusion or an eye for a market opportunity.

In the past year I've fallen in love with the writings and philosophy of the Frenchman Pierre Hadot (1922–2010), one of the most fascinating intellectuals of the New Age. Hadot greatly influenced Michel Foucault. He was also among the first of the French to delve into Ludwig Wittgenstein's doctrines.

Hadot believed that modern philosophy had become 'too professional, narrow-minded, and almost completely detached from life', and that it was barely a shadow now of what it had been in its glorious Athenian past.

Pythagoras, of course, thought philosophers should examine everything that happens in the world as observers on the side lines, like the spectators in a stadium. But how can they? It's impossible to ignore the fact that they are *part* of this world.

Modern academic philosophy is a theoretical discipline that has set the goal for itself of systematically organizing knowledge. Pierre Hadot argued that contemporary philosophy isn't really interested in how the philosophical study can improve the lot of life's citizens. I find myself in agreement with this, especially when I come across an article with a title like 'The Quasi-Linearity of the Space of Language and Its Reflections in Transcendental Perceptions in Object-Dense Metrics'. (Is there actually such an paper or did I make it up? What do you think?)

The use of complicated words indicates childishness and a desperate need to impress others.
after Michel de Montaigne

Ancient philosophy, wrote Hadot, taught the art of living, whereas modern philosophy has invented a sophisticated language accessible only to experts. He quotes a sentence of Seneca's to make his point: in the ideal world, 'Philosophy teaches action and not chatter.'

For Pierre Hadot a rational *life* is no less important than rational thinking. Seeing ancient philosophy as a spiritual exercise (*exercice spirituel*) that combines a person's intellect, emotions, imagination, and way of life (*manière de vivre*), he believed modern philosophy should likewise help our efforts to understand who we are and what we are doing here.

I strongly agree with Pierre Hadot. Philosophy, in my opinion, cannot ignore the need to try to answer these two questions: How do we see life? How should we live life?

CHAPTER 12

Tips from Epicurus: The Great Art of Small Pleasures

The Greek philosopher Epicurus lived in the 3rd century BCE. His doctrines deal with the 'theory of happiness', and he too was looking for the path to *eudaimonia*. However, his conception of *eudaimonia* was different from Aristotle's.

The Epicurean school that Epicurus founded sees pleasure and the absence of pain as its most important goal: according to him, peace of body and mind, and absence of anxieties constitute the path to *eudaimonia*. To be happy, according to Epicurus, one must be in a state of *ataraxia* (ἀταραξία; freedom from distress and anxiety) and *aponia* (ἀπονία; absence of physical pain). *Aponia* was regarded by Epicurus and his followers to be the epitome of bodily satisfaction, even though defined in terms of absence, not presence.

Epicurus nurtured his philosophy in a garden just outside Athens, which he purchased to set up a school for his disciples. The Garden has become a symbol of the hedonic escapism associated with the Epicurean school. Greek biographer Diogenes Laërtius relates that for many years after Epicurus' death, his followers used to gather in the woods on his birthday to commemorate their revered teacher.

Neither Judaism nor Christianity could embrace Epicurus and his teachings. Christians opposed his philosophy because he refused to believe in divine providence and the eternity of the soul. (Dante Alighieri even placed Epicurus and his followers in his Inferno – in the Sixth Circle of Hell (Canto X). In Judaism *epicoros* is the term used for heretics, sceptics, agnostics, and secular free thinkers.

Epicurus was prolific. According to Diogenes Laërtius, he wrote more than 300 letters, although very few have survived. *Principal Doctrines* is a collection of 40 sayings that summarize the Epicurean philosophy of life. As for his other writings, only excerpts have been preserved. A thread of extraordinary philosophical courage runs all through his work: Epicurus practised what he preached. He showed love for humankind, graciousness, and wonder for all that transpired under the sun. Pierre Hadot, in *La Philosophie Comme Manière de Vivre* (*Philosophy as a Way of Life*), wrote that Epicurus viewed the universe and human existence as the result of pure chance, and that's precisely why he considered each and every moment a miracle and lived his life with immense gratitude.

Epicurus taught that just as a person suffering from physical pain will turn to a doctor for treatment, so one who is suffering from mental pain should consult a 'doctor for the soul' – the role, in Epicurus' day, of the philosopher. The philosopher's job was to guide a person toward complete recovery – that is, to happiness. Some modern philosophers totally agree with this idea. One of them is Professor Lou Marinoff, who wrote a bestselling book, *Plato Not Prozac: Applying Philosophy to Everyday Problems* (2000), whose title speaks for itself.

I'm not an expert in this field, and therefore will only mention that 'philosophical counselling' has not yet found its place among accepted methods of treatment. In 2004 Marion found himself at the centre of controversy when his philosophical counselling clinic at City College, New York, was temporarily closed down on the charge that he was offering mental health counselling without a license or proper training. Marinoff responded with a lawsuit for what he claimed was a severe violation of his freedom of expression.

I don't know the details of Marinoff's clinical methods. But there are quite a few fields in psychology whose ideas correspond with aspects of philosophy. One notable example is cognitive behavioural therapy (CBT). Its founders, Aaron Temkin Beck (he passed away in 2021 at the age of 100) and Albert Ellis, clearly borrowed principles from Stoic philosophy. I shall devote the entirety of Chapter 14 to Stoic philosophy, but here will just mention that the foundation stone of classic CBT is the following insight (attributed to Stoic philosopher Epictetus, and covered in his guide *The Enchiridion*): *people are not troubled by things that excite them but by the perceptions and thoughts they form about these things.*

One of the techniques of CBT is to have the patient encounter the 'worst case scenario' their pathology may produce. In Stoic thought, this approach is called *præmeditatio malorum,* meaning foresight of troubles ahead. The Stoics suggested we think about the possibility of poverty, imprisonment, illness, even death in order to build up a sort of resilience to these hypothetical situations. Psychologists call this Stoic approach 'stress inoculation training'.

Epicurus compiled a 'four-part remedy' to heal the soul. Its Greek name has a wonderful ring to it: the *tetrapharmakos.*

EPICUREAN VERSION	INTERPRETATION
Don't fear God	*Regardless of whether God exists or not, we are not important enough for God to bother punishing or rewarding us. The idea that God is concerned with our affairs is the ultimate sin of arrogance.*
Don't worry about death	*We do not feel anything when we're dead. As long as we are here, death is not; the moment death arrives, we are no longer here. Since we will never actually meet death, why should we fear it?*
What is terrible is easy to endure	*Jeff 'The Dude' Lebowski bravely endured beatings from Mafia thugs because he was familiar with Epicurus' words of encouragement: the nature of pain is temporal; the greater the pain, the faster it passes.*

What is good is easy to get	*Here is Epicurus' prescription for well-being: friendship, liberty, good mood, and good thoughts. And here is Mr Lebowski's updated version: conversations with friends, bowling, smoking pot, and empty minds.*

We can either agree with Epicurus' theory or we can ask for 'another opinion'. However, even if we do decide to adopt his four principles, we'll find that applying them in real life is by no means easy.

Epicurus speaks of two types of pain that disturb our peace: physical and mental. The physical pain is manifested by hunger, thirst, and damage within the body (caused by illness or accident); mental pain is expressed in anxieties, worries, sadness, and the like. Mental pain, the philosopher argues, is more troubling than physical, because bodily pains prevail only in the present, whereas mental disharmony is usually related to present, past, and even future. Serenity, he tells us, comes when we feel no pain.

Beyond serenity of body and mind, Epicurus believed in pleasure. The way he saw it, *eudaimonia* represents an ongoing experience of pleasure alongside freedom from physical or mental pain. However, it's important to note that he didn't advocate the pursuit of every possible pleasure that comes our way. Absolutely not! Epicurus recommended a policy for long-term pleasure that may be called 'optimization under constraints'. In other words, it can be worthwhile to endure some pain if this will lead to greater pleasure in the future; conversely, it isn't worth partaking of some pleasures if they lead, in the long run, to major suffering and regret. (And I'll just add here that, in my experience, a house of pleasure is almost always built on the edge of a slope leading to addiction.)

Epicurus also argued that it's impossible to live a life of both pleasure and peace without acting wisely, honourably, and justly, and that it's impossible to show wisdom, honour, and justice without living a life of both pleasure and peace. I must point out that there's a high probability the pleasures Epicurus speaks of are very much different from what comes to mind when *we* hear the word. His concept of supreme pleasure was conversations with friends, studying philosophy, and walking in the Garden. I tend to agree with him.

Epicurus believed that some of our desires are natural and necessary, some are natural but unnecessary, and some are both unnecessary and unnatural. Alongside this, he warns against the damage that can be instilled by craven passions such as greed, pursuit of esteem and glory, and desire for decadent food, as well as overblown pretensions and the sin of pride.

I've prepared a list of desires. Your job now is to decide into which of the above three categories to place each one:

Desire to love and be loved, desire to know, desire to remain ignorant, sexual desire, desire for food, desire to be famous, desire for health (present and future), desire for money and social status, desire for appreciation, desire to impress people, desire for security, desire to be happy, desire for truth and meaning, desire to crave, desire not to crave, desire for eternal life.

Epicurus didn't believe that a life without sorrow is possible, and he didn't promise anyone they could reach the state of *eudaimonia* regardless of their circumstances in life. He acknowledged with the utmost compassion those wretched souls who suffer from severe malformation, disease, the scourges of old age, the protracted torment of dying and its accompanying anguish. He beseeched these people to find the courage to deal with whatever pain and upheavals fate brings them.

Epicurus himself suffered from serious illness for a large part of his life, but he didn't allow it to break his spirit.

CHAPTER 13

What Is Wisdom?

No one should postpone studying philosophy when young, and when grown, should not grow weary of its study. There is no time that is not appropriate – neither too early nor too late – to strive for a healthy soul. Besides, whoever says that the time is not yet right to philosophize, or that the time has passed, is like someone who claims that the time is not yet right to be happy, or that it is too late.

Epicurus, opening lines of *Letter to Menoeceus*

'Philosopher' is the term for someone who loves wisdom, whereas 'wise' is the term for someone who has already gained wisdom. Not everyone who loves wisdom, gains it. But could it be that there's no one at all who possesses wisdom?

Aristotle dedicated the Book 6 of *Nicomachean Ethics* to the virtue of intellect. In this short chapter I shall not try to follow the course of his thinking, but will write a little on how I view the matter of wisdom.

All the clever ideas possible (not those involving new technologies or fields of science) have already been said and documented throughout the course of history. They have appeared repeatedly in countless different versions by prophets, poets, writers, philosophers, scientists, and spiritual teachers from East and West. In all these sources, there is invaluable knowledge, in a vast and scattered archive, but it isn't at all easy to convert this knowledge from the infinite world library into personal wisdom. 'Wisdom' is fundamentally different from 'knowledge', which can be passed from person to person and from generation to generation. Not so wisdom. It's impossible to teach someone how to be wise.

I doubt if you'll disagree that there's a need for more wisdom in the world, to deal with the knowledge that we have. At one time we had wisdom, but little knowledge. Now we have a great deal of knowledge, but not enough wisdom to deal with that knowledge.

The English poet William Cowper (1731–1800) expressed it thus:

Knowledge and Wisdom, far from being one,
Have oft-times no connexion.

Lord Alfred Tennyson (1809–1892), one of the greatest English poets, described the difference between knowledge and wisdom in Canto 114 of his famous elegiac poem *In Memoriam* (lines 2437–64). He wrote, among other things, that the source of knowledge is earthly and lies within the mind, whereas the source of wisdom is heavenly and resides in the soul.

To be clear, knowledge helps us to get along in life; wisdom allows us to give life meaning and make it better.

William Blake (1757–1827) had a pessimistic view of our prospects in this respect, saying that 'Wisdom is sold in a desolate marketplace where none can come to buy.' Others have been more hopeful, at least implicitly, in setting what presumably they believe to be attainable goals. According to Maimonides, the aim of the world and everything in it is a wise, decent man.

All this still leaves us with the question, what *is* wisdom? I decided to dedicate an 'all-nighter' to the subject – thoughts at night are inevitably deeper than those arising during the day. Shortly after midnight I sat at the keyboard and the name 'Socrates' came to mind. If you recall, the divine oracle in the Temple of Apollo, at Delphi, had declared that Socrates was wisest of all men. According to Plato's *Apology*, Socrates wanted to determine how it came to be that the high priestess of the oracle, Pythia, had arrived at this judgment. Here's his conclusion: 'I'm probably smarter than other people for this reason: none of us really knows anything, but people believe they know something when in fact they do not. But I do not believe I know – I know I do not know.'

Many have adopted this appealingly modest idea. Tolstoy echoed it by saying that the pinnacle of wisdom is to understand you know nothing. Shakespeare wrote something similar in *As You Like It*: 'The fool doth think he is wise, but the wise man knows himself to be a fool.' Many more good people have shared this sentiment in a variety of versions.

However, does this point of view help us in life? It shouldn't be surprising that Ludwig Wittgenstein found much to criticize in the Socratic wisdom. Let's say that we realize we don't know how to define courage, beauty, or justice. What are we to do with this knowledge? How do we convert it into wisdom?

Make no mistake about it: saying 'I don't know' from time to time is basically a moral obligation. After all, a person unable to say these words will never learn anything. It's important not to turn the means – lack of knowledge that arouses curiosity and leads to learning – into an end, or maybe an endpoint: the idea of 'I do not know' as an implication of ultimate wisdom.

I very much agree with the words of French mathematician, theoretical physicist, and philosopher of science Henri Poincaré (1854–1912) who believed that doubting everything and believing in everything are both forms of mental laziness: both, in exactly the same way, end up exempting us from thinking.

While I'm reflecting, during my all-nighter, on the ideas of philosophers, writers, scientists, and poets on the question, 'What is wisdom?,' the 'Serenity Prayer' pops into my mind out of nowhere. Attributed to American theologian Reinhold Niebuhr in 1943, it became very popular after being adopted by Alcoholics Anonymous.

God, grant me the serenity to accept the things I cannot change,
courage to change the things I can, and the wisdom to know the difference.

(The Serenity Prayer was beloved by Dr Abraham J. Twerski, an Israeli-American Jewish rabbi who also worked as a psychiatrist specializing in substance abuse. He died in Jerusalem on 31 January 2021 of COVID-19 at the age of 90. Dr Twerski founded, among other institutions, the Shaar Hatikva [Gateway to Hope] rehabilitation centre for prisoners in Israel. YouTube abounds with many short video clips of Rabbi Twerski's wisdom and love for all.)

Notice that the Serenity Prayer appeals to God for help: it isn't worded arrogantly to depend on a human decision such as, 'As of today, *I* will have the serenity … etc.'

I re-read the Serenity Prayer in the realization that here, in a nutshell, is a fairly accurate summary of the central idea of Stoic philosophy (which I discuss in the next chapter).

To attune my thoughts, I started listening to a playlist of Domenico Scarlatti's sonatas on YouTube and got up from the keyboard. I walked around my basement among the many bookcases. I thought a little, flipped through some books, and thought a little more before returning to the keyboard. Here is the first draft of my proposed definition of wisdom:

Wisdom: *Knowing that you do not know what you do not know and that you do know what you do know; being an attentive student in the school of life; developing good judgment on issues related to daily behaviour and choosing appropriate goals and means; using whatever knowledge and experience you have gained throughout life to make better decisions, do worthier deeds and, in general, enhance the days that are still allotted you; understanding that intelligence is a*

necessary condition for wisdom but not at all enough;
realizing that cleverness and cunning are not wisdom;
knowing that a wise person cannot be evil nor an evil
person wise; being able to cast real doubt about the
beliefs and opinions you have adopted for yourself, and
also to doubt the action of doubting; accommodating
the vast amount of uncertainty that each moment of life
contains; knowing how to distinguish between 'good'
and 'bad' and yet 'not being overly righteous' and trying
not to preach morality; understanding that suffering is
the lot of all creatures and feeling compassion for them;
knowing that suffering is not always the opposite of
happiness and realizing that you are never as happy
as you think you are, and never as miserable as you think
you are; not arguing with fools; not living every day as
if it were your last – that's silly – but remembering that
every day that passes will never return; striving to be
humble while avoiding false modesty; marvelling just
as much at the sight of every flower or butterfly as at
the daily motion of the celestial bodies; understanding
there are many things you will never understand; not
allowing your spirit to grow old before your body;
not trying to be smart all the time, nor too smart any of
the time; finding meaning in life, or living life well even
if you haven't succeeded in finding meaning.

In short, living appropriately.

Some thinkers, instead of coming up with a list, have highlighted the paramount feature of wisdom according to their own priorities at the time. For example, Epicurus wrote, 'Of all the good things that wisdom gives us, the best is friendship.' My list has been compiled according to different principles, allowing love, friendship, courage, and all other virtues to have their own independent lives, rather than being proxies for wisdom.

After writing my definition of wisdom, I made myself a cup of coffee. Then, back at the keyboard, I immediately understood that behind each of my points were further layers of thought I couldn't begin, even in an all-nighter, to do justice to. Then, at second glance, it seemed to me that my list, presented above exactly as I spontaneously wrote it, is also not a bad answer to the question, 'What is maturity?' In fact, could it be that maturity and wisdom are closer to each other than I realized?

Then I also realized that the most important thing I wanted to say had somehow eluded me, probably because it's something that's impossible to express in words. I feel it, but I can't say anything about it, because it's shrouded in the dense cloud of a great mystery. I mentioned earlier (see page 20) Wittgenstein's famous saying, 'Whereof one cannot speak, thereof one must be silent.' To echo the Serenity Prayer, perhaps wisdom involves, among many other things, understanding and expressing what can be understood and intuiting and keeping silent about what cannot.

CHAPTER 14

The Inner Citadel: Stoic Philosophy

Stoic philosophy, founded in the 3rd century BCE by Zeno of Citium (now Larnaca, Cyprus), engages with three areas: physics, logic, and ethics. However, despite the great interest shown by the Stoics in the first two areas, there's no doubt that their popularity stemmed – and still stems – mainly from how they dealt with ethics.

Stoic philosophy is a kind of master plan for a better, more moral life, free of unnecessary suffering. One of the means of achieving this goal is to build mental and physical resilience. *Stoic philosophy in its essence is concerned to prescribe a way of life: it is not merely verbalized cogitations.*

Stoic ethics is a particularly powerful form of eudaimonism. As you may remember, Aristotle taught that, although proper values were a prerequisite for reaching *eudaimonia*, they weren't enough in themselves. Despite emphasizing the importance of the rational aspect of the soul, he didn't completely ignore the realities of everyday life. He acknowledged that 'the prose of the mundane may interfere with the melody of *eudaimonia*'. Aristotle thought it unlikely that a person can reach a state of *eudaimonia* if he lacks certain things – such as sufficient affluence to live a dignified life, a loving family, good friends, stable health, and even a reasonably well-presented appearance. Aristotle really didn't live in an ivory tower: he in fact declared that someone who is extremely lonely, ugly, or miserable will not be happy, even if they study philosophy day and night.

According to the Stoic school of thought, *having the proper virtues is a necessary condition to reach* eudaimonia *and also a suffic*ient one.

Epictetus describes it this way: a person can be sick and yet happy, in great danger and yet happy, be exiled and yet happy. They can die in bitter agony yet still feel happy as they take their final breaths.

The Stoics also took the view that emotions such as fear or jealousy stem from poor judgment, and that a wise person – someone who has attained moral and intellectual perfection – will not succumb to them. They believed (contrary to Aristotle) *that a wise person is completely immune to bad luck of any kind:* their virtues are not only a necessary and sufficient condition for happiness, as we have seen, they also have a fortifying effect against misfortune. It's important to add that, as far as I understand it, Stoic serenity – a fairly common expression used too simplistically nowadays – doesn't mean lack of emotion or insensitivity. Instead, to borrow a term from philosopher and risk analyst Nassim Taleb, it means the 'domestication of emotions'.

However, it's worth remembering that Epictetus actually stated that there isn't – and will never be – a real Stoic in the world. A Stoic is someone who sets out on a journey that only brings them closer to a goal that always remains unattainable. Indeed, the Stoic approach to life is not for ordinary mortals but for the very few who are noble of soul and steadfast in spirit, and who are indeed able to live according to rigorous principles. The 'Holy Trinity' of Stoic philosophy comprises these exceptional souls: Seneca (4 BCE–65 CE), nobleman and teacher to the 'mad' emperor, Nero; Epictetus (55–135 CE), emancipated slave, admired by Marcus Aurelius; and Marcus Aurelius (121–180 CE), Roman emperor.

Marcus Aurelius' *Meditations* is one of the masterpieces of philosophy. He wrote this in Greek and meant it for his eyes only: he didn't intend the book to be published and didn't even give it a title. Although *Meditations* is the common title, I've also seen the work called *To Myself,* which seems to me no less appropriate.

Apparently Epictetus wasn't a member of the tribe of writers: his philosophical ideas are preserved only thanks to his disciple Lucius Flavius Arrianus, who compiled them in the *Discourses* and *Enchiridion* (*Handbook*). The latter is a condensed aphoristic version of the teacher's doctrines. Epictetus learned Stoic philosophy from Gaius Musonius Rufus, who also never bothered to pick up a pen. However, parts of Rufus' lectures have been preserved, and here are a few extracts from them:

The pinnacle of shame: complaining about how weak our body is when we are in pain but forgetting how weak our soul becomes when we are addicted to pleasure. ...

> *I would rather be sick than live in luxury. Disease affects only the body; living in excess harms soul and body by making both the body weak and helpless and the soul cowardly and undisciplined.*

His disciple Epictetus wrote as follows:

> *If you are told that a certain person is speaking ill of you, do not excuse anything and do not explain anything, but answer as follows: 'It's clear that this person does not really know me, otherwise they would have mentioned the many more flaws and shortcomings I have.'*

Epictetus believed the main function of philosophy is to make one's happiness independent of other people and of external circumstances.

The Stoics listed four values that should be used as a compass in various situations, both in times of joy and calm and also in times of distress, confusion, and anxiety. According to their view, these virtues will light one's path to happiness and inner peace:

1) Courage/Fortitude
2) Moderation/Temperance
3) Prudence/Wisdom
4) Justice

These are the pillars of the ethical structure of Stoic philosophy. Stoics argue that whatever is really good must benefit its owner in all circumstances. For example, being rich isn't always good – we can imagine a case where a man with a lot of capital might decide to spend it on heroin, which won't benefit him at all. Things like money, according to the Stoics, are neither simply good nor bad, but 'neutral', because their nature depends on what a person will do with them. You may not believe this, but even health is considered 'neutral'. I'll leave it to you to imagine when health might be harmful.

Quite a number of Stoic dictums have raised an eyebrow or two. Philosopher, writer, and orator Marcus Tulles Cicero in his book *Paradoxa Stoicorum* (*Stoic Paradoxes*) (*c.*46 BCE) attempts to explain the validity of six famous Stoic sayings that actually seem to be contrary to mortal logic. The sayings are:

1) Virtue is the only good
2) Virtue is sufficient for happiness
3) All the vices and all the virtues are equal
4) All fools are mad
5) The sage alone is free
6) Only the wise person is rich

Four of the virtues already appeared in Plato's *Republic* (*c.*375 BCE) and are strongly associated with Aristotle's virtues (as expressed in *Nicomachean Ethics,* written *c.*350 BCE), which greatly influenced the Stoics.

Here I'll point out that, according to Stoic sages, wisdom is basically the ability to distinguish between good and evil and being aware of the dichotomy between things that are under our control and those that are not. Right at the very beginning of *Enchiridion,* Epictetus (at least according to Arrianus) states the following: 'There are things that are in our control and there are things we have no control over. The things we have control over are opinions, desires, aversions, and – in short – our actions. Things beyond our control are the body, property, reputation, and – in short – anything that is not dependent on our actions.'

Wisdom, therefore, is what will allow a person to live as best they can according to the three remaining values – that is, courage, moderation, and justice.

Justice, unlike the other values, is not a personal but a social value. For the Stoics, justice is not necessarily associated with the law and the courts: rather, it is characterized mainly by social behaviour, more specifically camaraderie, equality, respect, courtesy, generosity, and helping others. Marcus Aurelius assessed justice to be a value that exceeds the other three because its impact extends to society as a whole.

The gospel according to Marcus Aurelius

In Ecclesiastes it's said: 'For there is not one good man on Earth who does what is best and doesn't err' (7:20). The truth is that there's no one who never sins, either in action or thought. French historian Ernest Renan (1823–1892) believed that, of all human beings who had ever lived under the sun, Marcus Aurelius was the one who came closest to perfection.

Certainly Marcus Aurelius (or, to give him his full name, Marcus Aelius Aurelius Antoninus) (121–180 CE) is one the most fascinating figures in history. He was the last of the 'five good emperors' (a concept coined by Niccolò Machiavelli) and the best of them.

Marcus Aurelius ruled Rome from 161 to 180, the year he left this mortal world to join his ancestors. During his reign, the Empire had about 50 million inhabitants, about one-fifth of the world's population at the time. Under his leadership, it flourished and became more sophisticated, although it also suffered quite a few disasters, including droughts, floods, and epidemics. Marcus Aurelius functioned as a type of philosopher-king based on the model devised by Plato. He was also a skilled warrior and an accomplished strategist, scholar, and politician.

As we examine Marcus Aurelius' writings, let's not forget that he was the Emperor of Rome, the most powerful man in the world at that time. Everything was at his beck and call: he reigned supreme. With the flick of a finger he could send people to their deaths and destroy cities. He was able to enjoy every pleasure and indulgence the world had to offer.

If we judge Marcus Aurelius by his depth of thought, it's quite clear he wasn't at all equal to Aristotle, Plato, or Kant. However, in his own time a philosopher's greatness was measured primarily by his ability to apply to his life the concepts he preached in his writings. And here Marcus Aurelius is in a league of his own. The adage, 'Power corrupts and absolute power corrupts absolutely', does not at all apply to Marcus Aurelius. He clearly embraced all four of the Stoic virtues.

Pierre Hadot believed that Marcus Aurelius' book shows evidence of a particularly impressive spiritual/philosophical regimen, perhaps the most impressive ever.

Meditations (probably written during the last decade of his life) comprises 12 books. The entire first book is a profuse stream of gratitude. To give you some understanding of the spirit of the thing, here's an abridgment of its beginning:

From my grandfather Verus I learned to be gentle and humble and to refrain from anger and lust. From him also I learned about modesty and what manly character is. From my father I learned the value of compassion, devotion to friends, hard work, and indifference to fleeting fashions. From my mother I learned kindness and abstinence, not only from evil deeds but also from evil thoughts, as well as simplicity in living and rejection of the habits of the rich.

This continues for many pages. He expresses his thanks to everyone who has contributed to every virtue he has adopted: grandfather, mother, father, uncles, friends, philosophers; and then he thanks the gods (in much detail) for having given him good parents, siblings, friends, teachers, associates, and more. But like a thoughtful author, he claims that any failings he might have (as a person, that is) are his own.

What follows is a collection of insights I have gathered from the diary of this great emperor, sometimes with my own thoughts and interpretations thrown in. To get the most satisfaction out of what you're about to read, keep in mind that these ideas were written by the most powerful man in the world, as advice for himself, and that he successfully lived by them. (By the way, is it at all necessary to say that, as usual, I've allowed myself some poetic license?)

Insight 1

Start each day by telling yourself, 'Today I will encounter people who are selfish, or wicked, or ungrateful, or stingy, or rude, or traitorous, or sycophantic.' Remember, they behave this way solely because of their ignorance and their inability to distinguish between good and evil. But you know the difference between good and evil and therefore you will not be angry with any of them – humans are meant to cooperate – and it will not adversely affect your day.

Many have noticed the similarity between Buddhism and Stoic philosophy. My recommendation is a work by existential psychotherapist Antonia Macaro: *More Than Happiness* (2018).

In my opinion, one difference (of the many) between the two philosophies is that a Buddhist monk finds peace in a monastery located on a high mountain top, far from the hustle and bustle of people. The Stoic, on the other hand, walks the streets of Rome, haggles with sellers in the markets, is a loving family-minded person, participates in political debates, rebels against dictators, and maybe acts as an adviser to the Roman emperor – or perhaps he himself *is* the emperor, or actually a freed slave or a warrior or a carpenter. Nevertheless, even though the Stoic lives among the people, nothing manages to disturb their peace.

Insight 2

Your happiness depends on the nature of your thoughts. You are where your thoughts are – make sure they are where you want to be.

This is a sort of fusion of Marcus Aurelius' thoughts with those expressed by Epictetus, Seneca, Leo Tolstoy (who admired the wise emperor and often quoted him), and even Rabbi Nachman (1772–1810), founder of the Breslov Hassidic movement. I should point out that a version of this concept is also attributed to the Buddha. Here's the first verse of the *Dhammapada* (the gospel according to the Buddha):

Thought is the basis of everything.
Everything is created by thoughts, and everything is controlled by thoughts.
If a person's thoughts are not pure, suffering follows him as the cart wheel follows the ox's hoof.
Thought is the basis of everything.
Everything is created by thoughts, and everything is controlled by thoughts.
If a person's thoughts are pure, he will always be happy and happiness will follow him like a shadow.

Insight 3

You'll find respite from false hallucinations and always do the right thing if you think of every act in your life as if it were the last.

Musonius Rufus (see pages 213–14) claimed that it's impossible for a person to live properly if they do not, every day, think that this is their last day on Earth.

Do you remember that Tolstoy also suggested using one's knowledge of death as a guide to a proper life and imagining every encounter with others as if it were one's last? Tolstoy's compatriot, Aleksandr Solzhenitsyn, wrote something similar in *The Gulag Archipelago* (1973):'Purify your heart and, above all else, cherish the people in the world who love you and wish you well. Do not hurt them or scold them, and most importantly, never part from them in anger. After all, you just don't know: this may be your last encounter before your arrest, and you don't want this to be how you're engraved in their memory.'[24] (During Stalin's rule and the days of the purges, the chances of someone in Soviet Russia being suddenly imprisoned were so great that many people regularly walked around with a small suitcase filled with things they'd need if indeed they were arrested.)

Insight 4

Don't complain about life – it's a precious gift you're lucky to have. If you wish, you can leave life this very instant – the door is always open. Take this possibility into account and use it to determine what you do, say, and think.

The Stoics believed that complaining about life was a foolish, useless act, in any case. Epictetus put it like this:

Remember you're just an actor in a play.
The playwright gave you a role.
Why this role and not another? You will never know.
Your role may be brief; it may be extended.
Maybe the playwright meant you to play a beggar,
or a cripple, or a junior clerk, or a slave, or a man of
*   high stature.*
It is in your power to play your part magnificently;
but the choice of role is not yours.

'The door is always open.' I'm quoting Epictetus here, and this, of course, brings suicide to mind. The Stoics believed suicide was a dignified exit from life both when a person had no viable alternative and in cases of unendurable suffering.

Nero ordered Seneca to commit suicide. Seneca's wife, Paulina, expressed her desire to join her husband, but the Stoic philosopher forbade her to do so, on the grounds that life is an amazing, wonderful thing and it's a great privilege to live. He, however, *would* commit suicide, but only because he had no other choice.

Slavoj Žižek made an impressively profound observation. Jesus, suffering unspeakable torment on the cross, calls out: 'My God, my God, why have you forsaken me?' (in both Matthew 24:46 and Mark 15:34). In other words, God himself – incarnated as Jesus, Son of God – casts doubt on God's love, or even perhaps on his very existence. Žižek points out the terrible power of this circularity. It's mind-blowing if you think about it – you might want to take a break from reading for a little while.

Insight 5

Everything you think is just an opinion. And you don't need to have an opinion on everything.

This echoes a saying in social media, attributed to Aurelius, that expands on the idea: 'Everything you think is just an opinion and everything you see is just a point of view.' I like this sentiment, but its second part doesn't appear in the emperor's journal.

Insight 6

Never make any choice, even if it seems likely to benefit you, that will cause you to break promises or compromise your dignity.

Insight 7

*No one can insult you if you don't give your consent. No
one can annoy you if you don't give your consent. No
one can make you sad if you don't give your consent.*

The last three sentences don't actually appear in *Meditations*,
but I managed to discover them between the lines.

Anyone capable of angering you becomes your
master and you become his slave.
Epictetus

Insight 8

*Everything that occurs takes place exactly as it should.
You must be grateful for every moment and be worthy
of everything that happens to you.*

There is nothing accidental in nature. All things are
determined by the necessity of the divine nature to
exist and act in a certain way.
Baruch Spinoza

I once heard a wonderful lecture by Israeli writer Amos Oz
about S.Y. Agnon's novel *Temol Shilshom* (*Only Yesterday*) in
which Oz defined the essence of the Jewish faith in words
almost identical to those of Marcus Aurelius.

Epictetus taught that a person who hasn't yet learned
anything will blame others for the bad things that fall their
way; a person who has begun their studies knows that he
must blame himself; a wise person knows not to blame
anyone – neither themselves nor others.

Live so that you will always feel that you are in a superior position over life; do not be afraid of disaster and do not yearn for happiness; that which is bitter does not last forever and the bowl of sweetness will never overflow.

Aleksandr Solzhenitsyn, *The Gulag Archipelago*[25]

Insight 9

As long as you live, the sword of death will be hanging over your head. So don't be too elated about being an emperor. Restrain yourself and conduct yourself simply, be good, pure, thoughtful, a champion of justice, kind, and generous. Respect the gods and help the people. And do all this now.

Someone sitting on the highest throne is still sitting on his ass.

Michel de Montaigne, *Essays*

Insight 10

You will have much more time available if you stop being interested in what other people are doing or thinking. Rather, concentrate solely on your own thoughts and deeds and make them worthy, good, and right. How will you know if your thoughts are good and worthy? They'll be so if you're able to answer without hesitation and in complete honesty when you're asked what you're thinking.

Insight 11

Always note that everything is the result of change, and be comfortable with the idea that there's nothing nature loves more than changing an existing form to create something new. Time is like a river of transient events, and its current is very strong. As soon as an event unfolds, it's swept away by the current and something else takes its place. That will also be soon swept away. We should not be afraid of change. How can anything possibly happen without change?

The spirit of Heraclitus prevails in this sentiment.

Insight 12

The best revenge is: not to act like your enemies.

Avidius Cassius, a commander in Marcus Aurelius' army, rebelled against him. The generous emperor decided not to execute him but rather to meet with him and explain why what he'd done was wrong. However, before the meeting could take place, one of Cassius' centurions decapitated the rebel, even sending the amputated head to the emperor as a gift. Marcus Aurelius was shocked and saddened. Although his benevolence didn't help Avidius Cassius, he did succeed in saving the lives of almost all the members of the rebel commander's household.[26]

Insight 13

All things are intertwined, and this web of interconnections is sacred. What is not beneficial for the swarm is not beneficial for any of the bees.

This insight of Marcus Aurelius sums up an idea stated by Musonius Rufus: 'Agree with me that human nature is very similar to that of the bees. A bee is unable to live alone: it dies when solitary. The only way it can survive is to work and interact with other bees.'

There's a model in game theory that's a sort of extension of the 'prisoner's dilemma', called the 'tragedy of the commons'. The notion was popularized by Professor Garret Hardin in an influential article in *Science* magazine (1968). The tragedy of the commons is that the many problematic situations in the world – global warming, ocean pollution, overfishing, deforestation, overgrazing, traffic jams, susceptibility to epidemics – have come about because too many people think short-sightedly of their own good, feeling free to break the (unwritten) rules that have been set in the interests of the community. Often, when a group of people (or a party, company, or country) seek their own best choice without any care for the consequences of their action, the outcome may be disastrous for all.

Insight 14
Soon you will forget everything and soon everything will forget you.

Insight 15
Little is required for individual happiness. Continuously doing good deeds is a source of great joy. Nothing can beat true kindness.

Naval Ravikant, the Indian-American entrepreneur, argues in a podcast that passion is a contract that a person signs with themselves in which they promise themselves not to be happy until they achieve their desires; then a new passion appears. Stoics think that the endless parade of desires is an obstacle to happiness, just as Naval does.

Insight 16

A soul free of desires and anxieties is a person's inner fortress: there's nothing safer, it's an impenetrable refuge.

It is not this thing or that thing that hurts you, but your judgment of those things. You have the ability to reverse this judgment and replace it with another.

We are often more frightened than hurt. We suffer more from our imagination than from reality.

The Stoics distinguished between 'state of affairs' and 'events'. States of affairs are those things we have no control over, such as earthquakes or what other people think of us. 'Events' are things we do (in the Stoics' opinion) have control over, such as thoughts, feelings, and deeds. The only way to be happy is to completely ignore anything over which we have no control. Instead of wishing for things to happen the way we want, we should simply embrace everything as it happens.

If things happen in a way that does not suit me, I adapt myself to what is happening.
Michel de Montaigne, *Essays*

As you may remember, the Stoics believed that even fear is only an opinion, and whether to fear or not is a matter of choice.

One brief yet impressive book in my library is *Courage Under Fire: Testing Epictetus's Doctrines in a Laboratory of Human Behavior,* by Vice James Bond Stockdale, a US Navy vice admiral and aviator. Stockdale was a huge Epictetus fan and the *Enchiridion* always accompanied him on all his flights in the Vietnam War. He was captured by the Vietnamese and incarcerated in the infamous Hoa Lo military prison in Hanoi (the 'Hanoi Hilton'). I'll spare you descriptions of the torture the man went through in his seven-year incarceration. Stockdale reported that Stoic philosophy helped him to calm his fears and his despair.

He wrote that optimists didn't last long at the Hanoi Hilton. They would try to cheer themselves up by believing they'd be home for Christmas, or by Easter, and when that didn't happen they died of heartbreak. Optimism isn't a bad idea so long as life is floating on still waters. However, in moments of extreme crisis, Stoic philosophy brings better outcomes.

While in captivity, Stockdale deliberately wounded himself almost mortally, to convey to his captors that not only was he unafraid of torture, he was also unafraid of death. He won the Medal of Honor, the most prestigious of US military decorations.

Like Stockdale, Aleksandr Solzhenitsyn, winner of the 1970 Nobel Prize for Literature, also discovered the fragility of optimism when he was captive in a Soviet concentration camp, as described in his monumental book *The Gulag Archipelago*. I've already quoted from this work, as it's full of hard-won wisdom. Solzhenitsyn often echoes Stoic philosophy in his writings. Perhaps you need to be a Stoic to survive such extremities as Stockdale and Solzhenitsyn endured.

Stoic philosophy doesn't try to describe the world as less frightening that it is: it tries to make people more courageous.

This is what Epictetus said about death in one of his lessons: 'The worst thing about death is that everyone thinks that it's a terrible thing. But this is just an opinion. If death is indeed a terrible thing, Socrates would not have said the opposite.'

> There is nothing either good or bad, but thinking makes it so.
> **William Shakespeare, *Hamlet*, Act II, Scene 2**

Insight 17
Avoidance of action may result in injustice. Do what needs to be done.

Aleksandr Solzhenitsyn teaches us in *The Gulag Archipelago* that when we remain silent about evil, when we bury it so deep within us that no sign is seen on the surface any more, we are actually planting its roots, and in the future evil will rise above the surface and its intensity will be a thousand times greater.

Insight 18
Pain is the opposite of power, and so is anger.

In his *Meditations* Marcus Aurelius suggests we remember Epicurus' argument that pain is either tolerable or intolerable. If it's tolerable, we shouldn't complain; if it's intolerable, it won't last long. In any event, there's no need to feel anger.

Insight 19

Don't waste precious time arguing about the qualities of a good person. Be one.

And with regard to good and evil: anything that helps a person to be brave, wise, moderate, and just is good; anything that undermines these features is bad.

Epictetus asked his disciples not to explain philosophy but to live it. He felt a particularly deep contempt for those who speak eloquently but are far less lovely in their actions. Stoic philosophy isn't meant for admiration, but for assimilation.

Aleksandr Solzhenitsyn – I return to him again – thought the situation was more complex than the Stoics believed, and in *The Gulag Archipelago* wrote the following:

If only everything were so simple! If only evil and wicked people lived in one place and were cunningly committing cruel and criminal acts, and all one had to do was separate them from the rest of human beings and destroy them. It would be so easy. But the line between good and evil does not cross between people: it crosses through the heart of every individual. And who is willing to destroy part of their own heart? Even in a heart teeming with evil one will find one small bridgehead of good, and even in the purest, finest heart one will find a small permanently embedded trace of evil.[27]

Insight 20

If it's not right, don't do it; if it's not true, don't say it.

Insight 21

The obstacle in our path will become the path. Don't say, 'What a misfortune that this has happened to me.' Instead say, 'How fortunate that even though this has happened to me, I've managed to overcome it.'

Præmeditatio malorum, you may recall (page 198), is a Stoic exercise for dealing with the setbacks and misfortunes that may materialize during anyone's life. The idea is to imagine the worst case scenario and try to get used to it. Things may go wrong, things may be taken away from you – imagine this has already happened. The exercise is supposed to develop psychological resilience. And if the worst case scenario doesn't occur – thank your lucky stars and appreciate your escape.

I should point out that this isn't an easy exercise.

Insight 22

The human body and all its parts are a flowing river; the soul is a dream and a fog. Life is a battlefield far from home, glory is an illusion. So, what can guide us? Only philosophy.

We must defend our inner citadel and not allow anything inappropriate to penetrate.

Strive to live in harmony with nature and you'll arrive at your final destination of eternal peace like an olive that falls to Mother Earth, reaches her, and gives thanks both to her and to the olive tree.

I believe that Stoic philosophy is a lighthouse in the stormy ocean of life: while having no power to quell the waves, it can light the way.

CHAPTER 15

On Happiness and Other Small Things of Absolute Importance

The following pages present a ragbag compendium of ideas and reflections on the concept of 'happiness', with contributions from many people in all periods of history. Anything I've especially liked has qualified for inclusion. The ideas may be almost contradictory at times, but I imagine that you, my readers, won't mind this at all. Here and there I shall add a short commentary ... and there and here my commentary may not be quite so short.

> If you have to ask what jazz is, you'll never know.
> **Louis Armstrong**

In the same vein as the jazz giant's remarks, I could ask if someone who is actively seeking to learn about happiness

– what it means, what it looks like, how to go about finding it – can actually be happy in the end.

I wouldn't be in hurry to answer this question. I don't believe there's any information about happiness that will transform our lives into a paradise on Earth. However, that's not to say that thinking about happiness is useless: there's merit on both sides of the argument. At least, I hope, you'll find some pleasure in reading about the subject.

(I've tried to avoid the wearisome platitudes that abound on the Internet – for example, on sites that present a plethora of quotations. Instead, I've attempted to make use of my extensive library.)

Before we set out, I'd like to emphasize that the 'science of happiness' is not like the science of physics. There are no laws in this field, like Newton's laws or Maxwell's equations. In my research about happiness, you won't find any precise formulae. No doubt some will claim there *is* a formula, perhaps related to the number of miles a person walks and other, similar factors – perhaps along the lines of 'a person's happiness is equal to their height minus their weight divided by the average number of hours they spend surfing the Internet every day and the number of friends they have, multiplied by how many hours they sleep.'

An ancient guide to happiness
The Book of Ecclesiastes offer a bracing warm-up on the subject, so here's a selection of pertinent quotations:

How *sweet* is the light, what a delight for the eyes to behold the sun!
(11:7)

I withheld from my eyes nothing they asked for, and denied myself no enjoyment; rather, I got enjoyment out of all my wealth. And that was all I got out of my wealth.
(2:10)

Go, eat your bread in gladness, and drink your wine in joy; for your action was long ago approved by God. Let your clothes always be freshly washed, and your head never lack ointment. Enjoy happiness with a woman you love all the fleeting days of life that have been granted to you under the sun – all your fleeting days. For that alone is what you can get out of life and out of the means you acquire under the sun. Whatever it is in your power to do, do …
(9:7–10)

Even if a man lives many years, let him enjoy himself in all of them, remembering how many the days of darkness are going to be. The only future is nothingness!
(11:8)

A worker's sleep is sweet, whether he has much or little to eat; but the rich man's abundance doesn't let him sleep.
(5:11)

… and banish anger from your mind, and pluck sorrow out of your flesh!
(11:10)

Cast your bread forth upon the waters; for after
many days you will find it.
(11:1)

Thus I realized that the only worthwhile thing
is to enjoy yourselves and do what is good
in your lifetime.
(3:12)

Don't say, 'How has it happened that former times
were better than these?' For it is not wise of you
to ask that question.
(7:10)

So don't overdo goodness …
(7:16)

Ecclesiastes, though considered one of the most pessimistic
books in the Bible, in fact can serve as an exquisite ancient
guide for anyone seeking a path to a more appropriate and
rewarding life.

The most profound sentence in the world

This too shall pass.
Farīd ud-Dīn

This adage was popularized by none other than Abraham
Lincoln. In a speech delivered in 1859, he related the story
of a monarch from the lands of the East who gathered
together the great sages of his time and asked them to

find a sentence that would suit any situation. It had to be uplifting when life proved difficult and steadying when life was too euphoric. 'This too shall pass' was the maxim that supposedly met these requirements.

A version of the story was told by Persian Sufi poet Farīd ud-Dīn (or Attār of Nishapur) (c.1145–c.1220). The king requested an aphorism that would cheer him up when he was sad and restrain him somewhat when he was too jovial, and this was the result. It was said that the king even engraved the words on his ring.

Another variant including a king also appears in Jewish folklore, in which King Solomon is identified as having requisitioned such a ring.

Getting what we want?

If a person gets exactly what he wants,
his condition will not improve.
Heraclitus

What a fascinating perspective! I imagine most people wouldn't agree at all with this ancient philosopher's idea, but this doesn't mean that it's wrong or unworthy of discussion. Bear in mind that Oscar Wilde, in his play *Lady Windermere's Fan*, proclaimed that there are two tragedies in this world: the first is not getting what one wants and the second is getting it.[28]

This reminds me of another comment in a different play by the same author:

> When the Gods wish to punish us they
> answer our prayers.
>
> **Oscar Wilde, *An Ideal Husband*, 1893**

Let's explore this thought a little. Renowned psychologist and Harvard alumnus Dan Gilbert supports the view offered by Heraclitus – at least partially. Obviously, Professor Gilbert says, we don't always succeed in getting what we want – a person has many desires in their life, and can't attain them all. But often, even if we achieve our heart's desire, it actually proves to be quite disappointing. Sometimes, indeed, acquiring what we've longed for so fervently can lead to considerable suffering.

I highly recommend watching Professor Gilbert's TED Talk, 'The surprising science of happiness' (2013). This is one of the most frequently watched TED Talks ever. He challenges the idea that we'll be happy only if we get what we so desperately want; and that we'll be miserable if we don't.

Gilbert's book *Stumbling on Happiness* (2006) won the Royal Society Science Book Prize in 2007. 'Stumbling' in the title has carefully weighed connotations. Gilbert explains that it's impossible to predict what conditions in life will make us happy: we'll end up encountering these conditions only by chance, with luck – perhaps not far from our own doorstep, perhaps at some God-forsaken place at the edge of the world.

Often our 'psychological immune system' allows us to feel fine even when things aren't going as well as we'd hoped. Even after disaster has struck, this system in due course may somehow kick in to lift our spirits. On the other hand, if you think winning the lottery will make the victorious ticket-holder happy – think again. It isn't uncommon that a big win on a lottery fails to solve even a person's money problems. Worse, the winner may manage to spend every penny of their winnings and sometimes end up worse off than before.

By the way, some studies have shown that the lottery's second-prize winners are consistently better off than those who have won huge sums of money. I'll leave it to you to guess why this is so.

Similar principles can apply in the professional sphere. The prospect of failing at your job, and maybe even being dismissed, might feel like the end of the world, but those who jump or are pushed off the career ladder can, if they handle things well, end up just as happy as those who leave with everyone's blessing to pursue their dream. (In any case, nothing is really the 'end of the world' – except the end of the world, and may that never happen: fingers crossed! However, this doesn't mean there aren't things that are *worse* than the end of the world.)

Our emotional regulation usually improves over the years. Young children demonstrate extreme shifts in their emotions and are unable to control them efficiently – the smallest thing may trigger utmost despair or extreme elation. ('I wanted a red balloon, not a blue balloon!' will be accompanied by screaming and crying, and getting that red balloon will lead to sublime happiness and an engaging smile.) As we grow up, our emotional variance gets narrower: we become less dramatic. Reaching adulthood, we learn that most things aren't as terrible as we'd feared but also not as gratifying as we'd hoped.

Let's return to Dan Gilbert. He tells us we're wrong to think that a broken leg or a broken heart will make us more miserable than a problem that may seem smaller but is chronic. I don't know the technical definition of a chronic disease, but here's mine: a chronic illness is a medical problem that will vanish only with the disappearance of its owner. Over the years a person often accumulates not only chronic diseases but also chronic fatigue and sometimes also a chronic tendency to complain.

And me? My main complaint is this: *How is it that there's no chronic happiness?* Why can't a moment of extraordinarily powerful pleasure 'infect' us with chronic happiness?

Further thinking about happiness has revealed to me that Heraclitus' ideas are actually supported by many psychologists, from Daniel Kahneman to Sonja Lyubomirsky – all of them asserting something remarkably similar to what this ancient Greek claimed: that is, that the sentiment 'I'll be happy when … ' is almost never correct, no matter how the sentence continues. (The exception is the statement, 'I'll be happy when I'm happy.')

Renowned happiness researcher and author Sonja Lyubomirsky (b. 1966) wrote a book entitled *The Myths of Happiness: What Should Make You Happy, But Doesn't, What Shouldn't Make You Happy, But Does* (2014). If I were assigned the impossible task of summing up this book in one sentence, it would be this: Often, things we think will make us happy aren't what they're cracked up to be and lead to only short-term rewards, whereas more mundane things can satisfy our expectations and lead us to extended peace and tranquillity.

Have you noticed how this sentence echoes both Heraclitus and Gilbert?

At this point in our thinking, a little organization is needed, so let's ask Israeli-American psychologist Daniel Kahneman (b. 1934) for some help. Kahneman (who won the Nobel Prize in Economics in 2002) and his colleagues (Alan B. Krueger, David Schkade, Norbert Schwarz and Arthur A. Stone) coined the term 'focusing illusion' in an article they published in *Science* magazine in 2006 entitled, 'Would you be happier if you were richer? A focusing illusion'.

The main idea is that when people focus on judging a specific episode from the sum-total of episodes in their lives (health, relationships, income level, degree of appreciation, and so on), they tend to give too much weight to this specific aspect compared with all the other aspects that make up the whole. A sick woman will focus on her infliction ('I'll be happy when I'm healthy'), attaching immense importance to health. Similarly, a lonely man will place most weight on his relationships: 'I'll be happy when I find a suitable partner.' People tend to think that once they have what they're missing, their world will transform into something wonderful. However, after the sick woman recovers, she may encounter many other nuisances in her life – for example, lack of appreciation, poverty, or unruly kids. The man who resolves his loneliness issue may come down with health or other problems. 'I'll be happy when I'm rich' is a very common illusion, and I've no doubt that you'll know enough by now to explain why this *is* an illusion.

All this is not to say that health and relationships aren't important. They're very important. But if we believe Dan, Daniel, and Sonja, they're less important than we believe.

The 17th-century French moralist and satirist François de La Rochefoucauld (1613–1680) suggested the following: before embarking on a journey to follow one's dream, it's prudent to meet people who have had a similar dream and achieved it, then carefully examine if they're happy.

Anton Chekhov warned us – or perhaps he was actually encouraging us – that when an event occurs, only God can say if this is for good or for bad.

> The search for happiness is somewhat like picking mushrooms. It isn't easy to find a mushroom that looks good. You walk along, constantly scanning the area, bending down, then straightening up and bending again, soiling your hands. Often, on closer inspection, your mushroom turns out to be toxic.
> Maxim Gorky

Partial happiness

Christian theologian and thinker Augustine of Hippo (354–430 CE), in his book *The City of God*, claimed that any search for happiness in *this* world is doomed to certain failure. Happiness, in his opinion, can be experienced only in the *next* world. Christian optimism about the world to come is balanced in the scales against pessimism regarding the here and now. However, according to Thomas Aquinas, we can indeed attain happiness in this world – even though only 'partial happiness'– by giving charitably and maintaining hope and faith.

I breathe a sigh of relief at this assurance.

The Way

Vietnamese Buddhist monk Thich Nhat Hanh (1926–2022), during one of his recorded conversations (*The Art of Mindful Living*, on CD), said the following:

> *There is no way to happiness, happiness is the way;*
> *There is no way to peace, peace is the way;*
> *There is no way to enlightenment, enlightenment is*
> *   the way.*
> *The journey is the destination.*[29]

On almost every website, the Buddha invariably gets credit for the first line quoted above, but there's no evidence the Buddha ever said it. Very often he's cited rather wishfully for quotations that sound vaguely in line with his teachings.

An ordinary miracle

Thich Nhat Hanh taught that the true miracle isn't walking on thin ice or even walking on water: the true miracle is walking on the ground. He said that all day and every day we witness miracles that cannot be surpassed: the blue sky, white clouds, soaring mountaintops, green leaves, the ripple of water, a smile, a child's curious eyes, our own eyes. *Everything* is a miracle.

And since we're on the subject of miracles, here's something that amazes me every night and morning: sleep.

Sleep is the most ordinary thing and also the most extraordinary. Why? Every night, some time after sunset, a person gets into bed, tosses a little from side to side, and at some point, without even noticing, loses consciousness and regains it on the brink of a new day. Clearly a miracle, isn't it? It comes as no surprise, therefore, that immediately upon awaking in the morning a devout Jew will recite the prayer, 'I give thanks before You, the living and eternal King, for You have returned within me my soul with compassion; abundant is Your faithfulness!' The miracles of exiting this world at night and of homecoming or resurrection in the morning have impressed me every morning and night for decades.

There's also a koan (insightful riddle) in Zen Buddhism that asks, 'What is it that carries my corpse from place to place'?

I haven't yet answered this and I'm rather doubtful I ever will.

The opposite of happiness

One of the most amusing definitions of happiness is based on the idea that absence of specific emotions will give 'proof positive' that one is happy. These are the emotions that should be absent: sadness, nervousness, anger, rage, boredom, shame, jealousy, disappointment, anxiety, remorse, terror, disgust, despair, worry, lust, emptiness, guilt, dissatisfaction, revulsion, distress, and loneliness. I hope I didn't miss anything.

No research is needed to understand that only someone who is dead will be free of all such emotions. Therefore – if we accept this definition – the only people who are truly happy will be those who have passed from this world or have never entered it.

(It should be noted that Aristotle's *Nicomachean Ethics* devotes more attention to examples of what is *not* considered *eudaimonia* than to explanations of what is.)

Memories of happiness

Perfect happiness, even in memory, is not common ...
Jane Austen, *Emma*

If by chance you don't believe Lady Jane, please do this experiment: try to remember when you felt absolute happiness. If you can recall many instances in succession and you don't know where to start, you are especially blessed.

Psychologists who deal with matters of happiness distinguish between the person who 'experiences' and the person who 'remembers'. Sometimes, a pleasurable experience may become an oppressive memory, whereas an arduous or embarrassing experience may become a pleasant memory. In my book *The Most Beautiful Childhood Memory*, I relate a story that wonderfully illustrates the point – though this wasn't my intention. When I was five or six, my dad took me tobogganing. He decided the sensible thing to do would be to run alongside me on the slippery slope of the hill. He kept falling and getting up and falling again. All the kids made fun of us both – it was an embarrassing, unhappy experience, to say the least. Zero on the scale of happiness. However, now, 50 years later, I treasure this day as a particularly beautiful childhood memory that reminds me there was someone in this world who cared for me and loved me so much that he did really stupid things for me. The 'happiness score' of this incident became 10 with a huge plus.

Random acts of kindness

That incident aside, I've been able to come up with a few memories I could define as perfect happiness, pure and sublime.

Daniela, my partner, has successfully recalled many examples of perfect happiness. I'll relate to you one of them, concerning both my parents this time.

'For seven days and seven nights Job's friends sat beside him in silence, for they saw that his pain was very great' (Job 2:3). During the *shiva* (the seven days of mourning) after my mother's passing, we tried to reduce the almost insurmountable sorrow by talking incessantly, recalling more and more memories of her.

My parents loved Daniela deeply and she loved them no less. She told me that the first memory of them (of many) that came to her mind was actually a seemingly insignificant thing. One day, on her way back home (at that time, she wore the uniform of an Israeli Air Force officer) she experienced a particularly heavy downpour. She had no coat and no umbrella, and her uniform became so sodden you'd think she'd been swimming for hours in full attire. Before she'd even rung the doorbell, my parents, Sasha and Tania, opened the door into our warm and cozy home. My parents were there because, for many years and on a daily basis, they'd been serving as the most dedicated babysitters in the world to our daughters. My father swathed Daniela in a huge, comforting towel. Then, while Daniela was in the shower, Sasha and Tania got to work in the kitchen: Dad squeezed a full glass of orange juice so that the vitamin C would head off the chance of her catching a cold and Mom heated a pan of mushroom soup, cut up vegetables for a salad, and fixed up the mashed potatoes left over from the girls' lunch. ('Fixed up' meant adding a ton of butter and heating it up.) My wife added that when she sat down at the table for this little meal, she felt like she was a little girl again, protected and loved. A moment of perfect happiness.

> … that best portion of a good man's life,
> His little nameless, unremembered acts
> of kindness and of love.
> **William Wordsworth, 'Lines Written a Few Miles above Tintern Abbey', 1798**

I'll end this section with a fascinating idea about memory suggested by French dramatist Romain Rolland (1866–1944), who incidentally was the 1915 Nobel Laureate in Literature): 'Everyone, deep down within, carries a small cemetery of those they have loved.' This thought is a true insight and inspires me anew every time I think about it.

I almost never visit the cemetery where my parents are buried. That isn't where they really are. They are in the memories and hearts of those who knew and loved them.

Be healthy

> Orandum est ut sit mens sana in corpore sano.
> ('Pray for a healthy mind in a healthy body.')
> **Juvenal, *Satires*, X**

The phrase 'healthy mind in a healthy body' might be an excellent candidate for the title of 'most worn, battered, and chewed cliché of all time', and it isn't entirely clear to me what it means. It's a case of words being less useful out of context. Originally, in the writings of 1st-century Roman satirical poet Decimus Junius Juvenalis, this expression is preceded by the word 'Pray', which seems to make total sense. Getting up in the morning and saying a little prayer to Asclepius, the god of medicine, and his daughter Hygieia (or Hygea – her name is the source of 'hygiene'), the goddess of health, asking them to bestow mental and physical health upon the supplicant, doesn't seem to me like such a bad idea.

The Pythagoreans greatly revered Hygieia. Not only would they greet each other with a blessing for health: they occasionally made use of an emblem with the five letters of her name (there are actually six Greek characters but Pythagoreans used a five-letter version, *Υγεία*) on the points of a pentagram.

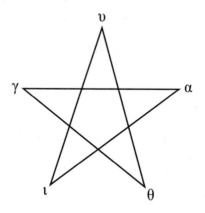

Similarly, speakers of Slavic languages, when they part from each other, often say '*будь здоров!*' ('Be healthy!'). Arthur Schopenhauer recommended the salutation 'Be healthy!', both when meeting and taking leave of someone. Wishing people continued health in this way reflects a deep-seated feeling that this is the foremost condition of our happiness.

Also of interest is that this German philosopher stated that a healthy destitute beggar is happier than an ailing king.

The waiting room

If one were to build the house of happiness,
the largest space would be the waiting room.
Jules Renard, *Journal*

In other words, happiness is found only in beginnings and in anticipation. Permanent residence in the House of Happiness is not possible for most of us. The eudaimonic happiness of Aristotle or the Stoics, and the Buddhists' Nirvana, exist only briefly. The ordinary person may live in this house only temporarily, and only on a rental basis. In fact, even during the rental period, they won't reside there continuously: they will leave, return, come back, with erratic timing. In any case, the House of Happiness is certainly not for sale for permanent residence.

Ivan Bunin, the Russian who won the Nobel Prize for Literature in 1933, wrote in his diary that anyone who hasn't completely lost the ability to wait for happiness is already happy.

To this I'll add that the expectation of happiness can sometimes give more joy than the happiness we so long for.

> Our happiness is often none other than preserving the right to silence our misfortune.
>
> Jules Renard, *Journal*

My advice is not to take advice (including this advice)

ADVICE, n[oun]. The smallest current coin.'
Ambrose Bierce, *The Devil's Dictionary*

These days, a lot of people's fingers are light on the trigger and they shoot advice in all directions.

Over the past decades, countless happiness guides and self-help books have been published, Many make grandiose promises, offering all kinds of recipes for improving our lives. I wonder when these advisers have got to know us so well that they so confidently believe they can transform us.

This doesn't mean that there are no worthy guides to happiness. There are, and we've already encountered some of them. There are also books that, while less worthy than the ones I've mentioned, still offer sage and helpful advice.

However, beware of over-simplistic guides. The most noteworthy warning sign is the magnitude of the promise that screams out from the title. For example, I'd never buy a book entitled *How to Be Happy Forever with Only Three Minutes of Daily Training,* or *Three Key Phrases That Will Help You to Influence People,* or *The Easy Path to Wealth and Joy.* However, I'm fully aware that it's impossible to formulate a criterion by which to judge whether a particular book is valuable or not, and any attempt to do so is foolish. I'm also aware that a book that to me may be superficial –

even silly – may be life-changing for someone else. Keep that in mind.

But still…

A few weeks ago I started watching a lecture on YouTube by a motivational speaker who needs no introduction. Right at the start, they offered this advice: 'Isn't life too short for us to suffer? Repeat after me: "From this moment on, suffering will no longer be our lot."' I've no idea what the speaker said next, because I turned the thing off. I don't believe the assertion – and, by the way, this video has garnered a great many views – that the only thing you need to do to stop suffering is *decide* to stop suffering. I just can't accept this. I don't want to underestimate the effect our thoughts have on reality – there are quite a few studies on this – but I'm well aware too that the relationship can work in the other direction. That is to say, our reality can have an enormous effect on our thoughts. For example, in times of great pain (whether physical or mental), the entirety of the sufferer's world may shrink down to the pain's narrow compass, so that the only thought that emerges is 'If and when will this end?'

People, of course, are different. Some reach for books or lectures on happiness out of desperation. Others, with leisure time to spare, may even treat such research as a leisure activity, from a place of more-than-average well-being. I'd even venture to say that if someone can be busy dealing with the issue of their happiness and has the leisure time and opportunity to listen to lectures or read a book, then, in a sense, their fate may already be considered well-favoured.

Returning to the idea of thoughts having the power to influence reality, I've witnessed people placing too much weight on this. It's easy to push this too far. Epictetus, you'll remember, said 'people are not troubled by things that excite them but by the perceptions and thoughts they form about these things.' This statement applies especially to those who are suffering as a result of what their brain tells them – for example, someone afflicted with OCD suffers from what is in their mind, not from the germs they seem to be so bothered by. But the statement does *not* apply to those whose source of suffering is external reality.

Unfortunately, however, the power of thought to solve physical problems is emphasized *ad nauseum* by motivational speakers and in countless self-help books. Are you really going to try to tell a distraught mother who has lost her son or daughter in an earthquake or war or terrorist attack that what's actually bothering her is her own interpretation of the event and not the event itself? I'm being intentionally extreme here, but there are countless examples, some more dramatic (unfortunately) and some less, that very much prove my point.

By the way, if you're a motivational speaker and you believe in the unlimited power of our thoughts upon reality, then why would you suggest to people they should stop suffering when you can give better advice: be happy? Being happy is better than not suffering. If only it were that simple …

You can advise someone suffering from a toothache to stop relating to their pain. You can advise someone suffering from depression to think positively. But their ability to do so is precisely the same as their ability to stop the rain, change the direction of waves in the sea, or be a just an inch or two taller.

On the other hand, if that lecture that I told you about (the one I abandoned after the first few sentences) was helpful to some of its listeners, and perhaps even changed their lives for the better, who am I to judge?

Sometimes I have a fervent desire to be open to things I don't much believe in, because I'm deeply suspicious of prejudice. However, the world of numbers and facts must be respected. Renowned astronomer Carl Sagan asked us to keep an open mind but warned us not to open it *too much* – otherwise our brains might fall right out.

If, as those speakers try to convince us in lectures, workshops, or books, it's so easy to stop suffering and be happy, then immeasurable happiness would have enveloped us all ages ago. The only mental ailment we'd be suffering from would be *excessive happiness*. Unfortunately, as we all know, this is far from the case.

Comparison is the thief of happiness

The title of this section is a variant of President Theodore Roosevelt's famous adage, 'Comparison is the thief of joy.'

The following point is so important, it deserves italicizing: *If people really wanted to be happy, they might succeed, but people don't really want to be happy. They just want to be happier than other people. This is clearly impossible, because we always imagine that other people are much happier than they really are, whereas we often appreciate our own happiness only in retrospect.*

The French poet Jacques Prévert expressed a similar idea. He pointed out that he noticed his own happiness only at the moment he heard the loud noise it made as he left.

Comparing oneself to someone else has never contributed to anyone's happiness. In this age of social networking the dangers are extreme: we can so easily compare ourselves to the entire online world. People of the younger generation who show addiction to social networks are often extremely anxious about what their fellow networkers think of them. Comparing oneself unfavourably with others can undermine enjoyment and even cause real suffering.

There's an ancient Arab parable about two friends, Sayid and Amir, who are strolling along the coast of Mogador in Morocco. Sayid draws a line on the sand with his walking stick and challenges Amir to shorten that line without touching it. Amir thinks a little, and then a little more. Finally, he draws a longer line next to Said's.

Sociological studies have found that money's effect on happiness stems less from the things it can buy (the so-called 'absolute income effect') than from comparing one's income to that of others, especially with regard to one's peers (the 'relative income effect'). This is a large part of the reason why people are no happier than their grandparents were, even though those in the 'first world' today live longer, are healthier and richer, have more leisure time, and are able to travel more. Those who constantly try 'to keep up with the Joneses' feel the strain.

Jordan Peterson's Fourth Rule in his book *12 Rules for Life* is: Compare Yourself to Who You Were Yesterday, Not Who Someone Else Is Today.

Comparing oneself to others is also one of the main reasons for FOMO (Fear of Missing Out) and FOBO (Fear of a Better Option).[30] These two phenomena almost invariably contribute to the misery of many 'first world' citizens.

Charles Bukowski (1920–1994), a poet and writer I'm particularly fond of, wrote: 'I never met another man I'd rather be.' Then follows the continuation: 'And even if that's a delusion, it's a lucky one.' Bukowski didn't gain literary recognition for many years, and in order to allow himself the spiritual freedom to write, he worked in a wide variety of menial jobs requiring no mental effort, such as dishwasher, truck driver, postman, guard, gas station attendant, parking lot attendant, and elevator boy. For a while, he worked in a factory that produced dog biscuits. Even though he eventually became successful as a writer, the epitaph on his tombstone reads, 'Don't try.'

Kurt Cobain, legendary lead singer of Nirvana, once said that a person's desire to be someone else is a disgraceful waste of the person they are.

In a consumer society there are inevitably two kinds of slaves: the prisoners of addiction and the prisoners of envy.
Ivan Illich, *Tools for Conviviality*, 1973[31]

Ivan Dominic Illich (1926–2002), an Austrian Catholic priest, theologian, and philosopher, is here responding to de La Rochefoucauld's opinion that there are a good number of people who'd be willing to do almost everything to arouse the envy of others.

In the world of the Internet, which is parallel to the real world, people travel to exotic places, eat at top restaurants, enjoy family meals, go to concerts, dive to the depths of the ocean or swim with dolphins, attend the graduation ceremonies of their offspring, and hug their children, grandchildren, and/or parents. A 'regular' person may think that the norm is an affluent, busy, fulfilled life for all.

I think the point bears repeating. Anyone who does not realize that one of the goals of posts made in the social media is to arouse the envy of others may end up experiencing mild to severe depression as a result of excessive surfing on the Internet.

> *It can be difficult to be happy if there are no witnesses to our happiness.*
> **after Jean-Jacques Rousseau and others**

> *But O, how bitter a thing it is to look into happiness through another man's eyes!*
> **William Shakespeare, *As You Like It*, Act V, Scene 2**

There's no one for whom everything is rosy and good. We all have problems. American self-help author Mark Manson wrote that happy people are simply those who have learned to deal competently with the problems that arise during their lives. You may remember you've met people who always seem to radiate happiness – I think it's just that we haven't known these people well enough or long enough to see them truly. Jealousy, therefore, is an incredibly pointless emotion: anyone we envy for their apparently wonderful life might in fact be undergoing a severe crisis or even tottering on the edge of an abyss.

They say
That there's a place,
Maybe Brazil,
Where a happy man lives.
Vladimir Mayakovsky (Russian-Soviet poet)

In today's world it can seem that (conspiracies and espionage aside) everything is visible, accessible, if we're willing to put some effort into the search. Even so, we may often get the impression that other people know more than we do about what's on offer. How can we be sure we haven't missed something unmissable? How do we know our decisions have been the best possible ones in terms of maximizing happiness? FOBO and FOMO accompany us everywhere. Can we not lock them in a box and throw the key into the sea?

This is not an easy thing to do, because once the genie has come out of the bottle it's not in any hurry to return.

By the way, *Kiasu* (驚輸) is the Chinese version of FOMO. It combines fear of missing an opportunity alongside particularly selfish behaviour. (Did you notice the beauty of the Chinese symbol?)

Our jealousy lasts longer than the happiness of those we envy.
François de La Rochefoucauld, Maxims

Everyone talks about how difficult it is to deal with unrequited love, but what about unrequited jealousy? What about someone who is constantly jealous of others and seems to get no jealousy in return ... Horrible!

The time has come to organize these ideas about 'jealousy' and its derivations, so I've compiled a modest lexicon:

Envy *Longing for something that belongs to someone else.*

Jealousy *Fear that someone else will get something you want for yourself. Romantic jealousy falls into this category.*

Ressentiment *Blaming external factors for one's disappointments, frustrations, and failures. This is blaming an imaginary enemy the 'ego' has created to disconnect itself from blame.*

Schadenfreude *Feeling pleasure or amusement when bad things happen to others. Schopenhauer believed that envy is part of human nature and stems from an emotion beyond our control. But to actually find satisfaction in someone else's distress is something directly from the devil's toolbox.*

Here's a random thought that just popped in for a visit. It's said that 'the misery of others is sometimes the consolation of fools'. I think misery of others may sometimes also be the consolation of the wise. If any of you, my readers, disagree with the last sentence, think how you'd feel if you were the only one suffering from disease and ageing, while around you the rest of humankind was enjoying eternal youth and endless pleasure. As usual, an honest answer will be welcomed.

Now let's move on to the idea (mentioned above) that we often appreciate how happy we were only in retrospect, once happiness has deserted us. My treatment of this idea will be short. Happy times are best savoured in the moment, when they are most intense. Doing ordinary things with the right person or people, at the right time and place, can be the epitome of happiness. Such wonderful moments don't come with flashy production values: they don't need to be hyped, as you might hype an exotic vacation. Just open your mind to the pleasures of the here and now, if you can. Nurture your gratitude, in a timely fashion. Greek author Nikos Kazantzakis had Alexis Zorba, the protagonist in *Zorba the Greek*, express the simple sentiment that we need very little to be happy – a glass of wine, some roasted chestnuts, and the murmur of the sea. It's true, however, that everyday pleasures in particular are often not recognized as wonderfully happy until we remember them later, with nostalgia.

> Happiness does not exist – that's obvious.
> Yet one morning you get up and find that
> it's disappeared.
> Anonymous woman, after one of my lectures

The search for lost time

> All my possessions for a moment of time.
> Queen Elizabeth I (on her deathbed)]

> *Ruit hora* ('Time is running away')
> Motto of Hugo Grotius (Dutch humanist)

I should like to suggest a nice little exercise here. The exercise is quite old and well-known, but that's no reason not to do it. Take a sheet of paper, a pen or pencil, and a straight edge, such as a ruler. Draw a pair of boxes – two columns, side by side, to write in. In the left column write the things you like to do or experience – in other words, the things that make you happy. In the right column, write down their opposites, the things that cause you discomfort. Do these two contrasting lists help you to arrive at a better understanding of what happiness is for you? (If you recall Sei Shōnagon's list on pages 8–9 and the long list I offered at the beginning of this book (pages 4–5), then this exercise should be really easy.

After completing the exercise, now ask yourself why you do the things in the right column at all? Can you find a way to limit your involvement in them. Can you devote more time to the things in the left column? It's really a waste of time and energy to be doing something you 1) don't like doing, and 2) don't have to do.

Two qualifications might be useful. First, there'll always be right-hand things you need to do in order to facilitate the left-hand things. To support my family, I have to prepare students for matriculation in mathematics and solve quadratic equations one after the other. I do these things because I really have no choice.

Secondly, carefully weigh the powerful forces of habit, duty, and external pressure. If associating with this or that person doesn't give me joy, why should I remain their acquaintance? Because they're a relative? Because otherwise they'd be offended? Because my wife would be offended? Because it's what I've done for years?

We can't choose what characteristics other people have, but we can choose to be only with people whose company we enjoy, whose good qualities outweigh their shortcomings, and who enhance our lives.

We complain that our days are numbered but we act as if they'll never end. Time doesn't waste time. Time doesn't rest, it plods on constantly, without holidays and without sick leave. Time progresses resolutely day by day and minute by minute on its journey toward our last moment. Maybe we don't know what to do with the time we have, but time knows very well what to do with us.

Seneca suggested looking at every new day as if it were a miniature version of life. The way I see this, he meant that just as the greatest sorrow would be someone reaching the twilight of their life and understanding that they'd wasted their allotted years, similarly we should try not to reach the end of the day to discover that it was just a 'normal' day, without any sparkle – just a day that would merge into the past and not be missed.

Modern technology has made interaction between people very easy but, as any economist knows, 'there's no such thing as a free lunch' and 'free cheese is found only in a mousetrap'. The price we pay for communication convenience is very high – perhaps even too high. The symptoms are familiar: people glued to their smartphone all day, even sleeping with it, social media stress, addiction to the Internet. Fake communication. What a waste of time! And I'm sure you've seen people texting while driving or checking their Instagram during a family meal. There are even reports of people experiencing a near-death experience when they lose their smartphone.

There's a mental disorder called 'nomophobia', an abbreviation of 'no-mobile-phone phobia' – that is, fear of being separated from one's smartphone. The problem is undergoing intensive investigation. Although nomophobia doesn't yet appear in the DSM-5 (*Diagnostic and Statistical Manual of Mental Disorders,* fifth edition), it's considered the most severe non-drug addiction. Teenagers using their smartphones at least 10 hours a day; people with low self-esteem using them more than the average person; unhappy people finding it difficult to remove themselves from social networks; extreme introverts and those who are especially extroverted (extremes tend to meet) – all these groups have a particularly high chance of falling victim to nomophobia. Researchers also know that adolescents' obsessive attachment to smartphones leads to anxiety, depression, EDD (empathy deficit disorder), and extreme narcissism. None of this is surprising. How sad!

The wheel of fortune

Good fortune is the joker in the deck of cards of life.
Anonymous

In modern Russian one word, *счáстье* (*schast'ye*) means both 'happiness' and (good) 'fortune'. This is similar to the double meaning of the German word '*Gluck*'. This is no accident. Though not found universally today, it turns out that in every Indo-European language, without exception, the word for 'happiness' is derived from the word from 'fortune'. Take, for example, English: etymologically, 'happiness' is derived from the ancient Icelandic root *happ* which means 'luck' or 'chance'.

Does this imply that our ancestors believed happiness to be, for the most part, a by-product of luck or good fortune?

Do you remember that Aristotle believed that without luck, nobody could reach the state of *eudaimonia*?

* * *

My favourite Greek goddess is *Εστία* or Hestia (Latin name Vesta), goddess of the hearth, but she isn't the goddess I'd build a temple for, because I already have one for her: her temple is my home. The only goddess I'd build a temple for (a spacious prayer hall with an extra-high ceiling and an organ with spectacular sound) is *Τύχη* or Tyche, goddess of fortune (whose Latin name is Fortuna).

On WhatsApp and the like I tend not to send long lists of blessings. That seems to me like a kind of grocery list made (my few trips to the grocery store have taught me this) to ensure I don't forget something. In my opinion one blessing, 'Best of luck!', fits the bill for anything. There's no need to wish someone a happy marriage or a successful interview or good health – all this is already included in 'best of luck'. It's important to understand that good fortune will mean good health, but health doesn't guarantee good fortune. It's probable, after all, that most of the passengers on the *Titanic* were more or less healthy. Did that help them? No, because their luck had run out.

Seneca taught that one must always keep in mind that Fortuna, goddess of luck, never gives gifts, only loans. Everything a person has – youth, health, good looks, property, fame, love, even life itself – is just a batch of loans that will one day need to be returned. Therefore, he suggested, we mustn't get too attached to anything: not to people, not to ideas, not to objects.

Never say about anything, 'I lost it' or 'It was taken from me,' but always say 'I returned that which never belonged to me.'
Epictetus

The Stoics had no problem with paradoxes such as, 'The righteous suffer and the evil prosper.' (By the way, this popular maxim is doubtful. This is how it is written in the Talmud, Tractate Brachot, page 7:1: 'Moses said before God: "Master of the Universe. Why is it that the righteous prosper, the righteous suffer, the wicked prosper, the wicked suffer?"') The Stoics believed that Fortuna 1) is not involved with either reward or compensation, 2) is brave – there's nothing she wouldn't dare do, and 3) has a macabre sense of humour (why *shouldn't* a person die from choking on a fish bone at their own wedding?)

A wise man once said that only the fortunate among us will end up in Paradise, if it exists: those who are unfortunate in this world will remain miserable in the next world too – they are the ones to fill all of Purgatory and Hell.

Black on white

Some people are born to look for flaws in everything. When they see Achilles, they see only a heel.
Marie von Ebner-Eschenbach (Czech-Austrian countess and writer)

Show people a white page with a black dot in the centre and ask them what they see: this has been done as a psychology experiment. Almost everyone answers that they see a black dot in the centre of the page. Not many will say they see a page that is completely white, except for a black dot at its centre. Some people will not only completely ignore the fact of the white that surrounds the black dot in every direction, they'll focus entirely on the black dot itself, pointing out that it's a perfect circle.

I decided to do this experiment in reverse. That is to say, I showed people a black page with a white dot at its centre and asked them to describe what they saw. Not one single participant – several dozen took part – answered that they saw a white dot without noting the fact that it's on a black page. The black background drew attention in a way the black dot had done; the white was only mentioned when it was exceptional (a dot). It seems to me that all this says something interesting not only about the point of view we have about life, but also about life itself.

Sometimes I've noticed, while experiencing the happiest moments of my life, a sadness creeping in without my understanding where it's come from. It isn't inconceivable that the source of this sadness was the knowledge that these beautiful moments won't last forever. The poet Lord Byron wrote: 'The memory of joy is no longer joy; the memory of pain is pain still.' In other words, memories of happy moments may not always make you happy, but memories of sad moments always make you sad.

Sometimes it's enough for one black cloud to appear in the azure sky of life to spoil everything.

Moments of joy cannot compete with catastrophic events and pleasure isn't a worthy opponent to pain.

The Romantic poet William Wordsworth wrote only one play, *The Borderers* (1842), and here's a line from it that's relevant to our discussion:

Suffering is permanent, obscure and dark.
And shares the nature of infinity.

Arthur Schopenhauer, discussing the supremacy of suffering over pleasure, notes that, with all due respect to the pleasure a lioness has when she satisfies her hunger by eating a gazelle, the suffering of the gazelle is immeasurable. Zhuang Zhou might remark that Schopenhauer was neither a lioness nor a gazelle, and therefore he couldn't have known what each might be feeling; whereupon the German philosopher would probably fly into a rage, raise his voice, and passionately argue that if anything is at all certain, it's suffering and pain, and both humans and animals feel it.

In one of his many lectures on YouTube, Jordan Peterson expressed one of the saddest ideas I've ever heard: no parent can be happier than their most miserable child.

It may not be surprising that we can clearly see a black dot on a white page but are less excited about a white dot on a black page: a glass of wine becomes lethal from a single drop of poison, whereas a glass of poison will not become drinkable with the addition of a drop of fine wine.

On the other hand, one small candle is often enough to illuminate the darkness.

Friend to Groucho Marx: 'Life is difficult!' Marx to friend: 'Compared to what?'

There are no sad loves
All loves are happy, even the loves that disappoint.
Lou Andreas-Salomé

I found this saying by Lou Andreas-Salomé in her book *The Erotic* (1910), which I think deserves more recognition than it gets today.

Happy Einstein

In 1922 Albert Einstein was invited to do a lecture tour in Asia. During his trip, he was informed that he'd won the 1921 Nobel Prize in Physics. However, instead of dropping everything to head to Stockholm for the award ceremony, he decided to keep to his original plan and proceeded to Japan.

When he arrived at the Imperial Palace in Tokyo, he was faced with thousands of people who wanted to witness the great scientist meeting the Emperor and Empress. Many also made the effort to attend his first lecture in the city, which lasted, so it's told, more than three hours.

He stayed at the Imperial Hotel, and while he was there the great physicist received some sort of letter or package. There are two versions of what happened next: either the messenger refused the tip that Einstein offered or Einstein didn't have any small change in his pocket. Either way, Einstein felt uncomfortable and wanted to reward the messenger anyway. So, the father of relativity took out a sheet of hotel stationery and wrote on it in German his theory of happiness: 'A calm and modest life brings more happiness than the pursuit of success combined with constant restlessness.'

How interesting from someone who'd just won the Nobel Prize: prioritize calm and humility over ambition.

Then Einstein took another sheet of stationery and wrote (it isn't clear how original the phrase is): 'Where there's a will there's a way.'

He advised the messenger to hold onto these notes, implying they might be quite valuable in the future. And indeed, so they were.

At an auction held in Jerusalem in 2017, the note on happiness was sold for $1.56 million! The second note fetched 'only' $240,000. And if you want to know who the seller was, yes, it was the grandson of the brother of the messenger of the Imperial Hotel in Tokyo.

This story about Einstein has made me long to write about Japan.

Ikigai

Let us visit the Land of the Rising Sun in the Heian period (794–1185). We already know (see page 7) that during this period three wonderful women lived in Kyoto: Empress Teishi (Sadako), author Murasaki Shikibu, and our old friend, author of *The Pillow Book*, Sei Shōnagon. During this era a philosophy called *Ikigai* was beginning to take shape. It's become very popular in recent years in Western culture. The approximate meaning of *Ikigai* is the 'reason to be and to live'. The term relates to whatever allows us to find meaning in our lives and, by doing so, be happy – and even live a long life. In fact, many residents of Okinawa, the island where *Ikigai* is most commonly practised, do live up to a triple-digit number of years. *National Geographic* journalist Dan Buettner is convinced that *Ikigai* and *Moai* (communal support for those to whom fate has been less kind) plays a crucial role in longevity (see his enjoyable Ted Talk, 'How to Live To Be 100+').

Ikigai's most basic principle – the Japanese version of *eudaimonia* – can conveniently be shown as a graphic display:

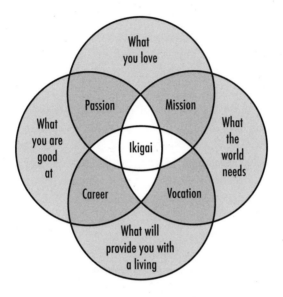

Do you want to find meaning in life? No problem. Turn the four items around the graphic into questions about yourself and answer them with utmost honesty: What do I love? What am I really good at? What can I do to make a living? What does the world need?

Take a sheet of paper and list your answers in four columns. Check if there's anything that appears in all four columns. If so – congratulations! You've found a meaning in life that will bring you happiness and longevity. If there's nothing that appears in all four categories, check if there's something that appears in three of them (one must be the things you can get paid for). If so – congratulations once again. If there's nothing that meets this requirement, the Japanese have no advice for you.

An interlude: Japanese proverbs

While you're doing this exercise, I offer a long riff on my favourite Japanese proverbs.

A frog that lives in a well knows nothing about the sea.

Remember Zhuang Zhou's story 'The Wise Man and the Frog?' The Japanese proverb sums it up – I don't know which came first, but would guess it's the Chinese philosopher who wandered over to the Land of the Rising Sun.

And here are two proverbs with meanings that are similar to each other:

Even monkeys sometimes fall from trees.

A kappa may also drown.

The meaning of both is that excelling at something doesn't mean you'll never make mistakes. Kappas (river-children) are exquisitely human-like mythological creatures who live in water and are known for their impressive swimming ability.

Ryūnosuke Akutagawa (1892–1927) is a Japanese writer I especially admire. His first name, Ryūnosuke ('Son of Dragon'), was given to him because he was born in the Year of the Dragon, in the Month of the Dragon, on the Day of the Dragon, and even in the Hour of the Dragon. Akutagawa believed that life was a kind of 'Crazy Olympics', because no one knows what sport they are supposed to compete in – so we're all just running back and forth in a stadium, with no clear purpose. In 1927, only 35 years old, he committed suicide. Akutagawa wrote many wonderful short stories. His most famous, 'In a Grove', provided the basis for Akira Kurosawa's award-winning film *Rashomon;* and I incorporated this story into my book *Thoughts for the Night*. One of his most enjoyable and thought-provoking stories is entitled 'Kappa'. The story is narrated by a psychiatric patient known as 'Number 23'. He claims to have visited the land of the kappa and befriended many of its inhabitants. The plot is a combination of science fiction and parody about bourgeois Japan in the early 20th century.

One of the craziest ideas in Akutagawa's writings is 'conversations with foetuses' – a Japanese version of our earlier discussion about whether it's better for a person to be brought into this world or not (see page 42). In this story we pass through the land of kappas who are about to go out into the world and are given one last chance to change their mind. Before making their decision, they are presented with an exhaustive probabilistic overview of everything that might await them throughout life – moments of happiness, despair, love, hatred, envy, anger, joy, ecstasy, agony, health, sickness, boredom, passion, all conveyed in detail. When you're seven you'll first see snow; aged nine you'll break you leg in three places; and so on, through all life's ups and downs.

After digesting this incredible amount of information about their fate, these kappa babies, still in their mothers' wombs but with a not insignificant amount of intelligence, must decide: to be born or not to be born? And what do most of them decide? Not to be born!

As the years pass, continues Number 23, the percentage of foetuses who choose not to be born becomes so high that some important kappas in key roles consider cancelling the opportunity to decide: the babies will go out into the world whether they want to or not. But this idea is rejected out of hand, because of its cruelty and the grave violation of the individual rights of kappas.

Wow! When I first read this passage about three decades ago, I couldn't sleep, it was so thoughtful and exciting.

One fascinating kappa is Tokku, a kappa poet who reveres German poet and writer Heinrich von Kleist – who wrote, among other things, the wonderful novella *Michael Kohlhaas* and committed suicide alongside his fiancée Henriette Vogel when only 34 years old. Tokku also greatly admires Austrian-Jewish philosopher Otto Weininger. (The young Wittgenstein read Weininger's book *Sex and Character* and was impressed by his genius, even though he disagreed with most of his views.) Weininger suffered from extreme misogyny. He was a homophobic homosexual and an antisemitic Jew. Clearly, intelligence and wisdom are completely different things: Weininger was brilliant but not wise. A wise man's heart doesn't have room for so much hatred and self-hatred. In 1902, at the age of 22, he converted to Christianity, and a year later committed suicide. (Italian Jewish criminologist Cesare Lombroso said that one of the most common symptoms in Jews who go mad is their desire to convert to Christianity. He added that grief over the decision to leave Judaism is one of the first signs of recovery. But I digress.)

In contrast to his love for von Kleist and Weininger, Tokku didn't at all like the patriarch of pessimism, Arthur Schopenhauer, because the German philosopher kept complaining about life and yet refused to end it willingly. (Akutagawa's description is so masterful that I have to keep reminding myself that Tokku is a kappa – an imaginary figure.) Tokku's highest admiration is for our old friend Michel de Montaigne. True, he didn't commit suicide: he prayed to die without suffering and hoped he'd meet death while planting cauliflowers in his garden.

As I was writing just now about the kappas, I recalled another Japanese proverb that's strongly connected to the previous two:

One who does not get out of his bed
will never stumble.

I offer now a phrase that isn't actually a proverb – 'friend to all'. The Japanese mostly use this as a derogatory term to describe someone who compliments everyone, tries to please everyone, smiles all day, but isn't really loyal to anybody. Aristotle called such a person 'too friendly'. I'm very wary of such people.

Now back to my proverbs:

Only a fool argues with a fool.

Laozi, in the *Tao Te Ching*, taught that the wise don't argue and anyone who argues isn't wise. To illustrate the spirit of this proverb, I'll tell a legend/parable/folk tale of indeterminate origin. As usual, my version will be freely improvised.

One day a donkey and a fox met.

'You know,' said the donkey, 'I've been thinking and thinking and I've realized that twice two is five.'

'You're wrong, it's four,' the fox replied.

'No, it's five!' the donkey insisted.

'Four,' said the fox angrily.

'Five!' said the stubborn donkey.

'Let's go and ask the lion,' suggested the fox.

The debaters went to the house of the lion, who ruled: 'The donkey is correct and you, Fox, are expelled for half a year from my forest.'

The donkey thanked the lion for the great wisdom and fair ruling. He left satisfied and happy, breaking into a sprightly trot.

The stunned fox approached the lion and asked him to explain his verdict.'Obviously, twice two is four! What do you take me for? I gave you such a severe sentence for your crime of arguing with an ass!'

Two brief remarks. 1) Donkeys are really delightful, intelligent animals and I've no idea why their good name has been trampled on in so many stories; 2) Here's a translation of a Japanese proverb that summarizes this parable, followed by a scriptural variant:

Anyone who argues with a fool is more foolish than the fool.

Do not answer a fool according to his folly, for fear that you be like him yourself.
Proverbs, 26:4

Finally we come to one of the most popular sayings in Japan, and I've no interpretation to contribute because it speaks for itself:

If you fall seven times, get up seven times.

I intentionally extended this section on Japanese proverbs. I hope you have by now completed the *Ikigai* exercise. (I did the exercise myself once and the result was that I should focus on giving lectures … but what about writing books? So here's the thing: I really like writing, but I'm not sure how good I am at this craft or if the world really needs my books. In any case I can't make a living from writing. So, based on *Ikigai*, I should stop right now and go give a lecture. Okay, I understand the point, but with all due respect to *Ikigai* I shall continue writing. I hope you'll continue reading.)

Hygge

If you haven't found yourself and your destiny according to *Ikigai*, don't despair! You still have options. For example, you can hop from Japan to Denmark and try out the Danish principle of happiness, called *Hygge*. Is this word somehow related to the word 'hug'? I've no idea.

The basic idea of *Hygge* is 'domestic cosiness', which is the realm of the goddess Vesta. *Hygge* has become a global trend, and in 2016 the term was chosen by the Oxford Dictionary – along with 'Brexit' and 'Trumpism' – as a 'word of the year'.

So what do the Danes recommend? Here's my interpretation, which, true to the principles of *Hygge*, does not take itself very seriously:

- Make every room in the house cosy and warm – the smell of coffee and fresh-baked cinnamon cookies will always elevate the atmosphere in the dining room, and an abundance of pillows on the bed will make the bedroom cosier.
- Light as many candles as possible in the house, at every opportunity (and don't forget to blow them out when leaving the house).
- Wear comfy, snuggly clothes at every opportunity, such as pyjamas with Winnie-the-Pooh or the Little Mermaid (tribute to local hero Hans Christian Andersen) printed on them, and woollen slippers with or without pompoms.
- Relax in front of a blazing fireplace with friends, or with a good book and a cup of hot chocolate.
- Eat fine chocolate at every opportunity.
- Be sure to have romantic candlelit dinners (candles with everything!) at least twice a week.
- Always prepare delicious meals with a preference for hot food with a lots of carbohydrates.
- Go for walks among snow-laden trees.
- Leave TV to sad people.
- If you want your friends to remain your friends, avoid talking about politics with them.
- Learn to express gratitude for everything there is; know how to enjoy simple pleasures; settle for little.
- Take time for hobbies; and adopt a dog.

A perfect formula, isn't it? How can you *not* relate to chocolate, candles, slippers with pompoms, and cinnamon cookies?

Well, you already know my opinion of recipes like this – if things were that simple, sublime happiness would be not only flooding the kingdom of Denmark, it would be running rampant throughout the entire world as well. But that's not the case. Which doesn't mean that there's nothing to learn from the Japanese or the Danes or anyone else for that matter – only that everything must be taken with a grain of salt.

Travel book writer Michael Booth spent many years in the Scandinavian countries. In his book *The Almost Nearly Perfect People*, which examines these Northern climes, he wrote about *Hygge* and noted that perhaps the real reason for the Danes' high levels of happiness isn't so much candles and woolly socks, but rather their tendency to be quite wealthy and very sexual, and not to work too many hours. He also notes that Denmark has one of the highest rates of antidepressant use in the world! Something seems rotten in the State of Denmark.

By the way, Booth doesn't spare criticism of *any* of these northern European countries. He comments on the rise of neo-Nazi power in Norway and on alcoholism, suicide, murder, and drug addiction in the Finns. His harshest criticism concerns the Swedes. But I don't want to get into any quarrel with Viking descendants, so I'll quit here.

It's true that Scandinavian countries always rank at the top of lists of 'happiest countries in the world', but is that a reason to envy them and emigrate there? I'm not in a hurry to do so. I'd settle just for a trip to see the Northern Lights and then come back home to where my life is really happening.

Happiness eventually arrives

Old age comes at that very moment when one says that one has never felt so young.
Jules Renard, *Journal*

Forty is the old age of youth; fifty is the youth of old age.
Victor Hugo

Old age is like the first snow. You wake up one morning and are surprised to see that everything is white.
Jules Renard, *Journal*

When I learned physics in school, I was taught that time flows uniformly. But I've a feeling time only flows this way in textbooks about classical physics. As you get older, time keeps accelerating. Anyone who has gone travelling knows that as their journey nears its end, the miles seem longer and longer, but this isn't the case in the journey of life – every year seems shorter than its predecessor.

Old age is one of the most unexpected of all things that can happen to a person.
Leon Trotsky, *Trotsky's Diary in Exile*, 1935

As we age, it's not uncommon for us to love life more – it's become a good old friend.

Think for a moment and try to answer this question honestly. At what age did you feel happiest? A decade ago? A quarter of a century ago? Today?

Many studies have shown that the intuitive belief held by many of us is that our level of happiness decreases over the years, but this isn't true – it's outdated information. According to the latest scientific researches, happiness increases as the years accumulate.

Grow old along with me!
The best is yet to be,
The last of life, for which the first was made …
Robert Browning, 'Rabbi ben Ezra'[32]

Indeed, many studies show that the curve describing the relationship between age and happiness is U-shaped. If I wanted to be a little more precise, I'd say that one's degree of happiness decreases with age until you reach the bottom of the curve – around 45 years for men and 50 for women – and from there everything just gets better. (Looking at the graph, we might be tempted to think excessive happiness might be a common cause of death.)

The consensus regarding this point is so great that if you Google 'age and happiness', countless U-shaped diagrams will turn up.

Having said that, I also noted on a graph on the World Economic Forum website something that seems to make a little more sense to me: that around age of 70, happiness begins to decline. This has made me feel a bit calmer.

I wonder what Mark Twain would have said about the more optimistic of the graphs – that is, the U-shaped happiness curve. Twain claimed not to believe that any sensible person who has reached the age of 65 would agree to live his life again.

Here are some hypotheses that may possibly explain why happiness increases with age. Perhaps grandchildren generate immense joy and compensate for the stress of lost vitality? Perhaps not having to work, and look at the face of the boss you hated so much, is a wonderful feeling? Perhaps at last you stop trying to impress everyone else and start saying whatever comes to mind?

With young people (similar to small children in many ways) the simplest things can lift their spirits to the highest peak or lower them into the deepest abyss. Perhaps seniors who are wise in the ways of the world, while not easily lifted to great heights of joy, will also not so readily sink into black bile. Maybe happiness increases because older people are more prone to savour even the minor gifts of life? I also think that in old age many stop searching for the meaning of life, simply because they've reached the understanding that there will be no further clues to enlighten them? I don't know if this increases happiness, but certainly it's comforting. However, could the the real reason be that older people are better able to regulate their emotions?

I've noticed that with age there's almost no change in a person's ability to control their thoughts, but there's a rather dramatic change in their ability to control their reactions. This is probably not because we've developed a stronger character but because the opponents we face – emotions and passions – have been greatly weakened by time.

Now it's time for 'recommended reading'. You might like to take a look at the 2010 article, 'A snapshot of the age distribution of psychological well-being in the United States' by Arthur A. Stone and colleagues.[33] The study focuses on our sense of mental well-being (WB), a concept in psychology that signifies a person's subjective assessment regarding the quality of his life in general (global WB) and emotionally (hedonic WB). Well-being is considered an essential ingredient in the mental health of individuals and groups. Interestingly, since that study, a third index has been added, and that's the sense of meaning that life has. In other words: *eudaimonia*! Aristotle strikes again!

Life. I understand it less and less and love
it more and more.
Jules Renard, *Journal*

Here's my definition of *eudaimonia*-happiness: a moment when when a person, in the last days of their life, can look back and say that, given the cards Fortune dealt them, they've successfully produced a not-very-bad version of themselves, and for that they are happy.

However, keep in mind that this is probably just a provisional definition. Over the course of my life I've created quite a few definitions for happiness, so I have no reason to assume this will be the last.

At this point, I thought I could move on to the next chapter, but suddenly I remembered an excerpt from a letter written by Franz Kafka (who was suffering from TB) to his beloved Milena Jesenská:

If a person can die from happiness, then surely this will happen to me very soon; but if a dying person can remain alive as a result of happiness, then I will remain alive.

To give some context: Milena had written Kafka in 1919 asking for permission to translate one of his stories, and this started an exchange of letters which became increasingly passionate. A year later, Kafka met with Milena in Vienna for a few days that he described as the 'happiest days of my life'. He called lying on the grass, his head resting on Milena's bare shoulder, the 'best moment in my life'. 'Happiness' is not a word one often encounters with Kafka, but such is the power of love.

Which brings me to the final chapter.

CHAPTER 16

A Few Words about Love

Some things never cease to amaze me. Is it not strange that in Western culture the story of Romeo and Juliet, a couple of naïve, confused children, serves as a model for the type of sublime love that's greater than life itself?

Let's take a good look at what happens.

The story begins like this: Romeo is madly in love with … Rosaline. Yes, Rosaline.

Rosaline? Who is that? Many people forget this detail, but at the beginning of the story Romeo is in love with Rosaline, Juliet's cousin. Here's what Romeo says about her:

The all-seeing sun
Ne'er saw her match since first the world begun.
William Shakespeare, *Romeo and Juliet*, Act 1, Scene 2

Moments before he meets Juliet, Rosaline is the one who has captured Romeo's heart, the one he cannot live without. He is willing to sacrifice everything for her love.

In fact, the main reason Romeo's friends drag him to the big ball thrown by the head of the Capulet family, where he first lays eyes on Juliet, is to contrive a meeting with Rosaline. They've seen their friend wandering the streets of Verona, sighing endlessly because of his unrequited love for her. They had no choice but to intervene, for they feared the young lover would lose his sanity. It seems that Romeo's friends knew about the boy's problematic character.

A split-second before Romeo falls in love with Juliet to the depths of his soul, he actually loves Rosaline to similar depths of the same soul. But then, at the Capulet ball, he notices that Juliet is slightly fairer than Rosaline, and immediately transfers his full measure of love to her.

Here's what Romeo says when he first sees Juliet:

Did my heart love till now? Forswear it, sight!
For I ne'er saw true beauty till this night.
Act I, Scene 5

What happened to Rosaline? Where has it gone, this great love he felt toward her?

By the way, we must ask this question. If what we have here is supposed to be a play about the (apparently) pure, exalted love between Romeo and Juliet, why did Shakespeare need the presence of another beloved within the narrative? That's pretty confusing, isn't it?

Let's continue a little more with the story of the young lovers of Verona. Juliet is a girl who 'hath not seen the change of fourteen years' – this is explicit in the script. Yet after spending just a few hours with Romeo, this young lady, one whose whole life supposedly lies before her, feels that her soul has cleaved to his and that she couldn't possibly live without him. Wow! Real madness.

Romeo's age isn't specified, but it can be assumed that he too is pretty young.

Juliet and Romeo meet briefly only twice before exchanging vows and promising to marry each other as soon as possible, with a clear preference for the very next day. From the moment they meet until the day they succumb, barely a week has passed (!), during which time Romeo manages to slay Tybalt. Later he also slays Paris.

Did Romeo have such anger-management issues that he couldn't prevent taking lives?

Do you remember how the play ends? Juliet drinks a potion to makes her fall into a deep sleep simulating death. Thinking Juliet is dead, Romeo obtains a vial of (real) poison. Again I ask – was Romeo so impulsive that he couldn't wait a moment or two and try to get his head together before imbibing the poison? A moment after he drinks his 'dram of poison', Juliet wakes up and discovers Romeo, the love of her life (or at least the love of her last week), lying dead beside her, whereupon she grabs the vial of poison so she too may drink from it and end her life. But, alas, the vial is completely empty. Romeo has left nothing to chance. Juliet therefore – oh! how romantic! – kisses Romeo on the lips, hoping there are still some drops of poison there so she can share his death with him. But once again – disappointment! – not a single drop of poison remains on her lover's lips. Left with no alternative, Juliet stabs herself with Romeo's dagger and dies. The curtain falls.

Is this tragic dimension what gives the story its charm? I don't know. To me, the dimension is tragicomic with a strong emphasis on comic.

One of my acquaintances, a great expert on Shakespeare, told me with considerable rage that although he and I had probably read the same words, we hadn't experienced the same play because, according to him, *Romeo and Juliet* is the most beautiful, moving love story ever written. I agreed on the matter of beauty, but reminded him that Socrates had already understood that beautiful words are often not true and that truth often strides forth without beautiful words.

For the sake of proper disclosure, I'll reveal to you that, for me, Rosaline is the true heroine in this play. So what if we don't even meet her? I sometimes imagine her as she briefly appears in Franco Zeffirelli's film of *Romeo and Juliet*, which came to the silver screen in 1968.

I imagine Rosaline meeting Juliet, and pleading with her not to listen to Romeo's declarations, because he's a fickle boy and not mature enough for a serious relationship. 'Listen,' Rosaline tells Juliet. 'There was a reason I told Romeo I'm never going to get married. I wanted him to leave me alone.' I can also hear Rosaline telling Juliet that there are other men no less worthy than Romeo who can also spout Shakespearean English.

Had Rosaline miraculously arrived in time for the final scene, she would have pleaded with Juliet not to take her own life. 'No man is worth it,' I imagine her saying. 'Especially not Romeo, who inside a week – or two days or two minutes – might meet a Yolanda or Adriana or Cordelia or Bianca and fall desperately in love, say a few beautiful English phrases, and throw you to the devil.'

Keep in mind that Juliet is Romeo's 'rebound love' and all modern psychological studies are suspicious of love of this kind. Now, I'm an avid Shakespeare fan – I even possess an antique many-paged notebook with a hefty lock into which I copy in my own handwriting, using a fancy pen, especially moving sentences that he penned. Even so, to me this story is almost a *parody* of love at first sight, because love, true love, love worth dying for, is certainly a love worth more than one look.

I know that it's customary to elevate romantic love to the status of a miracle, but in my opinion the real miracle is the serene, stable love that follows in its wake. This more mature love doesn't exclude romantic love; instead, it invites it along as a dear companion. Such tranquil love doesn't need fireworks. Its melody is devoid of drums and cymbals. It's as silent as a heartbeat and almost as essential.

Dante, Stendhal, and Goethe

Not venturing far from Romeo and Juliet's Verona, we shall move now to Tuscany, to beautiful Florence. We'll replace the greatest of English poets with the greatest of Italian poets. We'll also convert the fictional plot into a completely true love story. According to what's recounted in *La Vita Nuova* (*The New Life*), Dante meets Beatrice only twice in his lifetime, at an interval of nine years. Dante was married, as was Beatrice. Yet he loved her steadfastly to the end of his days, even after she'd died at the mere age of 26. The great poet relates that, during their second meeting, he almost died from the surfeit of joy and exhilaration he felt when she greeted him!

But what exactly did Dante love about Beatrice? Like Romeo, the author of *The Divine Comedy* knew only that his beloved was beautiful. But there's an important difference between our two lovers: Romeo was Shakespeare's brainchild, whereas Dante was an actual person. (By the way, Vladimir Nabokov believed that Hamlet, Lady Macbeth, and King Lear were more convincing than any flesh-and-blood person who has ever graced our world.) Unlike Romeo, Dante seemed to have discovered something important: that the most romantic love is unrequited love. Imagination is better than reality. He realized that through Beatrice he could enjoy a kind of self-love that would be painfully pleasant.

In Japan there are men who go a few steps further than Dante dared – they just buy themselves a little doll as a partner who will live with them in their house. They take the doll everywhere they go (it will fit in a jacket pocket), talk to her, and imagine this is their great love. They might even marry it. In their imagination, the doll loves, understands, encourages, and comforts them, and even buys them exactly the gifts they desire.

When French author Marie-Henri Beyle (1783–1842) (better known by his pseudonym Stendhal) visited Florence in 1817, he was astounded by the city's beauty. When he stepped into the Basilica of Santa Croce, where Michelangelo, Machiavelli, and Galileo Galilei are buried, he almost lost consciousness in the face of its sublimity.[34]

Any reader of Stendhal's book, *De L'Amour* (*On Love*) (1822), can't help noticing how much the writer is immersed in the 'I' of 'I love you.' Some call love 'couple egoism' or 'madness in pairs'. With Stendhal, there's no couple and no pair. His book traces the journeys of a lone traveller into the depths of love's emotion.

It isn't surprising, therefore, that Stendhal's favourite literary hero is Werther, the eponymous hero of Johann Wolfgang von Goethe's epistolary novel *The Sorrows of Young Werther* (1774). The novel reveals everything about Werther, but his acquaintance with Lotte, his lover, who is engaged to someone else and marries later in the book, is treated with the utmost superficiality. As I see it, Werther doesn't love the actual Lotte; like Dante, he's in love with an idealized representation he has created in his imagination. I would say that, even more than loving Lotte, Werther just loves to love.

Countess Matilda Dembowski, the inspiration for *De L'Amour*, was married with two children. There was no doubt that Stendhal's love for her would remain forever unrequited, but it was nevertheless a deep romantic love that would never die.

Romeo, Dante, Stendhal, Werther – I've mixed literature and reality – all fell in love at first sight. To my mind, love at first sight is a mixture of sexual desire and self-love. What can you possibly love about a person you don't know at all? I'll repeat myself and say that I'm much more impressed by love at one-thousand-and-first sight and all the 'sightings' that come thereafter.

The key question

A friend of mine, a former CEO of a large travel company, once told me that although the feedback questionnaires given to travellers who have just returned from a guided trip include many questions, he really only focuses seriously on one of them to determine the future of the guide. The question is, 'If you take another trip with our company, would you like to have the same guide?'

I think this is a pretty good way to answer the question 'What is love?' Loving couples who have come a long way together should ask themselves this: 'If we could miraculously live our lives again, would we want to repeat it with each other?'

The business of love

A businesswoman friend of mine shared with me her opinion that in the world of business one cannot stay still. A business that isn't growing and expanding will crumble and fail. I don't understand a thing about business matters, so I don't know how to assess the accuracy of her words. However, I thought this was another idea showing remarkable accuracy if applied to love. My observations of not a few of my friends over many years has taught me that if love isn't growing, it will fade away.

The sentence, 'I'm happy in my marriage', should be replaced by a longer but more accurate sentence: 'At the moment, I'm happy in my married life and very much hope to remain so.' The art of love is the art of perseverance.

Thoughts I have thought

- Love is the meeting between the most sacred and the most random.
- Love is a paradox that lives within a great mystery, on an island of courage, kindness, beauty, passion, hope, and holiness, surrounded by an ocean of profanity and mist.

- True love makes the world more expansive and more exciting. It's a shared pilgrimage toward all that's good, beautiful, and true.
- The mystery of love will forever be a mystery. Falling in love is a divine gift. A person cannot choose whom they fall in love with or when they'll fall in love.
- We might not be able to keep loving the way we wish to. We may, if we wish to, be unable to expel love from our lives in the blink of an eye.
- Although many swear they'll keep the flame of love dancing all through their lives, they may forget that, when love dies, desire to maintain it also withers away. No matter what, the freedom of human beings to choose in matters of love is scant to the point of non-existence.
- It's amazing to see what intimacy a couple can achieve over the years – it reaches the point where they can quarrel and become reconciled without saying a word.

About jazz and love

Recently, I've noticed that I really like playing jazz, which I do whenever there's no one else at home – just me and the piano. I won't play jazz in public because I'm not good enough, and also because it seems to me to be too revealing – suddenly everyone can hear what I'm thinking.

When I was delving into the mathematical laws behind the chords, progressions, and scales in jazz, I was reminded of Eryximachus, an eminent, well-educated Greek physician who was Socrates' cousin. Eryximachus believed that musical notes that are connected by love are definitely, and strongly, drawn to each other. If love doesn't exist between one note and another, we say that the music is lifeless. Jazz players talk of 'forbidden notes' – notes that aren't attracted to each other and will never be harmonious. A satisfying rhythm comes from the attraction between fast and slow. In Eryximachus's opinion, love lies at the core of the art of composition.

Music has a mesmerizing effect on the psyche. It's capable of subduing rampant emotions, awakening long-hibernating ones, or even planting in us emotions that didn't reside in our hearts at all, including love.

It's no coincidence that everyday language abounds in metaphors that associate love and music: 'This couple lives in perfect harmony,' 'There's some major discord in their relationship,' 'The liaison ended on a sour note.'

In one way or another, jazz teaches us that love has many facets.

Love and jealousy

It is written in the *Book of Zohar* that there's no love without jealousy. There will be those who absolutely agree with this statement, and those who are dubious. Certainly, it would be correct to say that jealousy must be harnessed to stop it getting out of control. Too much jealousy can turn any love, even one that seems to be secure within its fortress, into ruins.

By the way, Othello, contrary to what many think, was not jealous by nature. Anyone who reads Shakespeare's play is sure to notice the huge effort Iago invests in convincing Othello of Desdemona's betrayal! A truly jealous person doesn't need persuasion. They don't need proof or even a smidgeon of proof. Their imagination will do the job.

François de La Rochefoucauld (1613–1680) claimed (and he isn't the only one) that, in a true fanatic, jealousy will continue long after love has died. Tolstoy's novella *The Kreutzer Sonata* is about precisely this subject.

Sex and love

Watching Hollywood movies – and at other times too – one can become easily confused between love and sex. One of the reasons for this is the difficulty of showing love on the screen. Suppose Paul loves Paula very much and she loves him no less. How does this look on the big screen?

I've witnessed only one genuine attempt to portray love on the screen. This was in an old Russian TV series called *Seventeen Moments of Spring* (1973). The protagonist is a Russian spy in Nazi Germany toward the end of the Second World War. At Christmas the spy's wife, in the company of another man, has arrived at the café where her husband is. It's clear that, for reasons of security, the protagonist can't approach his wife. So he's sitting in one corner of the café and she in another corner, and for about five minutes they are simply exchanging glances that are supposed to show the viewer how much they love each other.[35] Director Tatyana Lioznova (Татья́на Лио́знова) had extraordinary courage; and knowing how much perseverance her viewers would need, she understood the need for background music to help them make it through the scene. The composer for the series was Mikael Tariverdiev (Мика́эл Тариверди́ев). I've performed a number of his works on my YouTube channel, including the one that accompanies the café scene.

Hollywood, however, treats love a little differently. Paul races to Paula, and she jumps into his arms. He tears off her clothes and she his. He presses her to the wall … and so on. This is how we are supposed to understand that love prevails between them.

The singer Madonna published a book entitled *SEX*. I haven't read it, but I peeked at the first sentence: 'Love is not sex and sex is not love.' Make no mistake about it, it's really nice when love and sex meet, and I assume it happens often. But you can love without wanting to press anyone to a wall; and, of course, the opposite is also true. Passion is not love.

In my youth I really liked the book *The Unbearable Lightness of Being* by Czech writer Milan Kundera. The book has many ideas about love. Here is one. Kundera – or, more correctly, his protagonist, Tomáš – goes against the Hollywood approach that fuses sex and love and concludes that desiring to sleep with a woman and desiring (literally) to *sleep* with a woman are not only different, they are almost diametrically opposed. In the opinion of the Czech writer (or at least his protagonist), sexual desire can be felt for (very) many women – Tomáš wants to sleep with pretty much every woman he meets. But the wish to fall asleep with someone, to sleep side by side and wake up in the same bed, is reserved for one's one and only love.

The art of love

After my father passed away I discovered my mother was suffering from dementia. The doctor who examined her announced that the dementia was advanced. Why didn't we come to him long ago? 'How could you have not noticed? Haven't you visited your mother recently?' The doctor seemed quite angry, as if it affected him personally. I had no answer. I visited my mother quite often, as did my brother and my daughters – her granddaughters – and my wife, and also her friends and neighbours. I asked around: no one knew she had dementia. No one had noticed anything.

At first I was too upset to think clearly, but as time passed, each time I visited my mother, who now lived alone, the severity and rapid deterioration of her condition seemed even more pronounced.

Then one day I was sitting in the old armchair in Mom's house, which until recently had been home to both my parents, and I began to understand what had happened. I started to recall incidents to which I hadn't attached any importance when they occurred, but that now told a story of love. I remembered how, more than once, when I asked my mother something, my father would answer instead – gently and sometimes in a tone of amusement. More often than not, he would end his answer with a kind of semi-rhetorical question, 'Right, Tan'ka?' (my mother's name was Tanya, but he preferred Tan'ka with a very soft *n*), and my mother would answer 'Right'. Maybe I should have suspected this effortless agreement, because my mother had not in the past tended to agree with my father without adding a modicum of reproach. I then recalled times when one of our neighbours would be engaging my mother in a conversation that seemed unnecessarily long, and Dad would interrupt, smile, and say, 'Tan'ka. Some tea perhaps?' Apparently, this was a task she was still able to perform. 'Tea is always better than chatter,' he'd say, and my mother would go into the kitchen, while my father changed the subject of the conversation so that he'd be in charge. More and more similar cases emerged from my memory, and I finally realized exactly what had happened.

Tal, my eldest daughter, recalled that one day my father had asked her to put labels on all the things that were on my mother's dresser. 'Tan'ka is constantly asking me for things, and I don't always understand what she means, so now I'll be able to see the label and know.' Tal, a psychologist, didn't suspect a thing! But now we understood that all those labels were for my mother, not my father.

My father's love for my mother was so great that he was able to enfold her in a huge blanket that wrapped itself all around her dementia. He thus managed to maintain her dignity right up to the day he died.

About a month before his death, my father began writing his memoirs. He could hardly see, but the project seemed too important to ignore. This is what he wrote about my mother:

I will now tell how I met my other half, the woman I have been with for almost six decades. She is the same one, thank God, who still helps me with all her heart and soul even in my most difficult times. At this time, now my health has fallen into deep abysses that I never imagined could exist, we are always together, to share the occasional joys that come our way and also the sorrows.

Here's how it happened. One day I met a girl with long hair in the great hall of the university library where I liked to go after finishing my work as a locksmith. She was slim and beautiful, a student in her last year at the Pedagogical Institute. She studied literature, and I really loved books. I still really love books, but now it's very difficult for me to read. We decided together to build our

home library while we were building our home. The first
gift I gave her was the complete collection of Tolstoy.

In his memoir Dad didn't even hint at my mother's illness .

When he passed away I knew my mother could not overcome her longing for him, and that she would join him soon. And so it was.

In Judaism, if a couple have lived together for many years and shared a great love, when God decides to repossess the soul of one of them, there's a prayer by which the surviving spouse asks God to have mercy and repossess his or her own soul as well. It's not uncommon for this prayer to be answered.

Endnotes

1   From the poem 'Ani Rotzeh Tamid Eynayim' ('I Always Want Eyes')
    in the chapbook *I Always Want Eyes* by Nathan Zach, Kibbutz
    MeUchad, 2019, in Hebrew. This translation by Linda Yechiel.

2   Freeman J. Dyson, *Infinite in All Directions: Gifford Lectures Given
    at Aberdeen, Scotland April–November 1985*. HarperCollins
    paperback edition 2004, with a new introduction by the author.
    Quoted by permission.

3   The houses of Hillel and Shammai were two schools of thought
    named after the sages who founded them during the last
    century BCE and early 1st century CE. The two schools had
    vigorous debates on matters of Jewish thought that were critical
    in shaping Oral Law and Judaism today. The opinions of Beit
    Hillel were usually more lenient and tolerant. In almost all cases
    Hillel's opinion is that followed by modern Jews.

4   The Talmud (specifically the Babylonian Talmud) is the primary
    source of Jewish religious law and formerly the centre of Jewish
    cultural life. It has two components: the Mishna (a compendium
    of Oral Torah) and the Gemara (comments by thousands of
    rabbis on the Mishna, as well as related writings that expound
    on the Hebrew Bible).

5   Bronnie Ware, *Top Five Regrets of the Dying: A Life Transformed
    by the Dearly Departing*, Hay House, 2019.

6   *The Wisdom of Solomon*, Watkins, 2018.

7   Tal Ben-Shahar's course on happiness was one of the most
    popular courses in the annals of Harvard University.

8   T. Gilovich and V.H. Medvec, 'The experience of regret: What,
    when, and why', *Psychological Review* (1995), *102*, 379–95.

9   If the subject really interests you, here is another article I
    recommend: T. Gilovich, V.H. Medvec, and D. Kahneman, 'Varieties
    of Regret: A Debate and Partial Resolution' *Psychological Review*
    (1998), *105*, 602–5.

10 See Helm W. Bennett, 'Friendship', *The Stanford Encyclopedia of Philosophy* (2008). For an online summary suitable for anyone interested in delving deeper into the concept, see plato.stanford. edu/archives/fall2021/entries/friendship/.

11 You can find my rendition of this work on YouTube. Simply search 'Haim Shapira. Rameau'.

12 These are the Rameau compositions for piano that I particularly like, with my favourite performers who have played them: *Les Tendres Plaintes*, Grigory Sokolov, Marcelle Meyer or Víkingur Ólafsson; *Le Rappel des Oiseaux*, Emil Gilels; *Pièces de Clavecin en Concerts: 11, La Cupis*, Víkingur Ólafsson; *Les Sauvages*, Grigory Sokolov; *Les Boréades: The Arts and the Hours*, Víkingur Ólafsson (transcribed Ólafsson); *Les Trois Mains*, Clément Lefebvre; *L'Entretien des Muses*, Marcelle Meyer or Víkingur Ólafsson; *L'Egyptienne*, Alexandre Tharaud or György Cziffra.

13 I devoted two chapters to Pythagoras's writings in my book *Eight Lessons on Infinity: A Mathematical Adventure* (Duncan Baird Publishers, 2019).

14 List Number 31, in Yevgeny Zamyatin, *We (Мы)*. The book was first published in English (trans. Gregor Zilboorg) in 1924 by E.P. Dutton, New York. The original Russian text was first published in 1952.

15 I wonder what Benedict (Baruch) de Spinoza would have said about this statement by Aristotle. Spinoza's book on philosophy, *Ethics*, whose full title is *Ethica, Ordine Geometrico Demonstrata (Ethics, Demonstrated in Geometrical Order)*, is based on Euclid's geometry.

16 Mohsen Joshanloo and Dan Weijers, 'Aversion to Happiness across Cultures: A Review of Where and Why People Are Averse to Happiness', *Journal of Happiness Studies*, June 2013.

17 Nozick's list: Ludwig Wittgenstein, Elizabeth Taylor, Bertrand Russell, Thomas Merton, Yogi Berra, Allen Ginsberg, Harry Wolfson, Henry Thoreau, Casey Stengel, The Lubavitcher Rebbe, Pablo Picasso, Moses, Albert Einstein, Hugh Hefner, Socrates, Henry Ford, Lenny Bruce, Baba Ram Dass, Gandhi, Sir Edmund Hillary, Raymond Lubitz, The Buddha, Frank Sinatra, Christoper Columbus, Sigmund Freud, Norman Mailer, Ayn Rand, Baron Rothschild, Ted Williams, Thomas Edison, H.L. Mencken, Thomas

Jefferson, Ralph Ellison, Bobby Fischer, Emma Goldman, Peter Kropotkin.

18 N.P. Li and S. Kanazava, 'Country Roads, Take Me Home … to My Friends: How Intelligence, Population Density, and Friendship Affect Modern Happiness', *British Journal of Psychology* (2016), 107(4), 675–97.

19 L. McGuirk, P. Kuppens, R. Kingston, R. and B. Bastian, 'Does a Culture of Happiness Increase Rumination over Failure?', *Emotion* (2018), 18(5), 755–64.

20 French philosopher Jacques Derrida liked the word *aporia* and used it in the contexts of 'undecidability' and 'deconstruction'.

21 Among the articles that can be found for free on the web, I recommend 'Understanding the Machine Experience Argument', 23 January 2017, at philosophicaldisquisitions.blogspot.com.

22 Peter Singer, 'Famine, Affluence, and Morality', *Philosophy and Public Affairs*, vol. 1, No. 3 (Spring 1972), 229–43.

23 Daniel Kahneman and Angus Deaton, 'High income improves evaluation of life but not emotional well-being', *PNAS*, 21 September 2010.

24 Aleksandr Solzhenitsyn, *The Gulag Archipelago: An Experiment in Literary Investigation* (*Архипелаг ГУЛАГ*), first published in Russian by the French publishing house Éditions du Seuil in 1973, and in English and French the following year. This passage and the ones on pages 224 and 230 are reproduced by permission: author's translation from Russian to Hebrew, translated into English by Linda Yechiel.

25 Solzhenitsyn, *op. cit.*

26 Roman historian Cassius Dio (155–235 CE) wrote 80 books on the history of Rome, among them a book about Marcus Aurelius. This monumental work can be found online in a version for Kindle. See penelope.uchicago.edu/Thayer/E/Roman/Texts/Cassius_Dio/home.html. If you're thinking of printing it out, be aware that there are more than 2,000 pages.

27 Solzhenitsyn, *op. cit.*

28 In 1903, about 10 years after Oscar Wilde, George Bernard Shaw wrote similar words in his play *Man and Superman*: 'There are two tragedies in life. One is to lose your heart's desire. The other is to gain it.'

29 Thich Nhat Hanh, *The Art of Mindful Living*, CD, Sounds True AE00499, 2000. Quoted by permission.

30 I wrote a chapter about FOMO and FOBO in my book *The Most Beautiful Childhood Memory*, Kinneret Zmora-Bitan Dvir, 2017 (in Hebrew).

31 Ivan Illich, *Tools for Conviviality*, Harper & Row,1973; paperback edition Marion Boyars, 2001. Quoted by permission.

32 These are the opening lines of the poem. It's about Rabbi Avraham ben Meir Eben Ezra (1089–1167), who was a biblical commentator, poet, philosopher, and mathematician (he preceded Fibonacci in the use of the decimal system) during the golden age of Spain.

33 'A snapshot of the age distribution of psychological well-being in the United States', Arthur A. Stone, Joseph E. Schwartz, Joan E. Broderick and Angus Deaton, *Proceedings of the National Academy of Sciences*, 1 June 2010, 107(22), 9985–90.

34 Stendhal Syndrome' is a psychosomatic condition characterized by accelerated heartbeat, fainting, confusion, and even hallucinations. It occurs when people are exposed to works of art or phenomena of sublime beauty.

35 My Hebrew editor and good friend Tirza Eisenberg pointed out to me that in the beautiful 1995 BBC series *Pride and Prejudice* (a version of Jane Austen's novel) we also witness exchanges of glances between the main pairs of protagonists, though they are of slightly less duration.

Acknowledgments

First and foremost, I should like to thank Etan Ilfeld for loving my books and having confidence in me and my writings.

I owe the greatest thanks of all to my friend Tirza Eisenberg, who worked with me on the Hebrew version of this book from its moment of conception as a vague idea until its publication. This is the ninth book we've worked on together, and not only does our collaboration improve each time, but I cannot imagine writing a book with any other editor.

I sincerely thank Erez Albo for our many conversations about Stoic philosophy. My hope is that one day we can collaborate on a book on this subject.

I should like to thank my faithful translator Linda Yechiel. My gratitude also to my friend Ofer Samocha, who read the text and made many worthy observations.

I'm gratefully indebted to the wonderful people responsible for writing the content of Wikipedia, which makes its extensive, valuable information about everything available to all.

My deepest gratitude to Watkins Publisher Fiona Robertson and Project Editor Brittany Willis, as well as everyone else who helped with this book: Laura Whitaker-Jones, Vikki Scott, Octavia Lavender, Emily Jarman and Francesca Corsini.

Many thanks, utmost respect, and sincere appreciation to Bob Saxton, who lovingly helped me to create a better version of this book.

I want to thank from the bottom of my heart my friend and agent Ziv Lewis and my international agent Vicki Satlow for helping my books to be published in dozens of countries.

Finally, thanks are due to Yoram Rose and Eran Zmora, chief editors of Kinneret Zmora Dvir Publications. They have believed in me since they read the manuscript of my first book and they continue to give me their trust to this day.

Contact shapirapiano@gmail.com with any comments.

Bibliography

The following is not a typical bibliography; it is a tiny list of some of my favourite books that influenced the writing of each chapter in *Notes on the Art of Life*.

CHAPTER 1: IN THE BEGINNING: THE POETICS OF SCIENCE
Richard Dawkins, *The Greatest Show on Earth,* Black Swan, paperback edition, 2009

CHAPTER 2: PEN, INK, AND FINE-QUALITY PAPER: THE ART OF WONDER
Sei Shōnagon, *The Pillow Book,* Penguin Classics, 2007

CHAPTER 3: ZHUANG ZHOU'S CRAZY WISDOM
Alan Watts, *Tao: The Watercourse Way,* Pantheon Books, 1975

CHAPTER 4: THE ARITHMETIC OF LIFE AND DEATH
Fung Yu-Lan, *A Short History of Chinese Philosophy* (Chapter 6), Free Press, 1997

CHAPTER 5: THE SOUND OF SILENCE
The Epic of Gilgamesh, Tablet XI, 'The Story of the Flood', www.ancienttexts.org/library/mesopotamian/gilgamesh/tab11.htm; also, trans. Maureen Gallery Kovacs, Stanford University Press, 1989

CHAPTER 6: A HARVEST OF REGRETS
Bronnie Ware, *The Top Five Regrets of the Dying: A Life Transported by the Dearly Departing,* Hay House, 2012
Leo Tolstoy, *The Death of Ivan Ilyich,* CreateSpace Independent Publishing Platform, 2011

CHAPTER 7: TENDER COMPLAINTS
Arthur Schopenhauer, *The Wisdom of Life and Counsels and Maxims,* Digireads.com Publishing, 2020

CHAPTER 8: DUDEISM AND TAOISM
Lao Tzu, *Tao Te Ching: The Way of Life*, Orkos Press, 2015

CHAPTER 9: ARISTOTLE'S BLOG ON *EUDAIMONIA*
John Sellars, *Aristotle: Understanding the World's Greatest Philosopher*, Pelican, 2023

CHAPTER 10: THE SECRET OF THE VIRTUES: ARISTOTLE'S ART OF FINDING BALANCE
Aristotle, *Nicomachean Ethics,* trans. Robert C. Bartlett and Susan D. Collins, University of Chicago Press, 2011

CHAPTER 11: THE APPEAL OF SOCRATES: WHAT IS PHILOSOPHY SUPPOSED TO DEAL WITH?
Robert Nozick, *The Examined Life: Philosophical Meditations,* Simon & Schuster, 1990

CHAPTER 12: TIPS FROM EPICURUS: THE GREAT ART OF SMALL PLEASURES
The Philosophy of Epicurus, ed. George K. Strodach, Dover Publications, reprint edition, 2019

CHAPTER 13: WHAT IS WISDOM?
Douglas J. Soccio, *Archetypes of Wisdom: An Introduction to Philosophy,* Wadsworth Publishing, 9th edition, 2015

CHAPTER 14: THE INNER CITADEL: STOIC PHILOSOPHY
Pierre Hadot, *The Inner Citadel: The Meditations of Marcus Aurelius,* Harvard University Press, revised edition, 2001

CHAPTER 15: ON HAPPINESS AND OTHER SMALL THINGS OF ABSOLUTE IMPORTANCE
Jennifer Michael Hecht, *The Happiness Myth: The Historical Antidote to What Isn't Working Today,* HarperOne, reprint edition, 2008

CHAPTER 16: A FEW WORDS ABOUT LOVE
André Gorz, *Letter to D: A Love Story,* trans. Julie Rose, Polity, 1st edition, 2009

Other Books
by Haim Shapira

Hebrew publications

In the Footsteps of Alice, Open University Press, 2006

Conversations about Game Theory, Kinneret Zmora-Bitan Dvir, 2008

About the Really Important Things, Kinneret Zmora-Bitan Dvir, 2009

Infinity: The Never-ending Story, Kinneret Zmora-Bitan Dvir, 2010

Ecclesiastes: The Biblical Philosopher, Kinneret Zmora-Bitan Dvir, 2011

Night Thoughts, Kinneret Zmora-Bitan Dvir, 2013

The Book of Love, Kinneret Zmora-Bitan Dvir, 2014

I Think, Therefore I Err (with Gil Gilboa Friedman), Kinneret Zmora-Bitan Dvir, 2015

The Most Beautiful Childhood Memory, Kinneret Zmora-Bitan Dvir, 2017

Notes on the Art of Life, Kinneret Zmora-Bitan Dvir, 2022

English-language publications

Happiness and Other Small Things of Absolute Importance, Watkins Publishing, 2016

Gladiators, Pirates and Games of Trust, Watkins Publishing, 2017

The Wisdom of Solomon, Watkins Publishing, 2018

Eight Lessons on Infinity, Watkins Publishing, 2019